HOMES
& GARDENS
COOKBOOK

HOMES
& GARDENS
COOKBOOK

BRIAN GLOVER

PAVILION

To my grandmother, Mary Jane Gore, who cooked with love

First published in Great Britain in 1996 by
Pavilion Books
26 Upper Ground, London SE1 9PD

Designed by Peter Bennett

Recipes marked with a ◉ are suitable for a vegetarian
diet. All the recipes in Sweet Pies and Tarts and Puddings
are suitable for vegetarians.

Food preparation for photography by Brian Glover,
with the exception of pages 75 & 98
(food preparation by Alison Birch).

A CIP catalogue record for this book is available
from the British Library

ISBN 1 85793 823 2

Typeset in 12pt Bodoni Book
Printed and bound in Spain by Artes Graphicas, Toledo S.A.

D.L.T.O: 159-1996

2 4 6 8 10 9 7 5 3 1

This book may be ordered by post direct from the publisher.
Please contact the Marketing Department.
But try your bookshop first.

CONTENTS

FOREWORD

Brian Glover first wrote to me in 1990 when he was a librarian at Exeter University. Something about his letter, the way he talked about food and his obvious passion not just for recipes but for the way in which food was produced caught my eye. I asked him to come and see me. I decided to take what was potentially a risk – after all, to employ a librarian as your cookery editor takes a real leap of faith: we've never looked back.

At that time Brian's pedigree was short, perhaps, but his knowledge and enthusiasm were just what every magazine editor is looking for. He had already won the 1988 *Independent/* Taitinger Cook of the Year Award, the 1989 *Daily Telegraph/*Krug Glyndebourne Picnic Competition, was a finalist in the 1988 *Observer/*Mouton Cadet Dinner Party Competition and was at the time taking part in the BBC series *Masterchef.*

We both felt that the *Homes & Gardens* food section should be for people who enjoy cooking, who do not want to be daunted by a complicated recipe, but who want to impress their friends with interesting taste sensations. We thought that the recipes should be one step ahead, offering a new perspective on traditional ingredients. Over the years Brian has achieved all this and more. Our food pages have always looked utterly mouthwatering and tempting. The ideas are clever, often witty, but never offputting. And yet Brian manages to pull off a great coup in that the cook always feels a warm sense of achievement.

Now that we have accumulated several years' worth of recipes, accompanied by stylish photographs, many people have asked us to produce some sort of index for Brian's recipes. What better record of all that Brian has done for *Homes & Gardens* than to put all his ideas together into this beautiful book.

I know you will treasure, use and enjoy it for many years to come.

Amanda Evans

Editor, *Homes & Gardens*

INTRODUCTION

I have always liked to cook. I enjoy the processes of cooking – the chopping, measuring, stirring and kneading. The whole activity gives me as much pleasure as the final result. Good cooking is not a mystery. If you enjoy eating, trying out new foods and dishes, if you are curious about new ingredients or a flavour you've never met before, you are well on the way to being a good cook. Enjoyment of, and curiosity about, food are two of the greatest motivators a cook can have. Skills and timing a cook can acquire and hone until they are almost second nature, but without enjoyment and curiosity I doubt whether anyone can become a really good cook.

This book is a selection of the best recipes I have contributed to *Homes & Gardens* magazine over the past five years, together with a few new ones. For the magazine I write about food seasonally, picking out ingredients and flavours that are at their best at a given time of year. Elsewhere, I have described this approach as instinctual: it is to do with the type of food we want to eat at different times of year. Modern production and distribution techniques mean that more and more choice is open to more and more people the year round. This is good, and modern cooking depends upon it. But the seasonality of food cannot be totally evened out, and I for one should never want it to be.

There are all kinds of recipes here. There are adaptations and variations on others' ideas as well as new 'inventions'. There are stylish entertaining and celebration ideas alongside recipes for homely soups, cakes and biscuits. There are dishes influenced by cuisines from around the world and others by the traditional food of the British Isles; there are simple recipes and dishes which will take more time to get together.

This is the way I like to cook and eat, without any allegiances or partialities except to the search for good quality and delicious flavours. Writing about cooking gives me the chance to pass on my enthusiasm for food and to encourage people to try new combinations of tastes or to rediscover old favourites which are part of our culinary heritage. This is what makes food writing so rewarding – the opportunity it gives to pass on enthusiasm and experience, and to encourage the love of quality and optimum flavour in the food we eat.

Almost inevitably, the recipes display a personal bias and taste. There is an emphasis on vegetables and fruit. There are, on balance, more fish recipes than meat and, lest this all sound rather puritanically worthy, a fair share of indulgent puddings and home bakery. Looking back over five years of recipes has been both rewarding and frustrating. Too often, in the rush from one magazine deadline to another, good dishes get overlooked and forgotten. It has been fun to rediscover recipes and try them again. But the sifting process has been frustrating too. When I cook, I taste constantly, and as my tastes change so do my recipes. There are, of course, certain recipes I wouldn't tamper with but most are not written in tablets of stone. Nor should they be. Often as I've worked on this book I have thought, 'What about a bit more spice here?', or 'Would a dash of that oil work there?' Tastes change and recipes should shift with them. The most important thing is to taste, taste, taste. You may want to add less sugar or more salt. You may want to serve a soup without cream or prefer a cake without an icing. Particularly with salt, sugar and chilli heat, people's tastes vary enormously. Take my quantities as a guide and adjust to your taste accordingly.

There are many people I should like to thank for their part in this book. First of all, to Amanda Evans, editor of *Homes & Gardens*, for her initial 'leap in the dark' and for her inspiration and advice ever since, and to Blossom Martis for her patience, enthusiasm and support. I would also like to thank all the art department at the magazine, especially Paul Ryan, whose trained eye has been instrumental in producing so many splendid photographs. Especial mention should be made of Helen Payne who, as stylist, is the unsung hero of the vast majority of the photographs that appear in the magazine and hence this book. Her eye and imagination for colour, shape and texture are unfailingly accurate and genuinely inspirational. Most of all I would like to thank all the photographers whose work appears in this book – it is they who bring the food to life for the readers of the magazine. By making food look beautiful and 'good enough to eat', they encourage people to try and experiment.

Many debts of influence and inspiration to other writers on food are acknowledged throughout this book. To any I have missed, my apologies. The bibliography at the end of the book lists the books to which I most consistently refer. Especially, I would like to thank Geraldine Holt for all her help and kind words of support when I started writing about food. At Pavilion, I would like to thank Trevor Dolby, Kate Quarry for all her patience in the face of my disorganization, computer illiteracy and frequent changes of mind, and Anne Johnson for her skill in unravelling my chaotic and inconsistent text. To my friends and colleagues at the University of Westminster, especially Pat Barclay, thank you for the forebearance and flexibility that have made this book possible. Last of all, but certainly not least, I would like to thank the friends who have tried out experiments and cooked my recipes and given their opinions and advice. Special thanks to Catherine, John, Fran, Jill, Gillian, Fiona, Ros and Melissa. They have all, in their several ways, had an effect on how this book has turned out.

Brian Glover, London, 1996

When it comes to the storecupboard, cooks fall into two categories: the hoarders and the minimalists. For hoarders autumn is the key time of year, when they go into a near religious frenzy of jamming, freezing, bottling and chutney-making. Their shelves (and worktops) are laden with bottles, jars and packets; there is always something being kept in a brown paper bag, 'just because it might come in handy'. The minimalists, on the other hand, have just one bottle of the smartest olive oil on view, and their shelves are textbook illustrations of orderliness and good planning. Many of us fall somewhere between these two extremes. I am by nature a hoarder who has had a modified minimalism forced upon him by restrictions of space. My kitchen is small, many would say tiny, and I have had to learn restraint and the absolute necessity of the annual clearout. Maybe this is no bad thing, but sometimes I recall the cool, walk-in larder in the farmhouse where I grew up and think it would be nice to have a bit more space.

I have learned to my cost over the years that storecupboard ingredients do not have indefinite shelf-lives. On many occasions I've delved to the back of the shelves for that bottle of a certain spice or sauce I know I have, only to realize on its triumphant discovery that it is well past its sell-by date, in all senses. There is no point in adding spoonfuls of paprika to your North African couscous if you brought it back from Spain three years ago and its colour has now faded from brick red to pale ochre. It will taste of nothing or, worse, it will lend a dusty, stale flavour to your carefully made dish. Certainly, if you're planning an important meal or a baking spree, it is always prudent to check what's going on in your storecupboard before you start cooking. If only I always heeded my own good advice.

The following categories suggest some of the ingredients I find essential or useful in the storecupboard and some ideas for making use of them. Dried pulses, grains, pastas and flours and sugars are important staples of the storecupboard which deserve separate discussion. See the introductions on pages 108–10 and 138–9.

THE BASICS

Salt is the most essential flavour enhancer we have. Mindful that many of us are trying to reduce the amount of salt in our diets, you should always taste a dish before adding more salt. For most cooking purposes I use a fine-grained sea salt. When you want large crystals of salt the soft flakes of Malden salt, crumbled between the fingers, can't be beaten. Black pepper has always been the most important of spices, accounting for over one-quarter of the world's trade in spices. Pepper is grown in India, Malaysia, Indonesia and Brazil. The best, if you're into such minute levels of discrimination, is said to come from the Wynad plateau in the Indian region of Kerala. Pepper should always be freshly ground or crushed.

OILS

Olive oils have come a long way since they were only to be found in small, anonymous bottles from the chemist. Now every supermarket worth the name stocks a range of olive oils. The best olive oils are made from the first cold-pressing of olives grown on trees from a single estate. This first pressing yields the thickest, fruitiest extra virgin oils. Like wine, olive oils vary according to geography, climate and soil. Most supermarket extra virgin oils are blended from several sources to produce a consistent product. Some green, unfiltered oils give a peppery 'catch' at the back of the throat. Other oils are yellow, smooth and fruity and still others, like the delicious Ravida oil from Sicily, have the scent of new-mown hay. I like to keep a bottle of supermarket extra virgin oil for cooking (heating diminishes an olive oil's scent and flavour, but enough remains) and a special cold-pressed oil for pouring on pasta, salads, cooked vegetables, grilled fish or as a simple dip for crusty bread. A pure olive oil, such as the French Plagniol brand, is useful for making mayonnaise or when an assertively flavoured oil would be overpowering.

NUT AND SEED OILS

When I want a bland oil for general cooking I use either refined sunflower or ground-nut (peanut) oil. Groundnut is the best deep-frying oil. Grapeseed oil is a good, light oil for using half and half with olive oil in a mayonnaise, as it reduces the chance of the mayonnaise splitting when chilled. Other nut oils make a delicious addition to salad dressings – add them, a drop at a time, to an olive oil dressing until you get the right balance. Look for dark, amber-coloured oils, as some light nut oils have had all the guts refined out of them. Hazelnut oil is good with lime and has an affinity with smoked fish and root vegetables. Walnut oil is excellent with orange juice, sherry or balsamic vinegar and works well on salads of chicory, beetroot, watercress and rocket. Toasted sesame oil is very strong and a few drops are good tossed with Chinese egg noodles or in a dressing for grilled aubergine. Try adding a few drops to a chickpea hummous to emphasize the sesame taste of the tahini. Pumpkin seed oil is quite delicious. Dark and toasty, it is good with sweet-sour

vinegars like Italian balsamic or Chinese Chinkiang rice vinegar.

Chilli oil is one of the most essential flavourings in the kitchen. But commercial chilli oils can be very hot and suspiciously bright red. It is easy to make your own and you can then determine how hot you want the oil to be. A couple of fresh, split red chillies or 5–6 briefly soaked dried red chillies, will be sufficient to flavour a 500ml/ 17fl oz bottle of oil. Use a pure olive oil or sunflower oil and add a few sprigs of rosemary or thyme if you like. The longer you leave the chillies in the oil, the hotter it will be. Other flavoured oils include Italian lemon-flavoured oil, made by pressing lemons with the olives, which is delicious drizzled on pasta with black pepper and chopped mint or in salad dressings with balsamic vinegar. Truffle and porcini mushroom-flavoured oils are also good with hot potatoes or home-made noodles. All flavoured oils should be added to cooked dishes at the last moment, even at the table, so that you do not lose the aromatic explosion as the oil hits the hot food.

VINEGARS

Vinegars can be made from any wine and, as a rule, the better the wine, the better the vinegar. Good wine vinegar should be well-aged and requires no added preservatives (quite the reverse, it is a preservative in its own right). Champagne vinegar is particularly delicate and mild. Sherry vinegar, aged in oak barrels, is full-flavoured and woody and is excellent in strong-flavoured salads and sauces. Cider vinegar is milder and sweeter. It is good in fruity salads and for quick, sweet/sour pickles of carrot, cucumber and red onion.

Balsamic vinegar is the most sought-after and expensive of vinegars and with good reason: it is delicious, not only in salad dressings but also for adding depth and character to sauces, stews and braises. A few drops will transform a dish of halved, lightly sugared strawberries. *Aceto balsamico tradizionale* is aged for years in wooden casks and as it ages the flavour deepens and concentrates. The commercially produced *aceto balsamico industriale* is not matured for so long, and may be sweetened with caramel, but can still be very good. There are many different grades. Age and price are good indicators of quality. One of the best is the Giuseppe Giusti brand from Modena.

Light rice vinegar is one of the most useful vinegars in the kitchen. Its mild, sweetish taste is particularly good in fruity salsas and excellent for shellfish salads and marinaded, raw fish dishes. Dark rice vinegar is quite different, similar to balsamic vinegar in colour and individuality, but with a quite different flavour and smell. Chinkiang vinegar, from north China, is one of the best. It is dark, smoky and deeply savoury. It is excellent in Oriental-style dressings and sauces (for a cold noodle salad, for example), but it also adds a delicious depth of flavour to salads of peppery watercress or rocket, or in a dressing for a salad of earthy, wild rice.

Tarragon vinegar is also excellent in mayonnaise and the classic *sauce béarnaise*. You can also make more exotically flavoured vinegars. Two of my favourites are saffron vinegar on a shellfish or seafood salad, and lemon grass vinegar, made by pouring hot, rice wine vinegar over some lemon grass stalks, split lengthways, and leaving them to steep for at least three weeks.

BOTTLED SAUCES, PASTES AND CONDIMENTS

Soy sauce – the Japanese Kikkoman brand is

best – is good not only for Oriental dishes and stir fries but also to add savour and bite to Western sauces and gravies. It is essential for marinades and good in salad dressings. I cannot imagine cooking without it. Similarly, I am fast becoming addicted to the taste of Thai fish sauce, which is usually labelled *nam pla* in Oriental food shops and large supermarkets. It is used across South East Asia and is manufactured from fermented fish. Salty, pungent, but without a definite fishy taste, I love it in Thai-style salad dressings, in fruity salsas and in seafood salads. I usually have a bottle or jar of some kind of chilli paste or sauce on the go too. American tabasco and north African harissa are good in marinades and in tomato dishes, and for adding a kick to mayonnaise to accompany fish stews. Mediterranean-style chilli pastes with garlic are excellent in pasta sauces or as a quick marinade for fish or chicken, with olive oil, coriander seeds and a little lemon or lime zest and juice. Other commercial pastes and pestos make useful storecupboard ingredients. Black or green olive pastes, green and red pestos, tapenade and pastes of sun-dried tomatoes, artichokes, mushrooms and sweet and hot peppers are all good with pasta or grains. Spread any of them on chicken or fish before adding a layer of herbed breadcrumbs and baking. Or try them underneath grilled goat's cheese on *brushette* and *crostini*.

Good mustards are essential. A straightforward Dijon mustard is good for adding to cheese sauces and to meat or poultry sautés. Mustard should be added to a dish towards the end of cooking, otherwise its essential 'kick' tends to disappear. I use tarragon mustard a lot, especially in salad dressings and marinades. It is good with beef, pork, chicken and rabbit. Another mustard I have recently discovered is flavoured with *herbes de*

Provence. It is delicious in the dressing for salads of grilled and cooked vegetables or for salads containing shavings of Parmesan or Pecorino cheese. Some old-fashioned mustard powder is good also for cheese sauces and soufflés, beef gravy or for dusting the fat of roast beef for a spicy crust.

HERBS AND SPICES

I don't use many dried herbs in my cooking. The essence of the sweet, summer herbs is their fresh, green fragrance. This is lost in drying. Tarragon and Greek oregano seem to be the only ones that survive the drying process with any credibility. The woody herbs dry more convincingly. Dried bay leaves, thyme and rosemary sprigs are good in slow-cooked stocks, stews and casseroles. A little dried sage is traditional in stuffings for pork. *Herbes de Provence* is a good mixture of dried herbs with spices and dried orange zest. That British peculiarity – mixed, dried herbs – belongs in the bin along with many an ancient *bouquet garni.*

I use a lot of spices in my cooking. My favourite spices are dried red chillies, coriander, cumin, cinnamon, nutmeg, cardamom, allspice, vanilla and saffron. I would call all of them essential. Food writers, myself included, are always advising the use of freshly ground spices rather than the ready-ground versions. The reason is simple: whole spices keep their flavour for far longer than ground ones. Even so, they do not keep indefinitely. As a basic rule, the harder and drier the spice, the longer it should keep. There are certain spices that one always buys ready-ground, and they should be bought in small quantities and used quickly: ground ginger, paprika, cayenne and turmeric come to mind.

Chilli does not just mean heat. Guajillo chillies are relatively mild; anchos and mulatos are hotter but with fruity and liquorice flavours respectively. Chipotle chillies are wood-smoked jalapeños and have a hot but deliciously smoky taste. These large dried chillies can be made into pastes by first toasting them, then soaking and puréeing with a little of the soaking water. Toasting spices brings out their fragrance and taste. Simply put the spice in a small pan over a medium heat for a few minutes. Stir constantly so that the spice doesn't burn. When the spice darkens a little and you get a blast of their delicious aroma, transfer to a plate then grind or crush when cool.

Chinese salted black beans keep almost indefinitely. A few mashed with a little sugar are delicious in stir-fries with soy sauce. Dried shrimps, dried fish pastes (known as *blachan* or *trasi*) and sweet-sour tamarind are essential for a whole range of South East Asian dishes. Other salty foods I like to have around are tins of anchovies, jars of olives and sun-dried tomatoes, and pots of salted capers.

I also keep some cans of coconut milk and some bottles of Italian passata – sieved tomato purée. Dried goods include a few dried mushrooms: Italian porcini (ceps), morels and Chinese black mushrooms (shiitake) dry best. Well-strained porcini soaking liquid makes a better stock than most cubes.

Besides actual storecupboard ingredients, there are a few fresh ingredients I shouldn't like to find myself without. Lemons in the fruit bowl. Onions and garlic in the vegetable rack. Unsalted butter, eggs and Parmesan cheese in the fridge. With unsalted butter you can gauge exactly how much salt you want in a recipe. When a dish is better for using lightly salted butter, I have indicated that in the recipe.

PRESERVED LEMONS

I love the sharp but mellow taste of lemons preserved in olive oil. The lemons age to a beautiful golden colour through the use of paprika. The method comes from Claudia Roden's indispensible book on the diverse cuisines of the Middle Eastern countries, *A New Book of Middle Eastern Food*. It is worth covering the lemons with plenty of oil, not only for preserving purposes, but also because the lemon-flavoured oil is so useful in marinades or simply as a brushing oil for grilled fish, chicken or pork.

Makes 1 x 1.2 litre/2 pint preserving jar

6 unwaxed, organic lemons, well
    scrubbed
3 tablespoons sea salt
2 teaspoons mild paprika
pure olive oil to cover (around
    600ml/1 pint)

Slice the lemons thinly and remove any obvious pips. Place the slices on freezer-proof trays and sprinkle with salt. Freeze overnight (or longer if convenient).

Thaw, then drain off the juices in a colander. Arrange the slices in glass preserving jars, sprinkling a little paprika between each layer. Then pour over sufficient olive oil to cover by at least 1cm/½ inch. Tap sharply on the work surface to get rid of air bubbles. Leave for at least 4 weeks before using and keep at least 1cm/½ inch oil over the lemon slices.

VARIATION
Add 1–2 dried red chillies to each jar for a spicier preserve.

PRESERVED LEMON AND RED ONION COMPOTE

Serve this compote as a relish alongside grilled chicken, pork or fish. Brush some of the oil from the lemons over the meat or fish and sprinkle with a spice mixture of coriander, cardamom and cumin before grilling.

Serves 4–6

3 tablespoons oil from the preserved
    lemons or olive oil
2 medium red onions, peeled and
    thinly sliced
1 teaspoon toasted coriander seeds,
    coarsely ground
1 clove garlic, peeled and chopped
10–12 slices preserved lemon, cut into
    strips
2–3 tablespoons sherry vinegar
brown sugar
a generous pinch of saffron strands
    (optional, but excellent with fish)
salt and freshly ground black pepper

Heat the oil in a medium-sized non-reactive saucepan over a moderate heat. Add the onions, stir, cover and 'sweat' over a low heat for 10 minutes, stirring occasionally. Add the coriander and garlic to the onions and cook very gently for a further 10 minutes, uncovered this time. Add the lemons, 2–2½ tablespoons vinegar and 1 teaspoon sugar. Soak the saffron, if using, in 2 tablespoons hot water for 10 minutes before adding, with its liquid, to the pan. Simmer, uncovered, until all liquid has evaporated. Season to taste with salt (probably not necessary), black pepper, and more brown sugar and/or vinegar to taste.

CRANBERRY, DATE AND KUMQUAT CHUTNEY

This sort of sharp, fruity preserve goes very well with cold meats, pâtés and terrines. Cranberries, with their high pectin content, do not need lengthy cooking in this chutney, so the fresh flavours of the ingredients are preserved.

Makes 3 x 350g/12oz jars

*300ml/10 fl oz cider or white wine
   vinegar*
275g/10oz golden granulated sugar
1 teaspoon cardamom seeds, crushed
1 teaspoon coriander seeds, crushed
1 small piece cinnamon stick
½ teaspoon dried red chilli flakes
175g/6oz peeled red onion, chopped
*4cm/1½ inch piece fresh ginger,
   peeled and finely chopped*
350g/12oz fresh cranberries, washed
*225g/8oz fresh dates, skinned, stoned
   and chopped*
*175g/6oz kumquats, washed and
   quartered*
shredded zest and juice of 1 lime

Place the vinegar, sugar and spices in a large non-reactive saucepan and cook over a low heat, stirring regularly, until the sugar has dissolved. Boil for 5 minutes then add the onion and ginger. Cook for 10 minutes. Add the cranberries and the rest of the ingredients and simmer, stirring often, until the mixture is thick and not at all liquid. This should take 25–35 minutes.

Ladle the chutney into warm, dry sterilized jars and seal while hot. Avoid using uncoated metal lids as the vinegar will corrode the metal.

Store for at least 3 weeks before broaching.

Cranberry, date and
kumquat chutney
served with rillettes
(page 34)

The following dressings are all sufficient for 1 salad, serving 4–6 people.

ORIENTAL-STYLE DRESSING

Use to dress warm noodles and serve with sliced grilled duck, or slices of Chinese cooked pork or wind-dried sausages. Or use on a salad of shredded raw vegetables – carrot, white radish (mooli), Chinese cabbage, celeriac, etc. Or try it on cooked vegetables, such as snow peas, baby corn and French beans.

1 teaspoon chilli oil
1 teaspoon dark sesame oil
2 teaspoons soy sauce
2 teaspoons rice or balsamic vinegar
salt, freshly ground black pepper and caster sugar
3 spring onions, trimmed and finely sliced
½ red chilli, de-seeded and thinly sliced

1 tablespoon finely chopped fresh coriander (optional)

Blend together the first 4 ingredients, adding sesame oil and vinegar to taste. Season with salt, pepper and a pinch of caster sugar (the soy will probably provide enough salt). Stir in the onions, chilli and coriander, if using.

ROASTED GARLIC DRESSING

Getting the flavour of garlic into a dressing can be a problem – not everyone appreciates biting into a piece of raw garlic. One solution is to use a garlic-infused oil or vinegar, another is to add a purée of mild, sweet roasted garlic, the flavour is deliciously mild, sweet and toasty. The purée may be prepared in advance as it keeps well in the fridge under a little olive oil. This dressing would go well with crisp salad leaves, such as Cos or Webb's, with watercress or rocket. Toss with some briefly cooked fennel, crisp croûtons and some grated Parmesan or Pecorino cheese. It is also good on grilled aubergine, pepper or fennel salads.

2 large heads of garlic
bay leaves and sprigs of fresh thyme
salt and freshly ground black pepper
7–8 tablespoons extra virgin olive oil
2 tablespoons white wine
1 teaspoon Dijon mustard
1 tablespoon lemon juice
chopped fresh thyme (optional)

Preheat the oven to 160°C/325°F/gas 3. Place the garlic in a small, oven-proof dish and tuck in a few bay leaves and sprigs of thyme. Season well and pour over 3 tablespoons oil and the wine. Cover tightly and cook in the oven for 1–1½ hours until the garlic is meltingly soft. Cool, squeeze the garlic out of its papery skin and then purée with its oil and the mustard in a liquidizer or processor. Gradually blend in the remaining oil, adding it in a thin stream as you would for mayonnaise.
 Then beat in the lemon juice.

Adjust seasoning to taste, adding a little chopped fresh thyme, if liked.

VARIATIONS
1. There are all kinds of pestos and pastes available now which can form the basis of salad dressings. Use a black olive or sun-dried tomato paste in a dressing for pasta salads. Herb pestos are good in dressings for rice salads, while a red pepper paste would make a lively addition to a dressing for a chicken or seafood salad.

2. Use a couple of grilled, skinned red or yellow peppers instead of the garlic, purée as above, adding the oil gradually.

N.B. Dressings based on vegetable purées are prone to separate. If this happens, blend in 1–2 tablespoons *crème fraîche* in the liquidizer or with a small whisk until smooth.

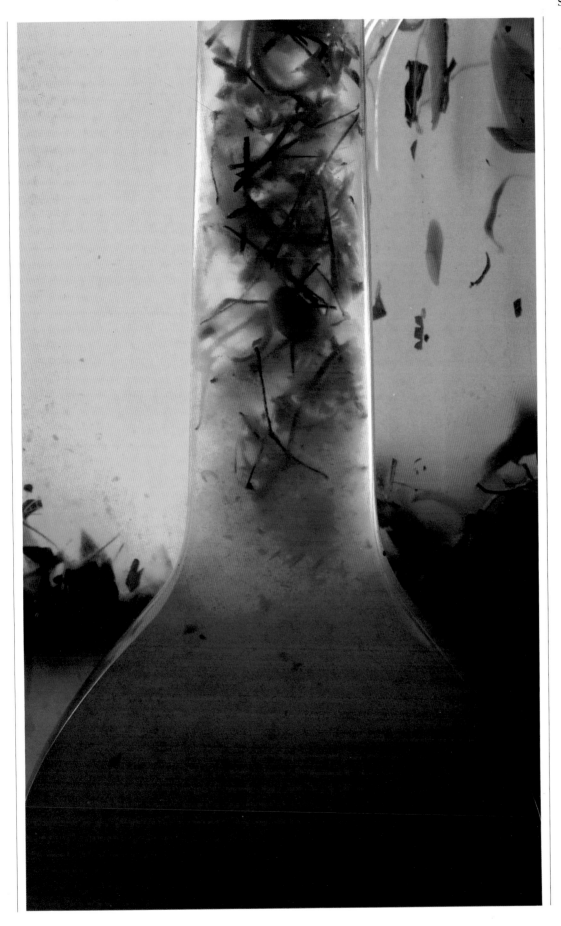

From left to right:
saffron and orange
dressing (page 18);
Thai-style oil-less
dressing (page 18);
and Oriental-style
dressing (page 16)

SAFFRON AND ORANGE DRESSING

This makes an excellent dressing for a seafood salad – try a mixture of just poached monkfish, turbot or brill with prawns, mussels and squid. Alternatively, use to dress a seafood rice salad, as the rice will absorb the dressing and turn a pretty yellow from the saffron.

a pinch of saffron filaments
5 tablespoons extra virgin olive oil
1 teaspoon sherry vinegar
½–1 tablespoon orange juice
finely shredded zest of ½ orange
a large pinch ground coriander seed
½ clove garlic, finely chopped
salt, freshly ground black pepper and caster sugar
1 tablespoon chopped fresh parsley or coriander

Place the saffron in a tiny bowl and soak in 1 tablespoon hot water for 15 minutes. In a bowl whisk together the oil, vinegar and orange juice. Whisk in the soaked saffron (and its liquid), the orange zest, coriander seed and chopped garlic. Season with salt, pepper and a pinch of caster sugar if liked. Leave to stand for at least 1 hour for the flavours to develop. Just before using, stir in the chopped fresh fresh parsley or coriander.

THAI-STYLE OIL-LESS DRESSING

A delicious fat-free dressing adapted from a recipe in Jennifer Brennan's *Thai Cooking*. This is a powerfully flavoured dressing for sprinkling on salads of papaya, pineapple and grated carrot, cucumber or white radish. It is delicious, too, on salads of thinly sliced rare roast beef, or pink duck breasts. Serve also with shellfish and fish salads. Make it as hot as you like with more or less chilli.

1 clove garlic, peeled
pinch of salt
½–1 red chilli, de-seeded and finely chopped
5cm/2 inch piece lemon grass stalk, finely minced
1 tablespoon fish sauce (nam pla)
2 tablespoons lime juice
1 teaspoon caster sugar
1 kaffir lime leaf, finely shredded
1 tablespoon shredded fresh coriander or mint

Crush the garlic in a mortar or food mill with the salt, then stir in the remaining ingredients and 2 table-spoons water. Adjust the seasoning to taste.

VARIATIONS
1. You can make this dressing as authentically Thai as you like by adding more garlic and/or chilli. Some ground toasted cumin or coriander seed makes a good addition, too.

2. A variation I like is to stir in 2–3 tablespoons of thick coconut milk (either canned or made from fresh coconut). Omit the water. This makes a much milder, creamier dressing, which is excellent on seafood salads.

BALSAMIC VINEGAR AND BASIL DRESSING

1 clove garlic
5–6 tablespoons extra virgin olive oil
½ teaspoon Dijon or herbes de
  Provence *mustard*
½–1 tablespoon balsamic vinegar
salt and freshly ground black pepper
2 tablespoons chopped fresh basil

Bruise the garlic with the flat blade of
a large knife and peel. Mix the oil,
mustard and vinegar in a small bowl
or screwtop jar then drop in the garlic. Leave to steep overnight or for
several hours. Just before serving, fish
out the garlic, re-mix the dressing,
seasoning to taste and stirring in the
fresh basil.

VARIATIONS
1. Make a delicious dressing by stirring in a few tablespoons of diced,
grilled and skinned sweet red or yellow pepper. Or use diced sun-dried
tomato with a little fresh or dried red
chilli and some chopped thyme.

2. Mix in a small, diced shallot and
use chopped fennel rather than basil.
Steep a few crushed fennel seeds in
the dressing too.

3. Use a mixture of walnut and olive
oils and some wholegrain mustard.

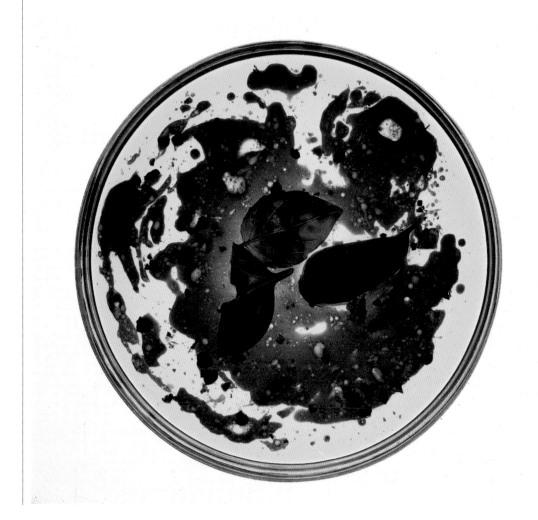

**Balsamic vinegar
and basil dressing**

MUSTARD SEED AND YOGHURT DRESSING

Serve this with salads of blanched, shredded celeriac and carrot. Or dress a mixture of chicory, celery and grated carrot.

2 teaspoons Dijon mustard
1–2 teaspoons lemon juice
5–6 tablespoons yoghurt
salt, freshly ground black pepper and
  caster sugar
3 spring onions, chopped
1 tablespoon groundnut oil
1 dessertspoon mustard seeds
pinch of dried red chilli flakes

In a small bowl whisk the mustard and beat in 1 teaspoon lemon juice. Gradually whisk in the yoghurt. Season with salt, pepper and a pinch of caster sugar. Adjust the seasoning with more lemon juice if liked. Stir in the spring onions. In a small pan heat the oil until hot, add the mustard seeds and chilli flakes and cook for a few seconds until they begin to pop. Immediately swirl the hot oil mixture into the yoghurt dressing.

VARIATIONS
1. The dressing is also delicious on a baby spinach salad, or try this variation.
First make the yoghurt mixture. Then heat the oil and mustard seeds, and pour this directly over a bowl of spinach leaves or of shredded mustard greens. Toss to wilt the leaves slightly, then mix in the yoghurt mixture. A few cumin seeds cooked with the mustard seeds are good, too.

2. Stir some chopped fresh mint or coriander into the dressing.

LEMON CURD

Surely lemon curd is the quintessential British preserve. It's delicious spread thickly on good bread or toast and makes an excellent filling for tarts and sponge cakes. Mixed with an equal volume of whipped cream it also makes an excellent filling for meringues. Freeze the same half-and-half mixture of curd and cream (preferably in an ice-cream maker) and you have one of the nicest ice-creams it's possible to make.

Makes 2 medium-sized jars

2 large, unwaxed, organic lemons,
  well scrubbed
100g/4oz unsalted butter, cut into
  small pieces
175g/6oz caster sugar
3 free-range eggs, size 2, beaten

Finely grate the zest from the lemons and place in a heatproof bowl with the butter and sugar. Squeeze the juice from the lemons and add to the bowl. Place the bowl over a pan of barely simmering water. Stir all the time until the butter melts. Strain the eggs into the mixture through a non-reactive sieve.

Cook for 10–15 minutes, stirring frequently, until the curd thickens considerably. Pot into small, warm, sterilized jars.

VARIATIONS
Use limes or Seville oranges instead of lemons. You will need 4 limes for the quanties above or 2–3 Seville oranges, depending on how big they are.

I often think that I prefer cooking and eating first courses to the main event of a meal. In a first course, the flavours can be more intense because you are serving smaller quantities and because it is the first thing you are going to eat. I like a meal made up of several small, starter-size dishes, especially if there is a theme, linking the dishes together (otherwise the whole thing can get a bit confusing for both eater and cook). It is a good idea to serve two complementary dishes as a first course – it makes the experience of eating far more interesting. Try, for instance, a cooked salad like that of Mushrooms and Squash *à la Grecque* with the Terrine of Rabbit on page 93, or serve the terrine with a fruity relish such as the Red Onion, Kumquat and Cranberry Relish on page 190.

EASY FIRST COURSES

Another good idea for a first course for informal eating is to assemble a collection of small dishes for people to help themselves. This is a particularly good idea for lazy summer meals. Visit a good delicatessen and buy some cured fish and salami or other cured sausages, and some raw, air-dried ham like *jamón serrano*, *prosciutto di San Daniele* or some of the excellent home-reared Cumbrian examples. Arrange on a large platter and add some olives, fresh vegetables like grilled asparagus and spring onions, raw radishes and cherry tomatoes. Add a few cooked salads like an Oriental Aubergine Salad (page 47) or grated celeriac in a mustard mayonnaise. Some little onions or mushrooms cooked *à la Grecque* are good, too. Serve the whole thing with some delicious, crusty bread and perhaps a bowl of golden yellow, home-made mayonnaise and you have a first course which becomes a social event as people help

themselves and pass the dishes round the table.

Almost every country, apart from Britain and North America, has a tradition of this type of eating. The Spanish and Latin Americans have their *tapas*, Italy her *antipasti*, the Greeks and Middle Eastern countries their *mezze*. Traditionally, Russian meals began with *zakuski* and the Scandinavians vie to produce the best *smörgåsbord*. The French enjoy *hors d'oeuvres* while most Asian meals are structured on a succession of small dishes rather than one main course with peripheral extras. This seems a natural way of social eating, kinder on people's digestive systems and the cook's nerves than our traditional three-course meal.

You'll find many other ideas for first courses elsewhere in this book. Many of the salads in the next chapter would make excellent first courses and dishes like Grilled Sweet Potatoes with Chilli, Lemon and Garlic Aioli (page 56) or Salmon and Couscous Fishcakes (page 112) are delicious as a start to a meal. Other good ideas for delicious first courses include the marinated fish salads on pages 67 and 69.

SOUPS

Soups are traditional first course material. But soup is wonderfully versatile. Soups can stimulate and delight; they can comfort and satisfy; they can whet your appetite for the meal ahead or fill you handsomely when you are hungry. A hot soup in the chill of a British winter will cheer and warm like no other food; in the balmy days of summer a chilled soup can cool you down and refresh. Soups are all things to all people. There are elegant soups to start a meal and meal-in-a-soup-bowl soups, which form a whole meal in themselves.

Previous page: roasted aubergine and garlic soup with tomato and chilli salsa (top, page 26) and tomato and orange soup with marjoram and garlic croûtons (page 28)

Then there are all the things you can put in soups or eat alongside them. For if there is one thing which some soups lack, it's texture. However delicious consommés, cream soups and puréed soups can be, they can also become boring to eat. Garnishes, croûtons, dumplings and bread give a change of texture, as well as flavour, and make soups a lot more interesting to eat. Of course, there are whole families of soups which have masses of texture and interest in themselves: these soups are on the boundaries between stews and soups. Even puréed soups are all the better for a bit of texture. A *mouli légumes* food mill will produce a less homogenized soup than a liquidizer. A food processor, too, will also produce a more interestingly knobbly texture.

ACCOMPANIMENTS

I like things you can add to soups and eat with soups at the table. They not only provide texture but they make eating into more of an event. Croûtons can be made from all kinds of bread. Bread made with a proportion of yellow maize flour is always delicious toasted, or try walnut bread or a light rye bread. Toss the cubed bread in oil (or oil and butter mixed) and bake in a medium oven (180°C/350°F/gas 4) for 8–10 minutes until crisp and golden. Croûtons can be tossed with all sorts of good things before baking. Try using chilli oil or adding a little ground spice – chilli, cumin, coriander. Toss the croûtons in herb pastes or pestos before baking or sprinkle with grated Parmesan cheese. Dumplings make a substantial addition to soups. Add chopped herbs to the dumplings to match the flavours in the soup and add a crisp garnish. Frizzled onions, crisp-grilled pancetta or bacon, deep-fried root vegetable 'crisps' or just some breadcrumbs fried in a little olive oil/butter mixture until golden are all good sprinkled over dumplings and soups.

Smooth salsas, flavoured oils and creams also make good additions to soup, allowing you to add a complementary or contrasting flavour (and colour) to the soup. In the recipes that follow, you'll find ideas for a spicy Tomato and Chilli Salsa, which is great in the Roasted Aubergine and Garlic Soup but also delicious in many other soups that need the kick of a little chilli heat. Try it in a chickpea or white bean purée or in a soup of potato and onion or squash. A simple purée of oil and a fresh herb is also delicious drizzled over a soup, or try folding some chopped herbs into a little whisked cream as in the Chervil and Pernod Cream on the top of the Rhubarb and Star Anise Soup. *Rouille*, a mayonnaise-style sauce spiced with hot peppers, garlic and saffron (see recipe on page 185), is traditional with the fish soups and *bourrides* of the Mediterranean region. But it is good, too, with vegetable soups that have the typical Mediterranean flavours of tomato, saffron, garlic and orange.

Little pastries, like the Russian *pirozhki*, are delicious accompaniments to soup. Make a buttery pastry, binding with sour cream or yoghurt. My favourite filling is mushroom, onion and sour cream, or you could try one of cabbage and hard-boiled egg. Serve them hot with a chilled beetroot soup or a hot, earthy mushroom soup. Or try little filo pastries, filled with curd cheese, spinach and onion.

Some soups, such as the Sorrel, Lemon Grass and Prawn Soup on page 24, rely on well-flavoured stock. There are recipes for basic stocks in the final chapter. For strong-flavoured soups you could use stock-cubes, but simple puréed vegetable soups are often better made with plain water, as stock can muddy the clean flavours of the fresh ingredients.

Chicken and fennel soup with tarragon and pancetta dumplings (page 27)

23

RHUBARB AND STAR ANISE SOUP

Serves 4–5

40g/1½oz butter
1 medium-sized onion, chopped
1 teaspoon finely chopped fresh ginger
3 star anise pods
450g/1lb young rhubarb, trimmed
1.2 litres/2 pints chicken or vegetable
    stock
salt, freshly ground black pepper and
    caster sugar
150ml/5fl oz double cream
2 teaspoons Pernod or other aniseed
    liqueur
1–2 tablespoons chopped fresh tar-
    ragon or chervil
sprigs of chervil and croûtons, to serve

Melt the butter in a medium-sized non-reactive saucepan over a low heat. Cook the onion, ginger and star anise slowly for about 10 minutes, stirring frequently and not allowing the onion to brown at all. Cut the rhubarb into 5cm/2 inch lengths, add to the pan and cook, turning the rhubarb in the buttery juices for a further 5–10 minutes. Add the stock and season with salt, pepper and 2 teaspoons sugar. Bring to the boil, cover then simmer for 10–15 minutes. Remove the star anise when the flavour is strong enough.

Cool a little then liquidize. Taste for seasoning, adding more sugar to taste. Reheat to just under boiling and stir in 2–3 tablespoons cream and 1 teaspoon Pernod. Whip the remaining cream with the other teaspoon of Pernod, season with a little salt, pepper and a pinch of sugar, then fold in the chopped herb (use less tarragon than chervil as the flavour is stronger). Serve the soup in warmed bowls topped with a spoonful of the cream mixture and garnished with sprigs of chervil. Some little croûtons, fried in butter and oil, are good too.

SORREL, LEMON GRASS AND PRAWN SOUP

Serves 4

750g/1½lb raw, large prawns, shelled
    (reserve the shells)
1 tablespoon vegetable oil
2.5cm/1 inch piece fresh ginger,
    peeled and sliced
2 x 10cm/4 inch lemon grass stalks,
    thinly sliced
2 cloves garlic, peeled and thinly
    sliced
1.2 litres/2 pints fish stock
salt and freshly ground black pepper
2 slim leeks or 3 spring onions,
    trimmed and finely sliced
50–75g/2–3oz fresh sorrel leaves,
    finely shredded
lime juice
1 red chilli, de-seeded and thinly
    sliced
2 tablespoons coriander sprigs

With a small, sharp knife, cut down the back of each prawn and remove the black vein that runs the length of the prawn. Set aside the prawns. Heat the oil in a roomy non-reactive pan until fairly hot, add the prawn shells, the ginger and half the lemon grass and garlic. When the prawn shells have turned bright pink, add the stock and bring to the boil. Add a teaspoon of salt and some black pepper. Cover and simmer the stock for 15 minutes.

Strain and return the stock to the pan. Add the remaining garlic and lemon grass, cook for 2 minutes then stir in the prawns and leeks (or spring onions) and cook for another few minutes, until the prawns turn pink and are cooked. Add the shredded sorrel. Taste and correct seasoning, adding more salt and/or lime juice. Serve sprinkled with chilli and coriander.

Sorrel, lemon grass
and prawn soup
with rhubarb and
star anise soup

ROASTED AUBERGINE AND GARLIC SOUP WITH TOMATO AND CHILLI SALSA

The salsa in this soup is great for adding a lift to other autumnal soups such as squash or pumpkin. It is also good as a pasta sauce.

Serves 4–5

*2 heads garlic, outside papery skin
    removed*
4 tablespoons olive oil
2 dessertspoons fresh thyme sprigs
*3 large aubergines (about 750g/1½lb
    in total weight)*
2 large red onions, peeled and sliced
*1.2 litres/2 pints chicken or vegetable
    stock*
salt and pepper

FOR THE SALSA:
4 ripe tomatoes
1 fresh red chilli, de-seeded
2–3 tablespoons extra virgin olive oil
*1 tablespoon sherry or balsamic
    vinegar*
a pinch of caster sugar
*2 tablespoons finely chopped fresh
    marjoram or basil*
a few sprigs of fresh thyme

Set the oven to 220°C/425°F/gas 7. Wrap the garlic in a small package of foil, adding half the oil and half the thyme. Place package on a baking sheet. Pierce the aubergines in a few places with a sharp knife and place on the baking sheet, then add the tomatoes and the red chilli from the salsa ingredients. Put the baking sheet into the hot oven. Roast the tomatoes, aubergines and chilli for 20–30 minutes – until the skins blister and begin to blacken. Remove and set aside. Leave the garlic to cook for a further 20–30 minutes until soft, then remove and set aside to cool.

In a large, heavy pan, heat the remaining oil over a medium heat, then cook the sliced onions and the remaining thyme for about 10 minutes to soften. Remove most of the skin from the aubergines (though a little doesn't matter), chop the flesh and add to the pan. Cook, stirring often, for another 5 minutes. Meanwhile, squeeze the garlic out of its papery skin and mash roughly with a fork. Add to the pan with the stock – season well with salt and pepper, bring to the boil, cover and simmer for 20 minutes. Cool a little then liquidize in a blender or through a food mill. Return to the pan and correct seasoning.

Now make the salsa: remove the skin from the tomatoes and chilli. Blend to a purée either in a pestle and mortar or in a small food mill. While working the mixture, gradually blend in the oil, then the vinegar. Season with a little sugar. Stir in the chopped marjoram or basil.

Reheat the soup until almost boiling. Serve the soup in bowls decorated with a swirl of salsa, and sprinkled with the sprigs of fresh thyme. Serve the remaining salsa separately.

CHICKEN AND FENNEL SOUP WITH TARRAGON AND PANCETTA DUMPLINGS

For a more pronounced aniseed flavour in this soup, add 1–2 teaspoons Pernod when reheating the soup. This is a whole meal in a soup bowl. Serve with good bread and perhaps a salad to follow.

Serves 4–5

1 x 1.5kg/3lb chicken, preferably corn-fed and free-range
3 bulbs Florence fennel
1 onion, peeled and quartered
3 leeks, cleaned and trimmed
herb bundle of bay leaf, tarragon and parsley
120ml/4fl oz white vermouth or dry white wine
2 potatoes, peeled (about 150g/5oz)
100g/4oz butter
salt and freshly ground black pepper
150ml/5fl oz single cream
dumplings and crisp-cooked pancetta (see recipe below)

Cut the breasts off the chicken and set aside. Cut up the rest of the chicken into rough joints and place in a large non-aluminium saucepan. Cut the stalks and outer layers off the fennel, chop roughly and add to the pan with the onion, 1 leek and the herb bundle. Reserve the rest of the fennel and any feathery tops.

Cover the ingredients in the pan with 2.5 litres/4½ pints water, bring to the boil, skim, and then simmer for 1 hour. Remove the chicken pieces, pick off the meat, and return the bones to the stock, cook for a further hour. Strain the stock into a clean pan, add the vermouth or wine and simmer, uncovered, for another 15 minutes. Meanwhile, chop the remaining fennel, leeks and potatoes into 2.5cm/1 inch pieces. Melt 75g/3oz butter in a large pan and cook the vegetables, covered, over a very low heat for about 15–20 minutes. Stir occasionally and do not allow to brown. Then add 1.5 litres/ 2½ pints of the stock, season well and simmer, covered, for 20 minutes.

Meanwhile, preheat the oven to 190°C/375°F/gas 5. Place the chicken breasts on a baking tray, dot with the remaining butter, season well and roast for 20–30 minutes until the chicken is cooked. Cool a little, then cut into smallish pieces, set aside a few nice pieces for garnish. Process or liquidize three-quarters of the soup (or put through a food mill) with the reserved poached chicken, then return to the pan, with the small pieces of roast chicken.

Add the cream and more of the stock if the soup seems too thick. (Cook the dumplings at this point.) Reheat the soup to just under boiling point and taste for seasoning. Serve the soup in warmed soup plates, with the dumplings garnished with the roast chicken pieces, the crumbled pancetta and the chopped fennel tops.

TARRAGON AND PANCETTA DUMPLINGS

100g/4oz self-raising, white flour
40g/1½oz fresh white breadcrumbs
50g/2oz shredded suet (use vegetable suet if you prefer)
100g/4oz thinly sliced pancetta or streaky bacon
2 teaspoons chopped fresh tarragon (or 1 teaspoon dried tarragon)
salt and pepper
remaining stock from the soup above

Mix together the flour, breadcrumbs and suet. Fry or grill the pancetta until crisp. Cool. Crumble half the pancetta into the flour mixture and stir in the tarragon. Season well then bind with 3–4 tablespoons cold water. Form into about 8–10 small dumplings. To cook, heat about 1 litre/1¾ pints stock (make up with water if necessary) to a simmer. Add the dumplings and cook gently, covered, for 15–20 minutes until risen. Serve with the soup, crumbling the remaining pancetta over the top.

TOMATO AND ORANGE SOUP WITH MARJORAM AND AND GARLIC CROÛTONS

Serves 4

450g/1lb ripe, meaty tomatoes
2 tablespoons extra virgin olive oil
1 large onion, red or yellow, sliced
1–2 cloves garlic, chopped
1 mild dried red chilli, de-seeded
*1–2 teaspoons coarsely ground
  coriander seeds*
425g/15oz can peeled, plum tomatoes
*salt, freshly ground black pepper and
  caster sugar*
1 orange
1–2 tablespoons fresh marjoram sprigs

FOR THE CROÛTONS:
½ Italian ciabatta loaf
1 clove garlic, peeled
salt
2–3 tablespoons extra virgin olive oil
*2–3 tablespoons chopped fresh
  marjoram*

Preheat the oven to 200°C/400°F/gas 6. Place the fresh tomatoes on a baking sheet and cook, uncovered, for about 45 minutes until the skins burst and begin to char. Remove from the oven and set aside. Heat the oil in a roomy non-reactive pan and cook the onion and garlic over a low heat until just beginning to brown (about 10 minutes). Add the chilli and coriander seeds, and cook for a couple of minutes more. Add both the roasted and canned tomatoes, season with salt, pepper and a pinch of sugar. Add 900ml/1½ pints water and the zest of half the orange. Bring to the boil and simmer for 15–20 minutes. Cool a little, then blend in a processor or food mill to make a purée, but try to leave a little texture in the mixture.

Correct the seasoning, adding orange juice to taste. Reheat and serve the soup in heated bowls with the croûtons and sprinkled with marjoram sprigs.

Now make the croûtons: cut the bread into 2cm/¾ inch slices. Preheat the oven to 200°C/400°F/gas 6. Crush the garlic with a little salt, then blend in the oil and marjoram. Spread the bread pieces with this mixture, then turn on to a baking sheet. Bake in the hot oven until light brown (about 10 minutes). Serve with the soup.

Potato and herb
pancakes with
smoked salmon and
crème fraîche

Beetroot, Coconut and Lime soup

This simple but delicious soup becomes even simpler if you use ready-cooked beetroot and ready-prepared coconut milk. The soup is superb either hot or cold – season it a little more vigorously if serving cold.

Serves 4

225g/8oz unsweetened desiccated
   coconut
4 medium beetroot (about 450g/1lb)
juice of 1 lime
salt and freshly ground black pepper
4 tablespoons crème fraîche or
   yoghurt, to garnish

In a large bowl pour 1 litre/1¾ pints of boiling water over the coconut and leave to cool. Cook the beetroot by boiling them in lightly salted water for 50–60 minutes. Cool the beetroot, skin and chop roughly. Blend the coconut with its liquid in a liquidizer or processor, then strain through a sieve, pushing hard to extract maximum flavour. Return the coconut milk to the liquidizer or processor with the beetroot and blend until smooth. Pour into a saucepan or bowl and season to taste with lime juice, salt and pepper. Either reheat if serving hot, or chill for several hours if serving cold. If serving cold blend the soup again before serving. Top with *crème fraîche* if serving hot, or yoghurt if serving cold.

Potato and Herb Pancakes with Smoked Salmon and *Crème Fraîche*

Grated potato pancakes make delicious but heavy eating. These pancakes, made with sieved potato and a minimum of flour, turn out as light as a feather and make a splendid partner to smoked salmon and *crème fraîche*.

Serves 5–6 as a first course

250g/9oz floury variety potatoes
salt and freshly ground pepper
2 eggs
120ml/4fl oz milk
25g/1oz plain unbleached flour
3 tablespoons mixed chopped chives
   and dill
a little oil or butter for frying
100g/4oz sliced smoked salmon
150ml/5fl oz crème fraîche
small jar salmon roe caviar (keta)
   (optional)
lemon wedges, sprigs of dill, and
   chopped chives, to garnish

Scrub the potatoes and cook in boiling salted water until tender, peel then purée through a food mill or sieve to give a light, dry purée. In a separate bowl, whisk the eggs and milk together, then whisk in the potato purée and sifted flour to make a thick batter. Season with a little salt and plenty of pepper. Stir in the chives and dill.

Heat a heavy, preferably non-stick, frying pan over a moderate flame and brush with a little oil or butter. Make pancakes using 1½–2 tablespoons of batter. Cook for about 2–3 minutes on each side until golden brown. Brush the pan with butter between each batch. The batter should make 10–12 pancakes. Serve on warm plates with the salmon and a spoonful of *crème fraîche* and salmon caviar, if using. Garnish with lemon wedges, sprigs of dill and chopped chives. Grind over black pepper before serving.

CRAB CAKES WITH ASPARAGUS AND SALMON CAVIAR

Both crab and asparagus are at their best in early summer and combine deliciously in this recipe. Prepare the crab cakes well in advance and finish cooking just before serving.

Serves 2–3

175g/6oz fresh, prepared crabmeat
1 tablespoon chopped fresh chervil or
*   parsley*
2 spring onions, chopped
1 teaspoon capers, chopped
100g/4oz fine white breadcrumbs
175g/6oz cooked asparagus
salt and freshly ground black pepper
2–3 tablespoons mayonnaise
plain flour for dusting
1 small egg, beaten
oil for shallow frying
3–4 tablespoons crème fraîche
4 teaspoons keta (salmon caviar)
fresh chervil and/or chives, to garnish

Place the first 4 ingredients in a bowl with half the breadcrumbs and mix together. Cut the tips off the asparagus with about 5cm/2 inches of stem, and set aside. Cut the remaining tender stem of the aspapagus into 5mm/¼ inch pieces. Add to the crab, season to taste, then bind the crab mixture with the mayonnaise.

Form into 4–6 small cakes. Dust in flour, dip in egg, then into the remaining breadcrumbs. Chill until ready to cook.

To serve, fry the cakes in shallow oil for about 4–5 minutes on each side. Drain on kitchen paper. Place 2–3 cakes on each plate, top with some *crème fraîche* and keta, and garnish with asparagus tips and chopped chervil and/or chives. Grind over some black pepper just before serving.

Crab cakes with
asparagus and
salmon caviar

SEAFOOD, FENNEL AND SAFFRON TARTS

Serves 8

225g/8oz shortcrust pastry (i.e. made
 with 225g/8oz flour)
large pinch saffron filaments
2 yellow peppers
2 small bulbs Florence fennel
3 tablespoons extra-virgin olive oil
175–225g/6–8oz lemon sole fillets,
 skinned
225g/8oz freshly cooked shelled
 mussels
2 eggs, size 3
350ml/12fl oz full-fat milk or
 milk/single cream mixed
salt, pepper and cayenne
8–16 large, raw unshelled prawns
salad leaves and a few unshelled,
 cooked mussels to serve

Preheat the oven to 190°C/375°F/gas
5. Roll out the pastry and use to line
8 x 10cm/4 inch tartlet tins (preferably with loose bases). Support the
sides with strips of foil and bake
blind for 10–15 minutes until lightly
coloured but not quite fully cooked.
Remove the foil strips and set aside.
Set the saffron to steep in 2 tablespoons hot water.

Meanwhile grill the halved and de-
seeded peppers, skin-side up, until
the skin blackens and blisters, place
into a paper bag or covered bowl and
allow to 'steam' gently for 10 minutes, then remove the skin and cut
the peppers into strips. Cut each fennel bulb into 8 wedges, reserving any
feathery tops until later. Brush the
fennel with half the oil and grill, turning once, until browned and softened.
Cut the lemon sole into strips and
mix with the mussels. Beat the eggs
and milk (or milk and cream together),
and season well, adding a pinch of
cayenne. Beat in the saffron and its
liquid and the chopped, reserved
fennel tops.

Arrange the mussels, sole and
grilled peppers in the flan cases and
add a couple of fennel wedges to each.
Distribute the saffron custard between
the tarts, arrange on a baking tray and
bake for 15 minutes. Brush the prawns
with the remaining oil and season well.

Remove the tarts from the oven
and quickly press 1 or 2 prawns on to
each tart, return the tarts to the oven
and cook for a further 10–12 minutes.
Best served warm, rather than hot.
Serve each tart with a few salad leaves
and garnish with some unshelled,
cooked mussels.

Seafood, fennel and
saffron tarts

SAGE-FLAVOURED CORN PANCAKES WITH CHICKEN LIVERS AND FRESH PARMESAN

Serves 4–5

175g/6oz maize (corn) meal
1 egg, size 2
7 fresh sage leaves, chopped
½ teaspoon crushed, dried red chilli
salt, freshly ground black pepper and
  caster sugar
1 tablespoon extra virgin olive oil,
  plus more for frying

FOR THE TOPPING:
25g/1oz butter
1 small red onion, peeled and
  chopped
1 clove garlic, peeled and chopped
1 teaspoon mild Hungarian paprika
225g/8oz chicken or duck livers,
  trimmed and sliced
4–5 tablespoons red wine
3 fresh sage leaves, chopped
finely grated zest of ½ lemon
2–3 tablespoons finely chopped parsley
salt and freshly ground black pepper
150ml/5fl oz soured cream or crème
  fraîche
50–75g/2–3oz piece fresh Parmesan
sprigs of parsley, to garnish

In a bowl blend together the maize meal, egg and 150ml/5fl oz water to make a thick batter. Mix in the sage and chilli, and season with ½ teaspoon salt, freshly ground black pepper and a pinch of sugar. Set aside while making the filling. Stir in the 1 tablespoon of oil just before making the pancakes.

For the topping: melt the butter in a small frying pan, cook the onion and garlic gently until soft but not brown (approximately 10 minutes). Raise the heat slightly, add the paprika and livers and cook the livers for 2–3 minutes until browned on the outside. Add the wine and cook briskly to evaporate the liquid. Turn off the heat. Add the sage, lemon rind and parsley, season to taste and keep warm.

Make small (7.5cm/3 inch) pancakes with the batter in a large, lightly-oiled non-stick frying pan. Cook for 2–3 minutes on each side over a medium heat. Brush the pan with oil between batches. Top the pancakes with the livers, a spoonful of soured cream or *crème fraîche*, and top with shavings of fresh Parmesan. Grind over some black pepper and decorate with parsley before serving.

Sage-flavoured corn
pancakes with
chicken livers and
fresh Parmesan

MUSHROOMS AND SQUASH *À LA GRECQUE* WITH TOMATO AND ORANGE

This is a fine autumnal-looking dish with the mellow orange and red of the squash and tomato and the brown of the mushrooms. It makes a marvellous counterpoint to the flavours of the Terrine of Rabbit on page 93, but is also a good starter in its own right. Butternut, acorn or onion squashes all have excellent firm flesh suited to this method or you could use courgettes (which won't have the marvellous colour, of course). This dish should be made the day before and allowed to come to room temperature before serving.

Serves 6

175ml/6fl oz dry white wine
6 tablespoons olive oil
1 teaspoon coriander seeds, crushed
2 sprigs fresh thyme
2 bay leaves
1 orange
salt, pepper and sugar
225g/8oz peeled and de-seeded
  squash
350g/12oz small mushrooms (button
  or a mixture of shiitake and
  chestnut cap)
225g/8oz flavoursome tomatoes,
  peeled, de-seeded and diced
2 tablespoons finely chopped fresh
  marjoram or basil

Put the first 5 ingredients into a pan with 150ml/5fl oz water, the finely shredded zest of half the orange and the juice of the whole orange. Bring to the boil, season with a little salt and pepper, and simmer for 5 minutes.

Cut the squash into slices or strips, and halve or quarter the mushrooms if they are large. Add the squash to the pan and cook for 5 minutes, or until the squash is just tender. Add the mushrooms and the tomatoes, and cook for 3–4 minutes. Remove the vegetables to a serving dish using a slotted spoon. Turn up the heat, and reduce the liquid by fast boiling until 4–5 tablespoons remain. Taste for seasoning, adding a little sugar if necessary, and pour over the vegetables, cool, cover and refrigerate. Bring to room temperature and stir in the marjoram (or basil) just before serving.

Mushrooms and squash *à la grecque* with tomato and orange; served here with terrine of rabbit with garlic and parsley

RILLETTES

Rillettes, that mainstay of many a Gallic *charcutier*, can be made solely of pork or you can use a mixture of pork and poultry or game. Duck, goose, turkey and wild rabbit are all delicious. This recipe is an excellent way of using poultry thighs or drumsticks left over from another dish. Season the meat well, cook slowly until it is meltingly tender and keep the finished texture light and slightly fibrous. Covered with 1cm/½ inch fat, rillettes will keep for up to 10 days in the fridge; if you're only keeping them for a few days, the extra covering of fat is not necessary.

Serves 6–8

350g/12oz fat belly pork
100g/4oz back pork fat
450–750g/1–1½lb poultry or game on the bone (see above)
salt and freshly ground black pepper
1 teaspoon freshly ground allspice berries, plus extra to taste
2–3 cloves garlic, peeled and halved
2 sprigs fresh thyme plus a little extra to taste
fresh bay leaves

Cut the pork and the fat into 2.5cm/1 inch cubes. Joint and skin the poultry or game. Place all the meat in a shallow, non-metallic dish. Mix together 1½ teaspoons salt and 1 teaspoon pepper with the allspice. Rub the spices all over the meat. Cover and leave in the fridge overnight or for several hours. Preheat the oven to 140°C/275°F/gas 1. Place the meat in a casserole with a tight-fitting lid, add 150ml/5fl oz water, the garlic, thyme and 2 bay leaves. Cover tightly (seal with foil if necessary) and cook in the oven for 3½ hours. Place a large sieve over a bowl and tip the meat into it. Allow to drain and cool, then remove the herbs and any bones.

Pound the meat with a pestle or the end of a rolling pin, then, using 2 forks, tear it into shreds. If you use a food processor to do this, be careful that you don't end up with too smooth a mixture. Adjust the seasoning. You may like to add more chopped thyme and garlic (if you do, don't store the finished dish for longer than 4 days or the garlic may turn sour.)

Pack into small jars or ramekins. Pour over some of the cooking fat, but don't add any of the meaty juices. Add a fresh bay leaf or two to each pot. Allow the rillettes to set and 'mature' for a day or two before eating. If keeping the rillettes for longer, cover the mixture with a 1cm/½ inch layer of melted fresh lard or dripping. Serve with crusty bread, baby gherkins (*cornichons*) and a fruity chutney. Radishes and black olives make good accompaniments, too.

When I was a child, salad for tea meant cold meats served with undressed lettuce, halved tomatoes and an occasional slice of cucumber. Beetroot soused in malt vinegar, hard-boiled eggs and spring onions were optional extras. For many decades this constituted the typical British salad. Now there seem few limits to what we can add to the salad bowl; the range of leaves increases every year, as do the types of oils and vinegars to dress them with. Salads are no longer just a tired garnish on the side of the plate but star attractions in their own right.

John Evelyn, the 17th-century diarist, is probably the most famous British salad maker. In his Salad Calendar, published in 1664, he lists well over 30 different types of salad leaves and herbs. Evelyn was heir to a great tradition of British salad making: the *grand sallets* of medieval and Elizabethan tables used many different kinds of leaves and vegetables, adding colour and flavour with edible flowers and sweet salad herbs. Evelyn's Calendar suggests mixtures of leaves and herbs for the salad bowl for every month of the year.

Hannah Glasse in *The Art of Cookery Made Plain and Easy*, first published in 1747, includes plenty of recipes for salads, including four versions of a dish she calls 'Salamongundy'. A salmagundi, as we now know it, brings together a variety of both cooked and raw vegetables and adds cooked poultry, fresh and cured meats, preserved fish, olives, capers and nuts. The whole would be dressed with oil, lemon and vinegar. The ingredients were either piled into a great, layered pyramid or arranged in separate bowls for guests to help themselves. It was decorated with herbs and edible flowers –

particularly nasturtiums, or 'Station-flowers' as Hannah Glasse calls them.

SALAD LEAVES

Evelyn's and Glasse's ideas for salad mixtures strike us now as quite modern. We too look to add variety to our salads with a whole range of ingredients. Modern John Evelyns such as Joy Larkcom, author of *The Salad Garden*, and Frances Smith, supplier of salad stuffs to many of the top London restaurants, have worked hard to encourage the use of Oriental and Japanese leaves and herbs, many of which are winter-hardy, in salads as well as the more familar chicories, lettuces and cresses.

Assembling a salad is a good exercise in contrasting textures and flavours. Partner sweet, crisp lettuces such as Cos, Romaine or the indispensable Little Gem with sharp or slightly bitter leaves such as young sorrel, red and white chicories, radicchio and curly endive. Other good, substantial leaves, especially suited to warm salads, are escarole, batavia and young spinach or ruby chard leaves. Bland, soft leaves such as lamb's lettuce are good with the peppery, smooth taste and texture of watercress. Other peppery leaves are salad rocket, the most popular, trendy leaf of the 1990s but one familiar to British gardeners in John Evelyn's day and before, red mustard leaves, nasturtium leaves (and flowers) and mizuna. For crisp, almost crystalline textures look to Iceberg lettuce, purslane, Japanese chrysanthemum leaves and Witloof chicory.

FRESH HERBS

Fresh herbs are excellent additions to a mixed salad. If you have a patch of ground or just a windowbox, a few herbs will transform your salads. Supermarkets sell an increasing

Previous page:
summer squash salad
with feta, lemon,
olives and mint
(page 43)
This page: oriental
aubergine salad
(page 47)

range of fresh herbs, but for best value buy large bunches of fragrant mint, flat-leaved parsley and dill from Greek or Cypriot greengrocers, or coriander, Kaffir lime leaves and Asian basil from Chinese or Asian food shops. Herbs can be used in whole sprigs, not just chopped into the dressing. Sprigs of flat-leaved parsley, fresh coriander, young sorrel and dill are excellent in salads. Chervil, a pretty, feathery herb with a mild aniseed taste, is a personal favourite. Other herbs are better roughly chopped or torn: basil, mint, fennel, chives. Aniseedy Sweet Cicely and cucumber-flavoured Salad Burnet are unusual herbs for the salad bowl. Edible flowers include chive flowers, nasturtiums, primroses and violets, though I think these should be used sparingly if the salad isn't to resemble a flower arrangement.

SALAD DRESSINGS

It is the dressing that makes a salad hang together. A basic salad dressing is made from good olive oil and wine vinegar in proportions that vary from authority to authority. The classic proportion is 3:1 of oil to vinegar (or lemon juice) but usually I use 5–6 tablespoons oil to 1 of good wine vinegar. A little mustard is essential too. But don't stop there: a salad should be dressed according to the company it is going to keep and the ingredients it's made from. Simply grilled fish requires a salad dressed with your best extra virgin oil, a squirt of lemon juice and a grinding of aromatic pepper. Chargrilled steak or lamb will take a much more assertively dressed salad: add herb and wholegrain mustards, garlic, chopped shallots and strong vinegars such as sherry vinegar and sweet-sour balsamic. A good, basic rule is that the strong-flavoured, substantially textured salad leaves or herbs can take assertive dressings. Subtler salad mixtures of young lettuces and sweet herbs need gentler treatment.

Not all dressings are based on the classic oil and vinegar vinaigrette. Several recipes in this chapter make use of Oriental and Asian ingredients for salad dressings. Thai salads are dressed with fragrant, sweet-sour mixtures of lime juice, rice vinegar and fish sauce (*nam pla*), they are sweetened with sugar and made hot with chilli. Other salad dressings in this chapter are based on dairy ingredients such as yoghurt and sour cream or their Asian counterpart – coconut milk.

Other good additions to salads include shaved or grated cheese, chopped nuts, crisp baked or fried croûtons, crumbled bacon or pancetta, or crisply fried onions, shallots or garlic (a favourite garnish to Thai salads). Many of these are now available ready-made from supermarkets but are quick and easy to make at home. Young goat's cheese, crumbled Lancashire or Wensleydale are excellent in spinach or watercress salads. Toasted nuts and seeds make a good final scattering on salads. Try matching the nuts or seeds to their appropriate oil. Pine nut oil and toasted pine nuts are delicious in rice salads or with smoked fish or Parmesan cheese. A little toasted sesame oil or pumpkin seed oil with the appropriate toasted seed is very good on Oriental salads of noodles and cooked vegetables.

Most salad recipes are open to variation and experimentation with different or unusual ingredients. Just remember the few basic 'rules' about keeping a contrast of texture and flavour. You will find many more ideas for salad dressings in Chapter 1.

Salad of grilled courgettes, fennel and feta cheese (page 45)

Asian pear, kiwi fruit
and avocado salad
with a citrus dressing

ASIAN PEAR, KIWI FRUIT AND AVOCADO SALAD WITH A CITRUS DRESSING

Asian or nashi pears are now quite common in our supermarkets and they have a wonderfully crisp texture, which makes them ideal in salads. If you cannot find them, substitute a crisp European pear (Rocha for example) or a Granny Smith apple, or even slices of honeydew melon.

Serves 4

FOR THE DRESSING:
1 teaspoon coriander seeds
5 tablespoons olive oil
shredded zest and juice of ½ orange
1 dessertspoon light rice (or cider) vinegar
shredded zest of 1 lime
salt, pepper and caster sugar
6 mint leaves, shredded
2 tablespoons soured or single cream

FOR THE SALAD:
about 100g/4oz salad leaves (red and white chicories, watercress, lettuces)
2 Asian pears, cored and sliced
2 kiwi fruit, peeled and cut into chunks
1 large ripe but firm avocado, peeled, stoned and sliced
½ red onion, peeled and thinly sliced
a few sprigs of mint and fennel

First make the dressing. Heat the coriander seeds in a small pan over a medium heat for a few minutes, then coarsely grind in a mortar or spice mill. Place in a bowl with the oil, a dessertspoon orange juice and the vinegar. Beat to mix. Blanch the orange and lime zests in plenty of boiling water for 3 minutes, then drain and refresh under the cold tap. Add to the dressing. Season to taste with salt, black pepper and caster sugar. Stir in the mint.

Wash and dry the salad leaves and arrange in a salad bowl. Toss the pears, kiwi fruit, avocado and onion with half the dressing. Arrange on the salad leaves. Beat the soured or single cream into the remaining dressing, adjust the seasoning, and drizzle over the salad.

Decorate with the sprigs of mint and fennel. Serve immediately, tossing the salad at the table.

See photograph overleaf

CHICKEN SALMAGUNDI

This salad – my interpretation of 17th- and 18th-century salads – makes a pretty dish to serve at a summer lunch. The side dishes can be as many or as varied as you wish: other suggestions are chopped salted herring or marinated anchovy, crisp, young radish or carrots, chopped nuts or olives. Serve the salmagundi with the Anchovy and Lemon Dressing on page 184.

Serves 4–6

1 x 1.5kg/3–3½lb free-range chicken, roasted or poached
1 crisp Cos, Romaine or Webb's lettuce
about 225g/8oz mixed salad leaves and herbs (rocket, watercress, young sorrel, Ruby Chard and nasturtium leaves)
12 hard-boiled quail's eggs or 6 hen's eggs

FOR THE SIDE DISHES:
225g/8oz French beans, topped and tailed
salt and freshly ground black pepper
6 tablespoons extra virgin olive oil
175ml/6fl oz cider vinegar or light rice vinegar
2 red onions, peeled
caster sugar
2 medium-sized cooked beetroot, peeled

TO GARNISH:
3 tablespoons chopped mixed chives and flat-leaved parsley
1 punnet salad cress
sprigs of fresh herbs (parsley, chervil, salad burnet, bronze fennel)
a few edible flowers (nasturtiums and chive flowers)

Carve the chicken into thin slices or strips or pull into fork-sized shreds, cover and set aside. Wash the lettuce and salad leaves, dry and refrigerate.

To make the side dishes: cook the beans in a large pan of salted water for 3–5 minutes until just tender. Drain, refresh under cold water then dry on kitchen paper and place in a bowl. Toss with 2 tablespoons oil, 2 teaspoons vinegar and salt and pepper. Cover and set aside.

Slice the red onions to make thin rings. Place in a colander, then pour over a kettleful of boiling water, shake to drain, then tip the onions into a small basin. Add 1 teaspoon sugar and 150ml/5fl oz vinegar. Cover and leave to stand for at least 30 minutes in the fridge. Cut the beetroot into strips and toss in a bowl with salt, pepper, 2 tablespoons oil and 2 teaspoons vinegar. Season with a pinch of caster sugar. Cover and set aside.

When ready to eat assemble the salmagundi: halve or quarter the eggs, depending on their size. Toss the torn lettuce leaves and salad herbs in the remaining oil and vinegar, and season. Arrange all the salad leaves on a large platter or in a large salad bowl. Arrange the chicken on the salad leaves. Drain the onion rings, which should now have turned a pretty pink. And arrange all the side dishes around the chicken, either in little heaps or in separate little bowls. Sprinkle each side dish with some chopped herbs. Finally, garnish with little bunches of salad cress, sprigs of fresh herbs and edible flowers. Serve immediately.

Chicken salmagundi
(page 39) with
anchovy and lemon
dressing (page 184)

PARSLEY SALAD

The best parsley to eat in whole sprigs is the flat-leaved kind. The assertive flavour of parsley is good matched with the strong flavours of capers, olives and anchovies. All these powerful tastes are balanced by the croûtons, which help soak up the dressing. This makes an ideal first-course salad.

Serves 4

1 clove garlic, peeled and bruised
6 tablespoons extra virgin olive oil
1 tablespoon salted capers, rinsed
6 large black olives, stoned
4 anchovy fillets, drained
½–1 teaspoon French mustard (one
    flavoured with herbes de Provence
    is especially good)
1–2 teaspoons balsamic vinegar
freshly ground black pepper
100g/4oz good white bread, sliced
40g/1½oz sprigs flat-leaved parsley,
    washed and dried
100g/4oz rocket and/or baby spinach
    leaves, washed and dried
40g/1½oz fresh Parmigiano
    Reggiano or Pecorino, cut into
    thin shavings with a vegetable
    peeler
2 tablespoons toasted pine nuts

To make the dressing, put the garlic and oil into a jar and leave to steep for a few hours, then discard the garlic (or, for a stronger flavour, chop and add to the dressing). Finely chop the capers, olives and anchovies. Place in a small bowl and blend in the mustard, then gradually add 3 tablespoons of the garlic-flavoured oil. Whisk in the vinegar to taste, then season with black pepper.

Heat the remaining oil in a roomy frying pan over a moderate heat. Cut the bread into 1cm/½in slices, then into rough croûtons. Fry the bread in the oil until lightly browned on both sides. Drain on kitchen paper. Place the parsley and rocket and/or spinach in a large salad bowl. Add the croûtons and toss with the dressing. Add the cheese and the pine nuts. Serve immediately.

Parsley salad

WARM SALMON AND PRAWN SALAD WITH A COCONUT AND LIME DRESSING

Thai fish sauce (*nam pla*) is the essential seasoning here and is available in Oriental and Asian food stores.

Serves 4-5

*about 175g/6oz mixed salad leaves
   (lettuce, watercress, young sorrel,
   etc)*
450g/1lb skinned salmon fillet
2 tablespoons sunflower oil
225g/8oz large shelled prawns
75g/3oz piece coconut cream, grated
*7.5cm/3 inch piece fresh lemon grass
   (optional)*
*2 tablespoons Thai fish sauce
   (nam pla)*
*finely grated zest and juice of
   1 lime*
*1 red or green chilli, de-seeded and
   finely sliced*
*salt, freshly ground black pepper and
   caster sugar*
*3 tablespoons finally shredded basil
   or coriander leaves*
*lime wedges, herb sprigs and chilli
   'flowers' to decorate*

Wash and dry the salad leaves and chill until ready to serve. Use to line a shallow serving dish. Cut the salmon across the grain to make 5mm/¼ inch slices. Heat the oil in a non-stick frying pan and fry the salmon briefly until just cooked. Then set aside. Add the prawns, cook for a few minutes, then add to the salmon. Add the coconut cream and the finely chopped lemon grass (if using) to the pan and allow the coconut cream to melt.

Turn off the heat and add the fish sauce, lime juice and zest, and the chilli. Season with salt, pepper and a pinch or two of sugar, and return the salmon and prawns to the pan, stir to mix then turn on to the salad leaves. Sprinkle over the shredded basil or coriander and garnish with lime wedges, herb sprigs and chilli 'flowers'.

Warm salmon and
prawn salad with a
coconut and lime
dressing

SUMMER SQUASH SALAD WITH FETA, LEMON, OLIVES AND MINT

Serves 4

450g/1lb small summer squash (patty pan or young green or yellow courgettes)
salt and freshly ground black pepper
3 tablespoons extra virgin olive oil
1½ teaspoons toasted cumin, coarsely ground
1–2 cloves garlic, peeled and finely chopped
½ teaspoon finely shredded lemon zest
½ teaspoon runny honey
1 tablespoon lemon juice, plus a little more to season
1 large or 2 small yellow peppers
2 tablespoons roughly chopped fresh mint
100g/4oz feta cheese, sliced
50g/2oz black olives, stoned
sprigs of mint, to garnish

Halve patty pan squash or slice the courgettes. Place in a bowl, toss with 1 teaspoon salt, then turn into a colander and leave to drain for about an hour. Rinse, then dry on a clean cloth. Heat the oil in a roomy frying pan which will take all the squash in a single layer, and cook the squash over a moderate heat until patched with brown and just tender. Add the cumin and garlic, and cook for 1–2 minutes more, then add the lemon zest. Cook for 30 seconds, then turn into a bowl and toss with the honey and lemon juice. Turn the grill to high, halve and de-seed the pepper(s) and grill, skin-side up, until the skin blackens and blisters. Pop into a bowl and place a plate on top and leave for 10 minutes for the steam to soften the pepper(s). Peel off the skin and slice the pepper, and add to the squash with the mint. When ready to serve, taste for seasoning, adding pepper and more lemon juice as required. Toss in the feta and the olives and garnish with sprigs of mint.

BEETROOT SALAD WITH WALNUT, ORANGE AND CORIANDER DRESSING

This salad makes an excellent accompaniment to cold roast duck or pork. Make sure you buy unvinegared beetroot or, even better, cook your own.

Serves 4

FOR THE DRESSING:
1 teaspoon coriander seeds, crushed
4 tablespoons walnut oil
50–75g/2–3oz walnut halves
1 teaspoon caster sugar
salt and freshly ground black pepper
1 tablespoon sunflower oil
1 tablespoon orange juice
1–2 teaspoons sherry vinegar
1 teaspoon finely grated orange zest
1 tablespoon snipped fresh chives

FOR THE SALAD:
4 small beetroot, cooked and skinned
large bunch watercress, trimmed,
  washed and dried
15g/½oz chervil or fresh coriander
  sprigs, washed and dried
a few young Swiss chard leaves
  (optional)

First make the dressing: heat a small frying pan over a low heat and 'toast' the coriander seed for a few minutes to release the fragrance, then tip into a bowl. Wipe out the pan and return to the heat. Add 1 tablespoon walnut oil and heat up. Add the walnut halves and fry very gently for a couple of minutes. Turn up the heat slightly, then scatter over the sugar. Cook, stirring frequently, for the sugar to caramelize (1–2 minutes). Turn on to kitchen paper then into a bowl. Season well with salt and pepper.

Blend together the remaining oils, orange juice and vinegar to taste. Add the orange zest and toasted coriander. Leave to stand for at least an hour for the flavours to blend, then season with salt and pepper and stir in the snipped chives. Cut the beetroot into strips or slices and toss with the dressing (preferably while still warm). Just before serving, toss in the watercress, herb sprigs and Swiss chard leaves (if using), then scatter over the toasted walnuts.

Beetroot salad with walnut, orange and coriander dressing

POTATO SALAD WITH ROCKET AND ANCHOVY

I love potato salads of all kinds. At its simplest a potato salad needs no more than the best-quality, freshly dug salad potatoes, scraped and boiled and dressed with your best extra virgin olive oil and a handful of chopped, fresh herbs (always include some fresh chives or chopped spring onion). If you can't get potatoes that good, you will need to add a bit more flavour. This recipe contrasts the earthy taste of potatoes with the crisp pepperiness of salad rocket. If you can't find good rocket, use a mixture of watercress and baby spinach and grind over a little more pepper.

Serves 6–8

FOR THE DRESSING:
5 tablespoons extra virgin olive oil
1 dessertspoon balsamic vinegar
½–1 teaspoon French tarragon
  mustard
salt and freshly ground black pepper
1 tablespoon snipped fresh chives
½ teaspoon finely shredded lemon rind

FOR THE SALAD:
1kg/2lb new, waxy-fleshed salad
  potatoes
1 small red onion, halved and sliced
  (or 5 spring onions, sliced)
100–150g/4–5oz salad rocket (see
  above)
a few young sorrel leaves, whole or

finely shredded (optional)
15g/½oz sprigs of flat-leaved parsley
  and/or fresh chervil
4 soft-boiled eggs, quartered
small tin of best-quality anchovy
  fillets, drained

Make the dressing by combining all the ingredients, adding mustard and seasoning to taste. Scrub the potatoes and boil in lightly salted water until tender. Drain and cool a little. Peel or not as liked, then slice into a roomy bowl and toss with the dressing while still warm. Add the onion. When ready to serve, toss in the rocket, sorrel (if using) and herb sprigs, add the eggs and anchovies and serve immediately.

SALAD OF GRILLED COURGETTES, FENNEL AND FETA CHEESE

Serves 4

4 medium-sized courgettes (about
  450g/1lb)
2 bulbs of Florence fennel
100g/4oz feta cheese
2–3 tablespoons chopped, mixed
  marjoram and flat-leaved parsley
sprigs of marjoram, to garnish

FOR THE MARINADE AND DRESSING:
5 tablespoons extra virgin olive oil
finely shredded zest and juice of
  ½ lemon
½–1 teaspoon dried oregano
salt and freshly ground black pepper
1 teaspoon cumin seeds, toasted and
  lightly crushed
1 teaspoon honey
1–2 teaspoons Pernod or ouzo

Cut the courgettes lengthways into 5mm/¼ inch slices. Trim and cut the fennel into wedges or slices, reserving any feathery tops. Mix together the ingredients for the marinade and pour into a shallow, non-metallic dish. Add the vegetables and turn to coat them thoroughly in the marinade. Set aside, covered, for up to 4 hours.

Heat the grill or grill pan. Remove the vegetables from the marinade and grill for about 5 minutes on each side or until tender and browned. Layer the vegetables in a serving dish, add the sliced or crumbled feta and scatter with the chopped herbs, including any reserved fennel tops. Pour over the remaining marinade and garnish with sprigs of marjoram. Serve at room temperature.

WARM SALAD OF ROASTED NEW POTATOES AND ASPARAGUS WITH RED PEPPER DRESSING

Roasting may seem like a rather brutal treatment for asparagus, which is more usually steamed or boiled, but this method concentrates the flavour of this delicious vegetable.

Serves 6–8

1kg/2lb new potatoes, scrubbed
about 225g/8oz fresh asparagus
about 200g/7oz mixed salad leaves
50g/2oz fresh Pecorino or Parmesan
  cheese, flaked or grated
sprigs of flat-leaved parsley and
  fresh basil, to serve

FOR THE DRESSING:
1 large ripe red pepper
9 tablespoons extra virgin olive oil
1 clove garlic
salt, freshly ground black pepper and
  caster sugar
2 dessertspoons balsamic vinegar
1 teaspoon chopped fresh thyme
16 basil leaves

First make the dressing. Halve and de-seed the pepper, then grill, skin-side up, until the skin chars and turns black. Place in a covered bowl or paper bag and leave for 10 minutes for the steam to soften the skin. Remove the skin, cut the pepper into small dice and place in a small bowl with 1 tablespoon oil. Set aside.

With the flat blade of a broad knife, bruise the garlic and peel, place in a screwtop jar with all the other ingredients except the basil leaves, season to taste, then shake to mix. Leave to stand for at least 1 hour for the garlic to impart its flavour. Heat the oven to 190°C/375°F/gas 5.

Cut the potatoes in half and combine in a bowl with half the dressing. Turn on to a baking sheet and cook, uncovered, for 40 minutes in the hot oven, turning the vegetables from time to time. Add the red pepper and torn basil leaves to the remaining dressing and set aside. Cut off the asparagus tips with 7.5cm/3 inch of stem. (Use the remaining stalk for soup.) Add the asparagus to the pota-toes and stir to coat in the oil. Cook for a further 10–15 minutes until the asparagus is just tender and the pota-toes cooked, stirring once. When ready to serve, toss the salad leaves in a roomy bowl with the rest of the dressing (remove and discard the whole garlic clove). Remove the pota-toes and asparagus from the oven and add to the salad using a slotted spoon, toss to mix, then quickly arrange on six serving plates (or serve from one large salad bowl). Sprinkle over the Pecorino or Parmesan and decorate with the herb sprigs. Serve immediately.

OTHER IDEAS FOR ASPARAGUS
1. Serve cold, steamed asparagus with an orange-flavoured mayonnaise or vinaigrette flavoured with a little orange zest and toasted, ground cumin seed.

2. Serve warm, roasted or grilled asparagus with *dukkah* – an Egyptian spice mixture of toasted hazelnuts, sesame seeds, cumin and coriander – seasoned with plenty of salt and black pepper. Serve lime wedges and olive oil for people to help themselves. Or dress cooked asparagus with a simple vinaigrette and top with flakes of Pecorino or Parmesan cheese.

3. Serve hot, steamed or boiled asparagus with an oil and lemon juice dressing with plenty of chopped chervil and skinned, de-seeded tom-ato. Serve each person with a still-warm, soft-boiled free-range egg (or several quail's eggs) – the asparagus dipped into the mixture of soft egg yolk and tomato vinaigrette is very delicious. This is easier to manage for 2 or 4 people than for a larger dinner (unless you allow people to shell their own eggs).

ORIENTAL AUBERGINE SALAD

See photograph on
page 36

Serves 4

2 aubergines (weighing about
  450g/1lb)
4–5 tablespoons groundnut oil
1 tablespoon toasted sesame seeds
1 tablespoon fresh coriander sprigs

FOR THE DRESSING:
1 tablespoon sesame oil
1 clove garlic, thinly sliced
1 mild fresh red chilli, de-seeded and
  thinly sliced
6 spring onions, trimmed and sliced
3 tablespoons soy sauce
2 tablespoons dark rice or balsamic
  vinegar
black pepper

Slice the aubergines lengthways in
5mm/¼ inch slices. Heat the grill and
pour the oil on to a baking sheet.
Turn the aubergine slices in the oil,
then grill, for about 5 minutes on
each side, until browned and soft.
Cool a little, then cut into long, nar-
row strips. Heap into a serving dish.

For the dressing, heat the oil in a
frying pan and cook the garlic for a
few minutes until beginning to
brown. Add the chilli and spring
onions and cook for 1 minute, stirring all the time. Add the soy sauce,
vinegar and 1 tablespoon water, allow
to bubble for a minute or so, then
pour over the aubergine. Season well
with pepper. Allow to stand, covered,
for at least 1 hour (it may be prepared the day before). Return to
room temperature before sprinkling
over the sesame seeds and coriander
sprigs.

Warm salad of
roasted new potatoes
and asparagus with
red pepper dressing

PRAWN, PAPAYA AND LYCHEE SALAD WITH LIME AND CHILLI DRESSING

This fragrant, sweet-sour salad would make an excellent opening to a rich meal. It is full of lively, refreshing flavours and looks beautiful too. The lime leaves add a delicious flavour and are sometimes available in big supermarkets and good Asian food stores. They freeze well, so it's worth buying a few when you come across them. Test the chilli for heat and add to taste.

Serves 4

1 ripe but firm papaya (paw paw)
225g/8oz fresh lychees, peeled
juice of ½ lime
350g/12oz large, peeled, cooked
*   prawns*
7.5cm/3 inch piece cucumber (peeled
*   if preferred), sliced*
50g/2oz young mangetout
25–50g/1–2oz alfalfa sprouts
*   (optional)*

FOR THE DRESSING:
juice and finely shredded zest of 1
*   lime*
2 teaspoons caster sugar
½–1 tablespoon Thai fish sauce
*   (nam pla)*
½–1 red chilli, de-seeded
1 teaspoon light rice vinegar
a few sprigs of coriander, basil,
*   sweet cicely or mint (or a mixture)*
2 Kaffir lime leaves, very finely
*   shredded (optional)*

Cut the papaya in half, scoop out the seeds, peel and slice. Peel and de-stone the lychees. Place the fruit in a bowl and sprinkle with the lime juice. Add the prawns and cucumber and arrange on four serving plates (or one large serving platter). Wash, de-string and finely shred the mangetout and arrange on the plate with the alfalfa sprouts, if using.

For the dressing: mix together the lime juice and sugar and stir in ½ tablespoon fish sauce. Blanch the lime zest in boiling water for 3 minutes, drain and refresh in cold water. Finely dice half the chilli and add to the dressing with the lime zest and vinegar. Taste, adding extra fish sauce, vinegar or sugar as you prefer. Cut the rest of the chilli into fine strips.

Arrange the herb sprigs on the salad, then spoon over the dressing. Finally, sprinkle over the shredded lime leaves, if using, and the chilli strips.

Prawn, papaya and
lychee salad with
lime and chilli
dressing

VEGETABLES

Whether I'm planning a special meal or simply something to eat for supper, I tend to organize my ideas around seasonal vegetables. And when I feel that I'll never be able to come up with another recipe or food idea ever again, a visit to my local vegetable market or the produce section of a large supermarket will always provide some much-needed inspiration.

As you may have gathered, I love vegetables, their shapes, colours and, most importantly, their huge variety of tastes and textures. I love the seasonality of vegetables, too. Don't get me wrong, I'm no culinary Luddite who wants to turn back the clock of modern distribution and marketing techniques. I, too, treat sweet peppers and aubergines as year-round produce. I, too, expect fresh herbs to be available whenever I want them. But there are limits. I don't want Brussels sprouts or parsnips in July, nor asparagus and sweetcorn in January. I have my hobbyhorses too. Why, if we can fly a mangetout halfway round the world, can we not buy decent fresh peas and broad beans in the shops? Why, when we are perhaps the best celery-growing nation on earth, is most of the celery in the shops green, sappy and virtually flavourless? Why do carrots rarely taste of carrots and tomatoes of anything at all? Admittedly, as a farmer's son, I grew up believing that all cauliflowers tasted like the ones my father was so inordinately proud of. Peas for dinner often meant that someone had picked them only a few hours earlier. But I still find it a strange compliment when people say, 'These carrots are delicious, they taste of, well, carrots.' People are so used to vegetables as purely bland fillers on the plate that they are surprised when they actually get ones that taste as they should.

COOKING VEGETABLES

There's no doubting that vegetables are versatile. They adapt to many different cooking techniques. They roast, grill, steam and fry. But we should be careful not to undervalue cooking vegetables by the method to which the French rather pointedly refer as *à l'anglaise* (i.e. in plenty of boiling salted water). I wouldn't want the first fresh-dug potatoes of the season cooked any other way than boiled, with perhaps a sprig of mint, and served with lashings of lightly salted butter. Young peas and broad beans, broccoli and cauliflower are best boiled. The freshest of fresh sweetcorn should be boiled too, though grilling will rescue older corn. On the other hand, certain vegetables should never even see water. Courgettes, aubergines and sweet potatoes come to mind. I'm not that fond of boiled carrots either.

Many vegetables grill surprisingly well. Some, like leeks and potatoes, need a preliminary cooking in boiling, salted water. Others grill from raw, brushed with olive or flavoured oil. Sweet potatoes and parsnips grill surprisingly quickly and grilling concentrates their delicious sweetness. Most of the Mediterranean vegetables grill well: sweet peppers and onions, courgettes, aubergines and fennel. Hold slices of sweet red or yellow onion together on a skewer and salt courgettes before grilling to get rid of some of their water. The first flush of English asparagus should be steamed or boiled, tips proud of the water, but later on asparagus grills well and has a delicious concentration of flavour. Some salad vegetables will also grill, like chicory and radicchio (especially the long *radicchio di Treviso*) and spring onions.

Previous page: pan-fried squash with onions, mushrooms, chilli and cumin (page 62)
This page: salad of peas and beans with a lemon and herb dressing (page 52); and fried baby carrots with cumin and mint (top, page 53)

Roasting also concentrates the flavour of vegetables. I like to roast mixtures of root vegetables, adding some spices and aromatics for flavour. A little vinegar or citrus juice will balance the sweetness of root vegetables cooked in this way. One of my favourite ways of cooking carrots is in a covered casserole with ground coriander seed, a little orange zest and muscovado sugar, a knob of butter and the juice of an orange. Cook for about an hour, stirring once or twice, while you have the oven on for a roast or casserole. Winter squash are excellent baked with butter, cream, or olive oil. Try chilli, sage or nutmeg as flavourings. Or bake cubes of winter squash with a coconut, garlic and lime paste.

POTATOES

Potatoes are probably my favourite vegetable. I love the first Jersey Royals with nothing more than lightly salted butter, I like grilled potatoes with grilled meat or fish and I adore a *gratin dauphinois*, either by itself or with roast lamb or beef. Roast potatoes are a great favourite too. Parboil peeled potatoes in salted water for 10 minutes. Drain thoroughly then shake the dry potatoes in the pan to roughen their outer surfaces. Heat about 5mm/¼ inch fat in a roasting tin at about 200°C/400°F/gas 6 until hot. Turn the potatoes in the fat, then roast, turning once or twice, for 1¼ hours or until crisp and golden. The best fats to use for roast potatoes are, in descending order, goose, pork, duck and beef. If you have none of these use a mixture of olive and sunflower oils with a little butter for flavour.

MASHES AND PURÉES

Mashed potatoes are the ultimate comfort food, but make a surprisingly good accompaniment to summer grilled fish, meat and poultry as well as the more expected winter roasts and casseroles. My favourite flavoured mash is Champ, which has lightly cooked spring onions and an unhealthily large amount of butter beaten in. But you can add other things to your mashed spuds. A little soaked saffron and some fish stock makes a good mash for fish; lots of extra virgin olive oil and some grated Parmesan makes a mash that goes well with beef and pork dishes and sausages. Better still are mixtures of potatoes mashed with other root vegetables. Potatoes add the right texture while parsnips, celeriac, Jerusalem artichokes or swede provide the flavour. Add a few whole garlic cloves as the roots cook and mash with either butter or olive oil and some warm milk or cream. Nutmeg and lots of freshly ground pepper make good additions.

You can make more exotic vegetables into mashes or purées too. Sweet potato and winter squash (onion squash is particularly good) are good baked, then scooped out of their skins and mashed with butter, olive oil or cream. Their sweet flavours respond well to a little citrus sharpness (orange and lime) and are good spiked with some chilli heat. Mix in some Tabasco or some chilli and garlic paste. Or make a purée of sweet potato with coconut milk and a teaspoonful of Thai green chilli paste. A little chopped fresh coriander is good with squash or sweet potato purées. Or try a brilliant orange purée of carrots with a little briefly fried fresh ginger and crushed coriander seeds, add a little orange zest and lots of freshly ground black pepper.

Elsewhere in the book you'll find far more ideas and recipes for using both commonplace and unusual vegetables. Look at the Fish Baked with Root Vegetables and Ginger on page 71; or the Sautéed Chicken Breasts with Salsify and Rosemary on page 82.

SALOF PEAS AND BEANS WITH A LEMON AND HERB DRESSING

The lemony dressing in this salad complements the green sweetness of fresh peas and beans, and fresh herbs add the right note of summer fragrance. Serve the salad as a first course with crusty bread or as an accompaniment to a shell-fish salad or cold roast pork or lamb.

Serves 6

salt and freshly ground black pepper
225g/8oz shelled broad beans (about
    1kg/2lb in their pods)
225g/8oz young, fresh peas (about
    750g/1½lb in their pods)
450g/1lb mixture of any or all of the
    following: fine French beans,
    mangetout peas, sugar snap peas or
    asparagus peas
225g/8oz young, fine asparagus
    (optional)
75–100g/3–4oz young pea shoots,
    sprouted beans or alfalfa
    (or a mixture)
2 tablespoons extra virgin olive oil
lemon juice

FOR THE DRESSING:
2 fillets of canned anchovies, drained
1 level teaspoon Dijon mustard
    (tarragon mustard is good)
2 tablespoons extra virgin olive oil
5 tablespoons soured cream or thick
    single cream
finely grated zest and juice of ½–1
    lemon
2–3 tablespoons chopped fresh herbs
    (chervil, parsley, mint)
2 tablespoons snipped fresh chives or
    2 spring onions finely sliced

Bring a large pan of boiling salted water to the boil. Throw in the broad beans and cook for 4–5 minutes. Drain, cool under the cold tap, then slip off the light green outer coat of each bean (if the beans are very young this step may be omitted). Top and tail the mangetout, sugar snap or asparagus peas and cut the stalk end from the French beans. Trim any woody stalk from the asparagus, if using. Cook all the vegetables either in boiling salted water or by steaming until just tender. The mangetout and sugar snap peas will need very little cooking, or use them raw.

When cooked, drain, then place in a roomy bowl and toss with the olive oil and a squeeze of lemon juice. Mix carefully so as not to break the vegetables.

For the dressing, crush the anchovies in a bowl or mortar until they are a paste. Gradually work in the mustard and 2 tablespoons oil. Then beat in the cream. Season to taste with black pepper (the anchovies should provide enough salt), then add lemon zest and juice to taste. Finally stir in half the herbs. Stir the remaining herbs into the peas and beans and arrange on a serving dish with the pea shoots or sprouted seeds. Pour over the dressing and serve immediately.

VARIATIONS
Add some cooked young carrots or Jersey Royal potatoes to the salad. Replace some of the olive oil with a lemon-flavoured olive oil if you like, but add sparingly as the lemon flavour can be quite strong.

See photograph on
page 50

FRIED BABY CARROTS WITH CUMIN AND MINT

This is a delicious recipe slightly adapted from Sophie Grigson's inspirational book on vegetable cookery, *Eat Your Greens*. I have added cumin seeds and chilli to her recipe as I love the spiciness and slight heat with sweet, young carrots. You could use fresh coriander instead of mint, too.

Serves 4

450g/1lb small, baby carrots, scraped and trimmed
3 tablespoons extra virgin olive oil
1–2 teaspoons cumin seeds, bruised in a mortar and pestle
¼–½ teaspoon dried red chilli flakes (optional)
salt, freshly ground black pepper and caster sugar
juice of ½ a lemon
2 tablespoons chopped mint

Halve the carrots lengthways if bigger than your little finger. Heat the oil in a heavy frying pan large enough to take the carrots in a single layer. Fry the carrots over a low to medium heat, shaking frequently until tender and patched with golden brown (about 20–25 minutes). Add the cumin and chilli, if using, after about 10 minutes cooking. Then add ½–1 teaspoon sugar and cook for 2 minutes more to caramelise slightly. Place in bowl, toss with the lemon juice and season with a little salt and pepper. Cool for a minute or two, then toss in the chopped mint. Serve immediately or allow to cool to room temperature and serve as a salad.

PARSNIPS COOKED WITH GARLIC AND GINGER

Many Indian regional dishes start by preparing a paste of ginger and garlic, sometimes adding onions and chillies, which cooks to form a delicious coating to the meat or vegetables in the dish. Sweet parsnips have a natural affinity with Indian spices.

Serves 4–5

750g/1½lb parsnips, peeled and trimmed
salt and freshly ground black pepper
5cm/2 inch piece fresh ginger, peeled and chopped
1 fresh green chilli, de-seeded and chopped
2–4 cloves garlic, peeled
4 tablespoons sunflower oil
1 teaspoon whole cumin seeds
1 teaspoon black nigella seeds (kalonji)
225g/8oz mushrooms, halved
1–2 teaspoons ground coriander
lemon juice
2 tablespoons chopped fresh coriander

Cook the parsnips in boiling salted water until almost tender. Drain, cool and cut into 2.5cm/1 inch pieces. Put the ginger, chilli and garlic into a processor or liquidizer with 100ml/3½fl oz water and blend to make a paste. Heat the oil in a large frying pan or wok over a medium heat and then add the cumin and nigella seeds. Now add the paste from the blender and cook for a couple of minutes. Add the parsnips, mushrooms and 1 teaspoon ground coriander. Add about 250ml/8fl oz water and salt to taste. Cover and cook, stirring occasionally, for about 10–15 minutes. Uncover and test the seasoning, adding more coriander, salt, black pepper and lemon juice to taste. Continue to cook until the sauce is thick. Serve sprinkled with the fresh chopped coriander.

SUMMER TURNIPS WITH ORANGE AND CORIANDER

Young white turnips make a delicious vegetable, especially with roast or grilled duck, pork or lamb. You could also cook young kohlrabi like this, making sure that they are no bigger than a golf ball. These vegetables have a natural pepperiness, which is emphasized in this recipe by the coriander and orange.

Serves 4–5

750g/1½lb young turnips or kohlrabi
salt and freshly ground black pepper
1½ tablespoons olive oil or melted
  butter
1½ teaspoons coriander seeds,
  coarsely ground
2 teaspoons sugar
the finely shredded zest of ½ orange
the juice of 1 orange
1–2 tablespoons chopped fresh
  coriander, parsley or mint (or a
  mixture)
1–2 teaspoons walnut oil (optional)

If the turnips are really young, leave unpeeled and just trim the tops (young turnip tops are delicious, blanch and add to these turnips towards the end of cooking). Older turnips and kohlrabi will need to be peeled. Cut the vegetables in halves or quarters, depending on size. Bring a large pan of salted water to the boil. Throw in the turnips and cook for 2–3 minutes (give kohlrabi a little longer). Drain.

Heat the olive oil in a deep frying pan until moderately hot and cook the turnips for 4–5 minutes until just beginning to brown. Add the coriander seeds and sugar, and fry for 2–3 minutes more, stirring, until the sugar caramelizes slightly. Add the orange zest and juice and 2 tablespoons water, and cook until the turnips are cooked and the liquid reduced to a sticky glaze. Keep the heat fairly low and stir once or twice. Add a little extra water if the turnips look like burning before they are tender. Season to taste with salt and pepper, then toss in the chopped herbs and walnut oil, if using. Serve immediately.

VARIATION
Turnips with meat glaze are delicious with roast beef. Parboil 750g/1½lb young turnips, then drain and sauté in 25g/1oz butter until tender and lightly browned. Add 2–3 tablespoons of the juices from the roast joint or of reduced beef stock. Cook to reduce the liquid to a sticky glaze. Toss in a little wholegrain mustard if you like, then serve immediately, sprinkled with a little chopped parsley and/or thyme.

GRILLED CHICORY

The slightly bitter taste of grilled Witloof and red chicory goes excellently with beef and pork. Red Treviso chicory would be ideal for this dish but is hard to come by. The familiar red, round *radicchio di Chioggia* is almost as good.

Serves 8

4 plump heads of Belgian Witloof
　chicory
4 heads radicchio or red Treviso
　chicory (radicchio di Treviso)
4 tablespoons extra virgin olive oil
salt and black pepper
1–2 teaspoons balsamic vinegar

Preheat the grill to high and line the grill pan with foil. Strip off any damaged outer leaves of the chicons and cut in half (or quarters if very large). Lay on the grill pan, pour over half the oil and season well. Grill for about 10 minutes, brushing with the remaining oil halfway through cooking. Serve immediately, sprinkled with the vinegar.

GRILLED POTATOES

These are not a product of the nineties fashion for grilling but a delicious method of cooking potatoes from the early part of this century and adapted from a recipe given in Arabella Boxer's fascinating *Book of English Food*. You can marinate the potatoes with chopped onion, garlic or herbs such as rosemary or thyme, but these are best removed before grilling as they can turn unpleasantly bitter if they burn under the grill.

Serves 4

750g/1½lb waxy variety potatoes
salt and freshly ground black pepper
135ml/4½fl oz extra virgin olive oil
1 tablespoon balsamic, sherry or wine
　vinegar
1 small onion or 2 fat cloves garlic
　and/or 1 tablespoon chopped fresh
　rosemary or thyme leaves

Scrub the potatoes and cook in boiling, salted water until just cooked. Drain, cool, then skin if you like (I quite like the skin left on). Slice the potatoes quite thickly (5mm/¼ inch). Then marinate with the olive oil, vinegar and the chopped onion (or garlic) and/or herbs.

Preheat the grill to hot and lay the slices on a stout baking sheet, brushing off most of the flavourings. (The odd bit of herb or onion doesn't matter too much.)

Season the potatoes with a little salt and pepper and grill for about 5–6 minutes on each side or until golden brown and crisp.

GRILLED SWEET POTATOES WITH CHILLI, LEMON AND GARLIC AÏOLI

Unlike ordinary potatoes, sweet potatoes (both orange and white varieties) do not need pre-cooking before grilling. They cook surprisingly quickly and caramelize deliciously because of their sugar content. In fact you need to watch them like a hawk as they finish cooking, because they can easily burn. Served with a spicy, garlicky aïoli sauce, these sweet potatoes make a superb first course or main meal with salad.

Serves 5–6

1kg/2lb sweet potatoes
6–8 tablespoons olive oil
salt and freshly ground black pepper

FOR THE AÏOLI:
3–5 cloves garlic, peeled and roughly chopped
salt and freshly ground black pepper
2 egg yolks
up to 300ml/10fl oz good-quality olive oil or a mixture of olive and grape-seed oils
juice and finely grated zest of ½ lemon
½ fresh red chilli, de-seeded and finely chopped
½ teaspoon mild chilli powder (optional)
¼–½ teaspoon finely ground toasted cumin

First make the aïoli. Make sure the eggs and oil are at room temperature. Crush the garlic with a pinch of salt in a large mortar and pestle or bowl, then stir in the egg yolks. Gradually whisk in the oil a drop at a time, and when about half the oil has been added the remainder may be added in a steady stream.

The aïoli is ready when as thick as soft butter, so you may not need all the oil. Season with pepper, then stir in the lemon juice to taste. Stir in the lemon zest, chilli, chilli powder, if using, and toasted cumin. Leave to stand a little for the flavours to mature. Then correct the seasoning.

Scrub the sweet potatoes and peel only if the skins seem thick and old. Slice into 5mm/¼ inch slices. Lay on a baking sheet and brush with some of the oil. Season with salt and pepper. Preheat the grill to hot, then cook the potatoes about 10cm/4 inches away from the heat. Grill for about 5 minutes on the first side, then 2–3 minutes on the other side, brushing once or twice with the remaining oil. Serve hot with the aïoli sauce.

CABBAGE WITH FENNEL SEEDS AND SAGE

Serves 6–8

1 large Savoy cabbage
1 medium onion, peeled
2 tablespoons olive or groundnut oil
1 teaspoon mustard seeds
½ teaspoon fennel seeds, lightly crushed
salt and freshly ground black pepper
5–6 fresh sage leaves, shredded

Cut the cabbage into quarters, discard the central core and shred the leaves finely with a sharp knife. Halve the onion and thinly slice. Heat the oil in a large saucepan, and fry the mustard and fennel seeds for 2–3 minutes. Add the onion and fry over a medium heat until softened and beginning to brown. Add the cabbage and turn in the oil.

Cover and cook for 2–3 minutes. Turn the cabbage thoroughly, season with ½ teaspoon salt and add 5 tablespoons water. Cover and cook until the cabbage is tender but still crisp, turning once or twice. Stir in the sage, season with pepper and more salt to taste, and cook a few minutes more before serving.

ROAST PARSNIPS WITH GARLIC AND CUMIN

Parsnips are a very British vegetable. The French, especially, look askance at the idea of eating them and mutter darkly about animal feed, but is there a better accompaniment to roast beef? Cumin is another flavour that goes well with beef and with the sweet taste of parsnips.

Serves 6–8

1.5kg/3lb parsnips, peeled
salt and black pepper
3–4 tablespoons beef dripping or
  vegetable oil
2 teaspoons whole cumin seeds
2 cloves garlic, peeled and chopped

Cut the parsnips into wedges and cook in boiling salted water for 5 minutes. Drain.

Preheat the oven to 220°C/425°F/ gas 7. Put the dripping or oil into a stout roasting tin and put in the oven for 10 minutes, then add the parsnips, turning them with a slotted spoon to coat in the oil. Season well.

Return to the oven and cook for 40 minutes, turning once or twice. Add the cumin and the garlic and cook for a further 10–15 minutes, turning once. Transfer to a serving dish with a slotted spoon and sprinkle with a little salt.

Grilled sweet
potatoes with chilli,
lemon and garlic
aïoli

POTATOES AND FENNEL BAKED WITH SAFFRON AND GARLIC

Serves 4

large pinch of saffron strands
750g/1½lb potatoes, peeled
3 bulbs Florence fennel
4 tablespoons extra virgin olive oil
1 teaspoon fennel seeds, lightly
  crushed
6–8 cloves garlic, peeled and halved
salt and freshly ground black pepper
175ml/6fl oz vegetable stock or water
1½ tablespoons sherry vinegar or red
  wine vinegar

Soak the saffron in 3 tablespoons hot water for 10 minutes. Set oven to 200°C/400°F/gas 6. Cut potatoes into medium-sized pieces, trim the fennel, reserving any feathery tops, and cut into quarters or thick slices.

Put the oil and fennel seeds into a large baking or gratin dish and add the potatoes, fennel and garlic. Turn the vegetables over to coat with the oil and fennel seeds. Season with 1 teaspoon salt and black pepper.

Mix together the saffron, the stock (or water) and the vinegar, and pour over the vegetables. Cover the dish with foil and bake in the hot oven for 30–35 minutes.

Remove the foil, turn the vegetables, and cook, uncovered, for a further 25–30 minutes, until the vegetables are tender and browned and almost all the liquid has been absorbed.

Sprinkle with a little more salt and the chopped fennel tops before serving.

ROASTED ROOT VEGETABLES WITH OLIVE OIL AND GARLIC

Serves 6–8

450g/1lb small red potatoes, peeled
350g/12oz piece peeled celeriac
450g/1lb carrots, peeled
3 medium-sized parsnips, peeled
salt and freshly ground black pepper
5 tablespoons extra virgin olive oil
1 head garlic, separated into
  individual cloves but not peeled
2 tablespoons balsamic vinegar or red
  wine vinegar
1 heaped teaspoon mild paprika
1½ teaspoons coriander seeds, roughly
  crushed
sea salt

Preheat the oven to 200°C/400°F/gas 6. Cut the potatoes and celeriac into similar-sized pieces. Cut the carrots and parsnips into wedges. Place potatoes and celeriac in a medium-sized saucepan with 1 teaspoon salt, cover with water, bring to the boil and simmer for 5 minutes. Drain, reserving 5 tablespoons of the water.

Put the oil into a baking dish and heat in the oven, then add all the vegetables including the cloves of garlic. Turn the vegetables in the oil to coat. Mix together the vinegar, spices and the reserved potato water. Season with ½ teaspoon salt and black pepper. Pour over the vegetables and roast, turning 2 or 3 times, for 1–1½ hours until tender and browned. Sprinkle with a little coarse salt before serving.

ROASTED SHALLOTS WITH CHESTNUTS AND BACON

When skinned, fresh chestnuts have the most delicious flavour and texture. Dry-roasted and skinned chestnuts can now be bought in jars and vacuum packs, and these make an adequate, easier alternative for hard-pressed cooks. The easiest way to peel shallots and small onions is to pour boiling water over them, leave to stand for a few minutes, then drain and the skin should slip off quite easily.

Serves 6–8

175g/6oz bacon or pancetta, in one piece
1 tablespoon olive oil or goose fat
450g/1lb shallots or small onions, peeled
1 teaspoon caster sugar
2 tablespoons sherry vinegar or red wine vinegar
450g/1lb skinned, cooked fresh or bottled chestnuts
freshly ground black pepper

De-rind the bacon or pancetta and cut into thick matchstick strips about 2.5cm/1 inch long. Heat the oil or fat in a frying pan and cook the bacon or pancetta until browned but not burned. Set aside.

Preheat the oven to 200°C/400°F/ gas 6. Fry the shallots (or onions) gently in the bacon fat until browned, add the caster sugar and cook for a few minutes until the sugar caramelizes. Add the vinegar and cook for 1 minute. Turn into a shallow roasting dish and cook, uncovered, in the oven for 30 minutes or until the shallots are tender and well browned. Add the chestnuts and bacon and cook for a further 5 minutes.

Grind over the black pepper just before serving.

MASHED NEEPS

Mashed neeps are traditionally served with haggis and malt whisky on Burns Night, which is on 25th January. But they are too good to reserve for just one night of the year. I like to add some potato. It helps the texture of the mash and softens the sometimes too assertive flavour of the swede. This mixture of swede and potato is known as Clapshot (don't ask me why). Excellent with sausages of all kinds, with game and with fried, dry-cure bacon.

Serves 4–5

450g/1lb swede, peeled
225g/8oz potatoes (Estima are excellent), peeled
salt, freshly ground black pepper
freshly grated nutmeg
50g/2oz butter
50–85ml/2–3fl oz single cream

Cut the swede and potato into similar-sized chunks and place in a large saucepan. Cover with cold water, add 1 teaspoon salt, cover and bring to the boil. Simmer, covered, for 20–25 minutes until the vegetables are tender. Drain thoroughly and mash (best in a *mouli légumes*). Beat in the butter and reheat gently, adding the cream. Correct the seasoning, adding lots of black pepper and some grated nutmeg. Serve immediately.

CELERIAC PURÉE WITH ALMONDS

This recipe is based on one from Frances Bissell's *Real Meat Cookbook*. As she points out, it makes a delightful accompaniment to roasts of all kinds.

Serves 6

1 large head celeriac (750g/1½lb),
    peeled
225–350g/8–12oz floury potatoes,
    peeled
4–6 cloves garlic, peeled
salt and freshly ground black pepper
75g/3oz butter or 6 tablespoons extra
    virgin olive oil
6–7 tablespoons milk or cream
freshly grated nutmeg
50g/2oz flaked or sliced almonds

Cut the celeriac and potatoes into similar-sized chunks and cook with the garlic, in boiling, lightly salted water until tender. Drain and purée with a potato masher, ricer or vegetable mill. Season well to taste, mashing in 50g/2oz butter (or 4 tablespoons oil) and the milk or cream. Add freshly grated nutmeg to taste. Pile into a heated serving dish. Fry the almonds in the remaining butter (or oil) until browned, pour over the celeriac and serve immediately.

See photograph on
page 65

CHAMP

In my opinion this Irish dish makes the best mash there is.

Serves 4–5

750g/1½lb floury variety potatoes
salt and freshly ground black pepper
250ml/8fl oz milk
1 bunch of spring onions, trimmed
    but with some green leaves left on
at least 100g/4oz slightly salted
    butter, chilled

Scrub the potatoes and cook in lightly salted boiling water until tender. Drain, then skin and, for the lightest mash, put through a *mouli légumes*

or use a potato masher (on no account use a food processor as this turns potatoes into glue). Place the milk in a saucepan with the finely sliced spring onions and half the butter, bring to the boil and cook for a few minutes. Stir into the potatoes, adding pepper and more salt if liked. Reheat over a gentle heat.

Mound into 4 small, heated serving dishes, make a hollow at the top of each and divide the remaining butter between them. Serve immediately with more butter.

PARSNIP AND GARLIC PURÉE WITH PINE NUTS

Serves 6

450g/1lb parsnips, peeled and
    trimmed
225g/8oz potatoes, peeled
4 cloves garlic, peeled
salt and freshly ground black pepper
freshly grated nutmeg
100ml/3½fl oz single or double cream
50g/2oz butter
40g/1½oz pine nuts, toasted

Cut the parsnips and potatoes into equal-sized chunks and cook them, with the garlic, in boiling, salted water until the vegetables are tender. Drain and mash thoroughly, seasoning with plenty of pepper and nutmeg. Mash in the cream and half the butter. Melt the remaining butter in a small pan, then add the pine nuts. Pile the parsnips into a warmed serving dish, make a slight hollow at the top and pour over the butter/pine nut mixture. Serve immediately.

GRATIN DAUPHINOIS

If I were asked, hand on heart, to name my favourite food, this dish would have to figure near the top of the list. The alchemy involved in transforming two simple ingredients – potatoes and cream – into something so deliciously comforting is well-nigh miraculous. Ideal with roast lamb or beef, it is also delicious by itself.

Serves 4–5

750g/1½lb medium-sized potatoes
  (Estima and Desirée are good
  varieties)
1 clove garlic, halved
50g/2oz butter
salt and freshly ground black pepper
300ml/½ pint double cream

Preheat the oven to 190°C/375°F/gas 5. Peel the potatoes and slice fairly thinly (about as thick as a 50 pence piece). Rub the garlic vigorously over the bottom and sides of a shallow, earthenware gratin dish of about 1.5 litre/2½ pint capacity. Leave some bits of crushed garlic in the dish. Butter the dish generously with just under half the butter.

Layer the potatoes in the dish, seasoning between each layer and dotting with a little butter. Finish with a neat layer of overlapping slices and dot with the remaining butter. Pour the cream over the potatoes. Cover the dish with foil and cook the potatoes for 35–40 minutes. Turn down the heat to 180°C/350°F/gas 4, uncover the potatoes and cook for a further hour until golden brown and tender. Set aside for 5–10 minutes before serving.

JANSSON'S TEMPTATION

As with all famous 'national' dishes, there are many points of view on how this Swedish dish of anchovies, potatoes and onions baked in cream should be made. Should the potatoes be coarsely grated or cut into matchstick strips? Should Swedish or Norwegian 'anchovies' be used (actually salted sprats) or the Mediterranean anchovies canned in oil? Whichever way you make it, it is a delicious supper dish. Serve a salad alongside.

Serves 4

15g/½oz butter
750g/1½lb waxy-variety potatoes,
  peeled
2 large yellow onions, peeled and
  thinly sliced
2 tins of anchovy fillets in olive oil
salt and freshly ground black pepper
300ml/10fl oz mixed single and
  double cream

Preheat the oven to 200°C/400°F/gas 6. Lightly butter a 1.5–1.75 litre/2½–3 pint gratin dish. Coarsely shred the potatoes or cut into thin matchstick strips. Make a layer of potatoes in the dish, followed by a layer of onions. Season with black pepper. Add a criss-cross layer of anchovies, then the remaining onions and potatoes. Season with salt and pepper, but remember the saltiness of anchovies.

Pour over just over half the cream and the oil from the anchovies. Bake in the oven for 40 minutes, then pour over the remaining cream, return to the oven and cook for a further 30–45 minutes until the potatoes are cooked and golden brown. Turn the heat down if the top threatens to brown too much.

PAN-FRIED SQUASH WITH ONIONS, MUSHROOMS, CHILLI AND CUMIN

Serve this as a superb accompaniment to simply grilled chicken or white fish. It makes a supper dish in its own right served with pasta, rice or couscous, with perhaps a little yoghurt or *crème fraîche* stirred through with grated cucumber and chopped fresh mint or coriander as a sauce. Squash cooked in this way is deliciously concentrated in flavour – use butternut, acorn or onion squash. Pumpkin is rather too moist to fry successfully.

Serves 4

2–3 tablespoons extra virgin olive oil
¼–½ teaspoon crushed dried chilli
3–4 sage leaves
450–750g/1–1½lb winter squash, peeled, seeded and cut into chunks
225g/8oz small onions, red or yellow, peeled and halved or quartered
1–2 teaspoons whole cumin seeds, lightly crushed
225g/8oz mushrooms (a mixture of chestnut cap and shiitake is good), whole or halved, depending on size
salt and freshly ground black pepper

Heat enough oil to just cover the base of a large (25cm/10 inch) frying pan. Add the chilli and sage and just warm through for a few minutes. Remove the sage. Then gently fry the squash and onions over a low to medium heat, turning occasionally, until the squash is golden brown and tender.

Add the cumin seeds, stir, add the mushrooms and return the sage leaves to the pan. Cook the mushrooms for 3–4 minutes, shaking the pan to coat all the vegetables with the cumin. Season well with salt and pepper and serve immediately.

BRAISED CELERY WITH CHESTNUTS AND PANCETTA

Serves 6–8

175g/6oz piece pancetta or thick-cut streaky bacon, de-rinded
1 tablespoon olive oil
4 small heads of celery, trimmed
2 large red onions, peeled
350g/12oz peeled chestnuts
3 sprigs fresh thyme
6–7 fresh bay leaves
2–3 tablespoons roughly chopped celery leaves
300ml/10fl oz chicken stock or water
salt and black pepper

Preheat the oven to 200°C/400°F/gas 6. Cut the pancetta (or bacon) into thick strips about 2.5cm/1 inch long.

Heat the the olive oil in a frying pan and fry the strips until brown and the fat has run. Remove the pancetta (or bacon) and set aside.

Cut the celery hearts into halves and the onions into wedges, leaving them attached at the base. Reheat the fat and gently fry the celery and onions for 5–8 minutes until lightly browned. Turn into a baking dish and add the chestnuts, herbs, half the pancetta (or bacon) and the stock or water. Season with salt and pepper. Cook, turning occasionally, for 30–35 minutes until the vegetables are tender and most of the liquid has been absorbed. Add the remaining pancetta (or bacon) and cook for a few minutes more.

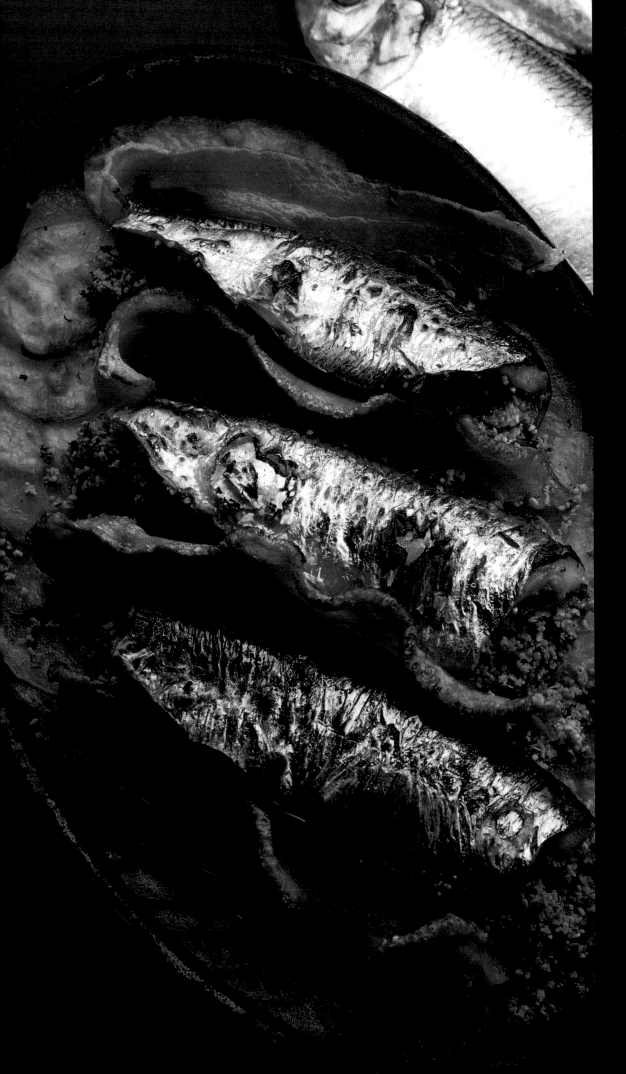

Fish has everything going for it: it cooks in minutes, it is low in fat, high in protein, mostly wild, thereby avoiding the disagreeable aspects of factory farming, easily digestible and it tastes good. So why do we not eat more of it? Anxiety, I suspect. We worry about preparing it (but a fishmonger will do all that for us if we ask), we worry about what kind to use (but if we stick to certain broad categories of fishy types most recipes are flexible on this), but most of all we worry about freshness. This last is a real problem. For an island nation we are sadly alienated from the produce of the seas around us. We are so used to de-natured food, food neatly prepared in cling-filmed packs, that we are disturbed by anything looking as though it was once alive. But once fish is filleted, skinned and wrapped in packaging, it is difficult to know whether it is really fresh or not. It is easier if we can see a whole fish, its eyes and its skin, and a sense of smell helps, too.

TESTING FOR FRESHNESS

Good tests for freshness are a clear, shiny eye with no trace of cloudiness or sunkenness; skin that is sparkling and sleek, not dull or dry. Fresh fish should smell of little apart from a faint whiff of salt water. It should definitely not smell fishy. Fillets of white fish should be firm, pearly white and not at all yellowish or flaccid. Always choose the best-looking, freshest fish on the day. Adapt your plans and cook another dish rather than buy second-rate fish.

COOKING FISH

The good news is that once you've got your fish home the cooking is easy. There is only one rule – never overcook. Indeed, it has

become fashionable to serve some fish – notably salmon and tuna – still pink in the centre, and there are a host of delicious fish dishes in which the fish is not cooked at all, ranging from the raw fishy delights of Japanese sashimi to the Latin American and Polynesian ceviches of fish 'cooked' (i.e. turned opaque) in citrus juice. These latter are delicious and almost my favourite way of eating really fresh fish. Cut 450g/1lb of skinned, firm white fish (sole, cod or brill are good) into thin slices. Marinate in a glass or china dish with the juice of 2 limes and a little chilli oil for 3–4 hours. When the fish is opaque, drain it, then lay on a serving dish and spoon over 150ml/5fl oz thick coconut milk mixed with a little fresh lime juice and a spoonful of Thai fish sauce. Scatter over some shredded lime zest, shredded red chilli and a few coriander leaves.

GRILLING

When it comes to applying heat to fish, keep it simple and brief. Unlike meat, fish will not become tough if cooked at a high temperature but you will ruin it if you cook it for too long. Grilling is one of the best cooking methods. Brush the fish with a little oil (the oil from the Preserved Lemons on page 14 is excellent) and sprinkle with some flakes of sea salt and perhaps a little crushed coriander seed or toasted cumin. Cook about 13cm/5 inches away from the heat for 4–5 minutes on each side. For whole fish an oiled grilling frame makes turning much easier. Searing on a ridged, cast-iron grill pan is also a good and healthy way to cook fish, giving it a delicious, charred outer surface to contrast with the soft, just-cooked flesh within. Whole fish of around 750g/1½lb barbecue well – try wrapping the fish in vine leaves, the husks from ears of sweetcorn or, if you can get them,

Previous page: herrings baked with oatmeal, bacon and potatoes (page 66) This page: grilled mussels with walnut and parsley (page 73)

banana leaves in place of the more usual foil. These leaves will impart a subtle, sappy flavour to the fish as it cooks and keep it moist. Or try grilling or baking whole fish on a bed of dried fennel stalks, which will give the fish a smoky, aniseedy flavour.

BAKING

Fish will also bake in a hot oven. Fillets or small whole fish are delicious cooked *en papillote* – in an envelope of foil or baking parchment. Set the fish on a bed of just-cooked vegetables so that the fish cooks in the steam and juices and remains moist. Another extremely popular method of cooking fish is to bake it in a protective covering of seasoned breadcrumbs or perhaps wrapped in thinly sliced bacon, pancetta or prosciutto.

POACHING & FRYING

Poached fish is excellent for seafood salads or terrines. Traditionally, fish is poached in *court bouillon* – water flavoured with wine, herbs and vinegar – or use fish stock for poaching, especially if you are planning to serve the fish with a sauce made from the poaching liquid. Poached fish should barely simmer, just the occasional bubble should rise to the surface. With large whole fish – salmon for instance – poaching does give a very good result, but I find baking in the oven, wrapped in foil with herbs and seasonings, is much less work. Fried fish is delicious but can be tricky to manage without the fish breaking up. Small fish and whitebait can be deep-fried, just dipped into milk and seasoned flour. Herrings and sardines are delicious coated in coarse oatmeal before frying.

A delicious way of serving fried fish is *en escabèche* – the fried fish is soused in wine vinegar, citrus juice and spices. It makes a delicious summer lunch or the first course of a larger meal.

SAUCES FOR FISH

Modern sauces such as salsas of raw fruit and vegetables or thick vinaigrettes with herbs and tomatoes make delicious, simple accompaniments to fish. Then there are the whole range of classic, mayonnaise-based sauces which are so good with baked, grilled or fried fish. A classic *sauce tartare* adds chopped gherkins, capers and herbs to a lemony mayonnaise, or try a rich, golden garlicky aïoli with simply poached fish and boiled potatoes. For a lighter sauce, stir herbs and diced, salted cucumber into *fromage frais* or *crème fraîche*. Fine white fish – sole, turbot, halibut and salmon trout – are good with a classic, buttery hollandaise sauce or try a variation made with orange juice and zest, known as *sauce maltaise*, with simply fried fillets of flat fish. You can make cream sauces by reducing a little fish stock and vermouth (Noilly Prat is the best known) in a pan, then whisking in any cooking juices from the fish, a little thick cream and chilled butter. Chopped fresh herbs should be stirred in at the last minute – chervil, sorrel or a little blanched, chopped watercress are particularly delicious. And to go with cod in breadcrumbs or fish cakes, you can't beat a classic parsley sauce (page 186) or a variation made with shredded fresh sorrel. For oily fish such as mackerel, herring and sardine, avoid creamy sauces and instead go for sharp or salty accompaniments. Gooseberries make a traditional sauce for mackerel or try some barely sweetened rhubarb or a sorrel purée. Fruity sauces go well with salmon and salmon trout too, though in this case a little cream to soften the acidity would not go amiss.

Seared fillets of
salmon with tomato
and chive vinaigrette
(page 73), served
with Champ (page
60)

HERRINGS BAKED WITH OATMEAL, BACON AND POTATOES

I like dishes such as this one where everything is cooked together in the one dish – they have a certain comforting integrity to them. The stuffing is based on the Scottish mixture of oatmeal and onion, called skirlie. This would make a complete supper dish with either a green vegetable or a salad to follow.

Serves 3–4

*750g/1½lb waxy variety potatoes,
    peeled
50g/2oz butter
salt and freshly ground black pepper
450ml/¾ pint vegetable or fish stock,
    or a mixture of white wine and
    water
40g/1½oz bacon fat or butter
1 medium onion, peeled and chopped
100g/4oz medium oatmeal
2 tablespoons chopped parsley
6–8 herring, each weighing about
    200g/7oz, boned
225g/½lb streaky bacon*

Preheat the oven to 190°C/375°F/ gas 5. Slice the potatoes thinly. Generously butter a 5cm/2 inch deep gratin dish, then layer the potatoes in it, seasoning well with salt and pepper and dotting with butter. Heat up the stock (or wine and water mixture) and pour over the potatoes. Cover with foil and cook for 30 minutes in the hot oven. Remove the foil and continue to cook for a further 15 minutes.

Meanwhile melt the bacon fat (or butter) in a medium-sized frying pan over a lowish heat, and fry the onion gently until it begins to turn brown. Add the oatmeal and continue to cook, stirring often, until the oatmeal absorbs the fat and begins to darken, but do not allow it to brown too much. Season with salt and pepper and cool a little. Stir in the parsley.

Open up the herrings, skin-side down, and season with a little salt. Divide the oatmeal mixture between the fish, then fold over to re-shape the fish. Remove the potatoes from the oven and lay the fish on top of the gratin. Tuck the slices of bacon between each fish. Dot with a little butter or bacon fat, then return to the oven for 20–25 minutes until the potatoes are cooked and the bacon is beginning to crisp.

VARIATIONS
1. Oatmeal is a traditional Scots partner for herring. Try brushing fillets of herring with a mixture of melted butter and mustard, then dipping in fine or medium oatmeal. Either grill or fry in bacon fat or vegetable oil.

2. Any of the Mediterranean-style stuffings for sardines work well with boned herring. Try a mixture of breadcrumbs, chopped mint, grated lemon zest, olives and toasted pine nuts. Season vigorously with salt and pepper.

MARINATED SALAD OF MACKEREL WITH ORANGE AND AVOCADO

This way of cooking fish *en escabèche* – by briefly frying then marinating in a bath of vinegar or citrus juices – is one of my favourite ways of serving fish as a cold first course. In season you could use bitter Seville oranges in this recipe. At other times of year, use sweet oranges with some lemon or lime juice.

Serves 4–6

3 medium-sized mackerel, filleted
2 tablespoons plain unbleached flour
salt and freshly ground black pepper
2 teaspoons ground coriander seed
6 tablespoons extra virgin olive oil
1 red onion, peeled and sliced
2 carrots, peeled
1 clove garlic, peeled
50ml/2fl oz orange juice (see above)
2–3 tablespoons white wine vinegar
a few fesh bay leaves and thyme
  sprigs
pinch of caster sugar
1–2 ripe avocados
1–2 tablespoons chopped fresh
  coriander

Wash the mackerel fillets and cut in serving-size pieces, if liked. Season the flour with salt, pepper and half the coriander seed. Dip the fillets in the mixture to coat both sides. Heat 3 tablespoons of oil in a roomy frying pan over a medium heat and cook the fillets on both sides until golden brown. Set aside in a non-metallic shallow dish.

Add the remaining oil to the pan and cook the onion, the sliced carrot and the garlic for 5–6 minutes until lightly coloured. Add the remaining coriander seed and cook for another minute. Add the orange juice (or mixture of orange and lemon or lime juices) and vinegar to the pan with the bay leaves and thyme sprigs. Cook for a few minutes until the carrots are just tender. Season to taste with salt, pepper and caster sugar if liked. Pour the contents of the pan over the fish, and cool, cover and chill. Leave to marinate for several hours.

Then stir in the peeled, stoned and sliced avocado and the chopped fresh coriander. This salad will keep well for a couple of days in the fridge. Add the avocado and coriander just before serving.

Marinated salad of
mackerel with
orange and avocado
(page 67)

ESCABÈCHE OF MULLET WITH PRESERVED LEMONS

Many types of fish may be served *en escabèche* (soused). Try cod, haddock, trout or very fresh mackerel instead of red mullet. Ask the fishmonger to scale and fillet the fish, but have him leave the skin on.

Serves 6 as a first course, 3 as a main course with salad

1 teaspoon ground cumin seeds
2 teaspoons coriander seeds, coarsely
    ground
salt and freshly ground black pepper
3 x 225–275g/8–10oz red mullet,
    scaled and filleted
2 tablespoons plain, unbleached flour
olive oil
1 medium-sized aubergine, cut into
    long wedges
1 large red pepper, seeded and sliced
1 large red onion, peeled and thinly
    sliced
1 large clove garlic, peeled and
    chopped
12 slices preserved lemon (see page
    14)
5 tablespoons sherry vinegar or
    balsamic vinegar
2–3 tablespoons chopped fresh parsley
    or coriander

Mix together the cumin seeds and 1 teaspoon of the coriander seeds. Add 1 level teaspoon salt and ½ teaspoon black pepper. Rub this spice mixture into the fish and leave in the fridge for 1 hour. Dust the fish with flour and fry in 4–5 tablespoons oil for approximately 5 minutes or until cooked and slightly browned on each side. Place the fish in a non-metallic dish.

Add a few more tablespoons of oil to the pan and fry the aubergine for 5–6 minutes, again until browned and cooked through. Add to the fish. If necessary, add another couple of tablespoons of oil to the pan and cook the pepper and onion together over a medium heat until soft. Add the garlic, the remaining coriander seeds and the lemon slices, and cook for another few minutes. Then add the vinegar and 5 tablespoons water. Boil rapidly until the liquid is reduced by about half. Spoon the contents of the pan over the fish and aubergine. Season with a little salt and lots of black pepper. Cool, cover and refrigerate. Leave to souse for at least 12 hours (preferably 24), turning the fish once in the marinade. Mix in the chopped parsley or coriander just before serving at room temperature.

Escabèche of mullet
with preserved
lemons

FISH BAKED WITH ROOT VEGETABLES AND GINGER

Cooking fish in a parcel of baking paper (*en papillote*) is an excellent method, as none of the flavour or juiciness of the fish is lost. Try whole, scaled fish like red mullet, small snapper or tilipea, or fillets of delicate white fish such as whiting, hake or lemon sole. Cleaned fresh scallops, cut in half, or fillets of trout would also be delicious.

Serves 4

2 medium-sized carrots, peeled
100g/4oz peeled celeriac
1 bulb Florence fennel, trimmed
25g/1oz butter, or 2 tablespoons oil
1 leek, trimmed and thinly sliced
4cm/1¼inch piece of fresh ginger,
    peeled and cut into fine strips
salt, freshly ground black pepper and
    caster sugar
4 small whole fish or 4–8 fillets
    (see above)
4 bay leaves
4 sprigs of fennel, fresh or dried
4 stalks fresh lemon grass or 4 sprigs
    of lemon thyme

Cut the carrots, celeriac and fennel into thin matchstick-sized strips. Heat the butter (or oil) in a frying pan over a medium heat. Cook the carrots, celeriac and fennel for a few minutes.

Add the leek and ginger, and cook gently for a further 3–4 minutes. Season well, including a pinch of sugar to taste.

Cut 4 x 35cm/14 inch circles or heart shapes from baking parchment or foil, fold each shape in half, open up then distribute the vegetables between the pieces of paper. Lay the fish on the vegetables, season, then top with the bay leaves, fennel and the lemon grass (cut in half) or lemon thyme.

Fold over the paper, then fold and twist the edges to create an

Fish baked with root
vegetables and ginger

airtight seal. Place the parcels on a baking sheet.

Preheat the oven to 190°C/375°F/gas 5. Bake the parcels for 10–20 minutes (use the shorter time for scallops and the longer time for whole fish). Allow each person to open their parcel at the table.

VARIATION
Cook the fish on a bed of fennel and sweet pepper cooked with a little skinned, de-seeded tomato, onion, garlic, ginger and basil. Add a few stoned black olives and a sprig of rosemary or thyme to each parcel. A little orange zest or crushed coriander seed would also work well.

Scallops with Wild Rice and a Vanilla and Lemon Grass Sauce

Keep this dish for a special *dîner à deux,* or at most as a starter for four people. This recipe is based on one invented by food writer Silvija Davidson and partners the scallops with wild rice that is also flavoured with vanilla. The carrots add both colour and a natural sweetness of their own. Excellent, ready-prepared fish stock can now be found in most large supermarkets.

Serves 2–4

6–8 fresh, shelled scallops, cleaned
salt and freshly ground black pepper
350ml/12fl oz fish stock
2 vanilla pods
2 stalks lemon grass, split in 2
100g/4oz wild rice
2 medium-sized carrots, peeled
50ml/2fl oz double cream
15g/½oz butter
1 tablespoon olive oil
sprigs of fresh chervil or flat-leaved
  parsley, to garnish

Separate the corals from the main, white muscle of the scallops and cut the white part into 2 or 3 pieces, depending on thickness. Place on a plate and season with salt and pepper. Set aside. Put the stock, 1 vanilla pod and both stalks of lemon grass in a non-aluminium saucepan and bring to the boil. Turn down the heat and simmer, covered, for 15–30 minutes. Meanwhile, rinse the wild rice and place in a saucepan with the second vanilla pod, a teaspoon of salt and 600ml/1 pint water. Bring to the boil, turn down the heat and simmer, covered, for 40–45 minutes or until cooked.

Cut the carrots into long, thin matchsticks and set aside. Strain the fish stock, set the vanilla pod aside, and return the stock to the rinsed-out saucepan. Reduce by fast boiling until you have about 150ml/5fl oz left, then add the carrots and continue reducing until the stock is quite syrupy. Split the vanilla pod lengthways and scrape the seeds into the stock. Add the cream to the stock and boil briskly to produce a thickish sauce. Taste and correct the seasoning, add the scallop corals to the sauce and keep warm. Drain the rice, and add the seeds of the vanilla pod to the rice as above. Toss with the butter and keep warm. Brush a non-stick frying pan or griddle with the oil and heat over a medium-high heat until hot. Sear the scallops for about 30–60 seconds on each side. Mound the rice on warm plates, then top with the scallops. Finally spoon over a little sauce and a few corals. Garnish with chervil (or parsley).

SALMON WITH GRILLED ASPARAGUS AND A LIME AND CUMIN HOLLANDAISE

Salmon trout is also delicious cooked in this way.

Serves 4

4 x 175–225g/6–8oz salmon fillets,
  left unskinned
salt and freshly ground black pepper
4 tablespoons extra virgin olive oil
450g/1lb thick-stemmed asparagus

FOR THE SAUCE:
1 small shallot, finely chopped
2.5cm/1 inch piece fresh ginger,
  peeled and finely chopped
6 tablespoons white wine
1 lime
3 egg yolks
175g/6oz unsalted butter
¼–½ teaspoon finely ground toasted
  cumin
wedges of lime to garnish

Season the fillets with salt, and brush with half the oil. Set aside. Trim the asparagus of the woody, bottom portion of stalk, and, if tough, peel the lower 7.5cm/3 inches of stalk with a swivel vegetable peeler. Set the asparagus on the grill pan and brush with a little of the remaining oil.

Prepare the sauce: in a small, non-aluminium pan put the shallot, ginger and white wine. Boil down until about 1 tablespoon of liquid remains. Meanwhile finely shred the zest of the lime and blanch in plenty of boiling water for 1 minute. Drain and rinse under the cold tap. Set aside a few strands for garnish, chopping the rest finely. Put the egg yolks in a basin and whisk in the cooled, reduced white wine mixture. Set the bowl over a saucepan of barely simmering water, ensuring that the bottom of the bowl does not touch the water. Add the butter, about 25g/1oz at a time, allowing each piece to melt into the sauce before adding the next.

When all the butter is in, cook until the sauce is thick and glossy, but do not allow to get too hot. Stir in the chopped lime zest, and season to taste with cumin, salt, pepper and lime juice. Turn off the heat and keep the sauce warm over the hot water.

Meanwhile, preheat the grill. Grill the asparagus, brushing occasionally with the remaining oil for 6–8 minutes, turning the asparagus once or twice. Adjust the heat so that the asparagus does not char too much. (Cover the tips with foil if they seem to be browning too much.) Heat a non-stick frying pan over a medium heat until hot. Add the salmon fillets, skin-side down, and cook for 4–5 minutes. Turn and cook for another minute. (Alternatively, both asparagus and salmon may be barbecued over charcoal. Oil the grill rack well, or grill the fish in a special, fish-shaped barbecue frame.) Serve the salmon on heated plates with the asparagus and garnished with lime wedges. Serve the sauce, sprinkled with the reserved lime zest, alongside.

Salmon with grilled
asparagus and a lime
and cumin
hollandaise

See photograph on
page 65

SEARED FILLETS OF SALMON WITH A TOMATO AND CHIVE VINAIGRETTE

Serves 4

4 x 175–225g/6–8oz fillets salmon
salt and freshly ground black pepper
1 bunch (about 15g/½oz) of fresh
    chives
6 tablespoons extra virgin olive oil
225g/8oz ripe, flavoursome tomatoes
juice and finely grated zest of ½ lime
a pinch of sugar (optional)
1 tablespoon chopped chervil or basil
sprigs of chervil and/or basil, to
    garnish
mashed potato with butter and spring
    onions, to serve (see Champ, page
    60)

Remove any stray bones from the fish, salt lightly and set aside. Put a few chives on one side and coarsely chop the rest. Warm the chopped chives, 5 tablespoons of oil and 5 tablespoons water in a small non-aluminium saucepan. Liquidize, then strain the mixture back into the pan through a sieve. Skin, halve and seed the tomatoes. Cut into small dice.

Add the tomatoes to the chive liquor in the pan and heat gently, just to warm through – on no account should the mixture come near boiling. Season to taste with lime juice, salt and pepper. You may also need a pinch of sugar, depending on the tomatoes. Stir in the remaining chives, finely chopped, the lime zest, and the chervil (or basil). Set aside to infuse while you cook the fish.

Brush the fillets with the remaining tablespoon of oil. Heat a large, heavy, ridged or non-stick frying pan over a high flame until hot. Put in the fillets, skin-side down, and cook for 2 minutes, turn and cook for a further 2 minutes. Turn again and cook, skin-side down, for a further minute. The fish will be only just cooked in the centre.

Serve on heated plates, spooning the vinaigrette around the fish. Garnish with herbs and serve with Champ (page 60) – potato mashed with milk, butter and chopped spring onions.

See photograph on
page 64

GRILLED MUSSELS WITH WALNUT AND PARSLEY

Serves 4

1.75kg/4lb fresh mussels
salt and freshly ground black pepper
2 large cloves fresh garlic, peeled
large bunch fresh parsley (about
    25g/1oz)
75g/3oz shelled walnuts, blanched
    and skinned
2 tablespoons walnut oil
4–5 tablespoons extra virgin olive oil
lemon juice
50g/2oz fresh white breadcrumbs

Scrub and clean the mussels, discarding any that remain open after scrubbing. Bring about 2.5 cm/1 inch salted water to the boil in a large pan. Throw in enough mussels to make a single layer, cover and cook for 30 seconds to 1 minute until the mussels gape open, then remove and repeat with all the mussels. Discard any that remain closed after cooking. Discard half of the shell and place the mussels in an ovenproof dish or dishes.

In a processor, chop the garlic, parsley and walnuts, add the walnut oil and 3 tablespoons olive oil. Blend again, season well with salt, pepper and lemon juice. Place the breadcrumbs in a bowl, then add the garlic/parsley mixture. Toss to mix and adjust the seasoning. Place a small spoonful of the mixture in each mussel half. Scatter any remaining mixture over the top. Sprinkle with the remaining oil. Heat the grill, then grill the mussels about 13cm/5 inches from the flame until golden brown.

BAKED FILLETS OF FISH WRAPPED IN AIR-DRIED HAM WITH CHICORY AND PARMESAN

Several kinds of fish are suitable for this treatment. John Dory and halibut would make delicious, if expensive, choices. Halibut has dense, meaty flesh that can be dry, but this way of cooking keeps it deliciously moist. I also like the red tilapia (St. Peter's fish) and snapper, which are becoming quite common in fishmongers and the larger supermarkets. Hake, cod or grey mullet are also excellent cooked in this way. Ask the fishmonger to scale mullet, tilapia and snapper but to leave the skin on; other fish is better skinned.

Serves 6

6 large or 12 small heads of Witloof
  chicory
salt and freshly ground black pepper
6 x 175–225g/6–8oz fillets fish (see
  above)
6 slices air-dried, Parma-style ham
6 tablespoons medium-dry white wine
6 tablespoons olive oil
50g/2oz white breadcrumbs
50g/2oz freshly grated Parmesan
2 tablespoons finely chopped parsley
herb sprigs, to garnish

Halve the chicory lengthways and steam over salted, boiling water for 5 minutes. Drain very well, and lay in a baking dish large enough to take both the fish and the chicory. Season the fillets, wrap each in a slice of ham (cutting the ham in half lengthways if necessary) and set aside.

Set the oven to 200°C/400°F/gas 6. Mix together the wine and oil and spoon a little over each chicory half. Bake for 10 minutes in the oven, basting with the wine/oil mixture halfway through cooking. Remove from the oven. Mix together the breadcrumbs, Parmesan and parsley, and season well. Press over the chicory halves. Place the fillets in the same dish and baste with the remaining oil/wine mixture. Bake for 10–15 minutes, basting once, until the fish is cooked and the breadcrumbs brown and crisp (if necessary finish browning the chicory under a hot grill). Serve on hot plate, spooning a little of the cooking juices over each fillet. Garnish with herb sprigs. Serve with Sauce Ravigote.

SAUCE RAVIGOTE

Serves 6

25g/1oz watercress, thick stalks
  removed
25g/1oz mixed fresh herbs – a
  mixture of tarragon, parsley,
  chervil and chives
1 small shallot, peeled and chopped
3 anchovy fillets, drained
2 small gherkins, chopped
1 tablespoon capers, rinsed
1 teaspoon finely grated lemon zest
1 hard-boiled egg yolk
4 tablespoons extra virgin olive oil
2–3 teaspoons tarragon vinegar
freshly ground black pepper

Whizz the first 7 ingredients in a processor, then mix in the egg yolk. (Or chop the ingredients very finely before mixing in the crushed egg yolk.) Blend in the oil very gradually, then season to taste with the vinegar and freshly ground pepper. For a milder sauce, stir in a few tablespoons of *crème fraîche*.

Baked fillets of fish wrapped in air-dried ham with chicory and parmesan, served with Sauce Ravigote

GRILLED FILLET OF COD WITH PARMESAN BREADCRUMBS

Fish is one of the quickest foods to prepare and cook. Seek out the freshest-looking fish you can find – it should be firm, pearly white and sweet-smelling. You could use haddock or whiting or the grander halibut instead of cod for this dish.

Serves 4

*4 fillets of fresh cod, skinned, each
    weighing about 150g/5oz
salt and freshly ground black pepper
4 tablespoons black olive paste
75g/3oz white crustless bread
15g/½oz fresh parsley
50g/2oz freshly grated Parmesan
4 tablespoons extra virgin olive oil
fresh herbs, to garnish (optional)*

Preheat the oven to 200°C/400°F/gas 6. Season the fillets with salt and pepper and spread 1 tablespoon of olive paste over each. Place the bread and parsley in the food processor or blender and whizz briefly to make breadcrumbs. Tip into a bowl and stir in the Parmesan, season with a little salt and plenty of black pepper. Stir in 3 tablespoons of the oil, mix thoroughly then spread over the fillets. Set the fish on an oiled baking tray, sprinkle with the remaining oil and cook in the oven for 15–20 minutes until the fish is just cooked. Serve with a tomato and avocado relish (see below) and some mashed potato. Garnish with fresh herbs, if liked.

VARIATIONS
There are lots of possible variations on this dish. Try using a purée of sun-dried tomatoes or grilled peppers instead of the olive paste, or mix some fresh herbs and chopped gherkins into a good bought mayonnaise and use that.

TOMATO AND AVOCADO RELISH:
*4 ripe tomatoes, skinned, de-seeded
    and chopped
1 ripe avocado, peeled, stoned and
    chopped
6 spring onions, cleaned and chopped
15g/½oz fresh coriander, chopped
1 small green chilli, de-seeded and
    finely chopped*

*½–1 teaspoon ground cumin
1 tablespoon cider or rice vinegar
2–3 tablespoons vegetable oil
salt, black pepper and caster sugar to
    taste*

Mix all the ingredients in a bowl. Season to taste with salt, freshly ground black pepper and sugar.

Grilled fillet of cod
with Parmesan
breadcrumbs served
with tomato and
avocado relish

GRILLED TUNA WITH TOASTED CORN SALSA

This sweetcorn salsa, inspired by several salsa recipes from Mark Miller's wonderfully quirky book on the cooking of the South West states of America, *The Coyote Café*, makes a great accompaniment to all kinds of simply grilled fish. I particularly enjoy it with 'meaty' fish such as tuna, swordfish or shark which are becoming increasingly popular.

Serves 4

4 x 75–225g/6–8oz steaks of fresh tuna
salt and freshly ground black pepper
1 teaspoon toasted, ground cumin
1–2 tablespoons chilli oil (or olive oil
    with a little ground, dried chilli)
juice of ½ lime
lime wedges and coriander sprigs, to
    garnish

FOR THE SALSA:
2 cobs fresh sweetcorn, de-husked
1 small red onion, peeled and finely
    chopped
4 pieces of sun-dried tomato in oil,
    drained and finely chopped
8 cherry tomatoes, quartered
½–1 fresh red chilli, de-seeded and
    finely chopped
½–1 teaspoon toasted ground cumin
finely grated zest and juice of ½–1
    lime
2 tablespoons chopped fresh coriander
1–2 teaspoons light rice vinegar
1–2 tablespoons extra virgin olive oil
    (or the oil from the sun-dried
    tomatoes)
salt and freshly ground black pepper

Trim any dark patches from the tuna, as these will taste bitter when cooked. Season with salt, pepper and cumin and brush with the chilli oil. Set aside while you prepare the salsa.

Heat the grill to maximum. Brush the corn with a little oil, then grill, turning 3 times until the corn turns brown in patches (about 5–7 minutes). Cool, then remove the kernels from the cobs, using a small sharp knife. Place in a bowl and add all the remaining ingredients (start with the lesser amount of chilli, etc). Leave to stand for at least 30 minutes, then taste, adding salt, pepper and more cumin, lime, chilli and vinegar to taste.

When you are ready to cook the fish, either preheat an overhead grill or heat a ridged, cast-iron grill-pan. Brush the fish with the lime juice, then cook for about 4–5 minutes on each side, brushing with the oil and lime juice when you turn the fish. Serve with the salsa, garnished with lime wedges and fresh coriander sprigs. A pilau of couscous with plenty of chopped fresh mint stirred in makes a lovely accompaniment.

Grilled tuna with
toasted corn salsa

If there's one dish guaranteed to make even the most forward-looking of trendsetting cooks come down with a bad case of nostalgia it's roast chicken. The simplest of dishes, you'd be forgiven for thinking, nothing could be easier than to stick a chicken in the oven and roast it for 1–1½ hours, basting once or twice towards the end. What's all the fuss? The fact is that as we approach the second millennium it is the simplest things that have become the most difficult to achieve and roast chicken has become a good example of this phenomenon of 'the simpler, the more complicated', at least in the culinary sphere.

FIND YOUR CHICKEN

First of all, of course, there's the question of the chicken. Nothing less than a 100 per cent, free-ranging, naturally fed bird will do. Period. We have all seen just one too many documentaries about the sickening conditions in which factory-farmed birds are kept. But it is not just a question of conscience or liberal revulsion, it is one of taste. Stressed birds, fed on processed foodstuffs and getting little or no exercise or natural light, do not produce chickens that are good to eat. They produce bland or tainted flesh with little or no texture. No amount of butter, stuffing or tender loving care will make a battery bird taste good. This immediately takes chicken out of the everyday, cheap food category. Many supermarket free-range birds are still reared on a pretty intensive scale. Some taste better than others. Well-reared, genuinely free-range chickens cost money. It saddens me, though, that good chickens now have to have designer labels, quite literally. French *poulet label rouge* or *poulet de Bresse* are pampered birds sold at a high prices in fancy food shops. A good roast chicken is no longer a fitting symbol of the simplicities of *la cuisine de grand-mère*. A good chicken is now a luxury item.

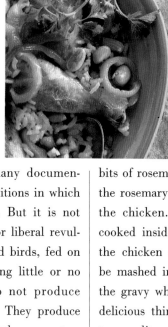

ROASTING CHICKEN

A chicken of this luxury status deserves the best treatment. Roast it with good, unsalted butter; herbs such as tarragon or lemon thyme and perhaps a little garlic. Tarragon and chicken have one of those natural affinities that make otherwise sensible people talk of marriages made in heaven. Putting divine match-making aside, it is a delicious combination. Try creaming the butter with some chopped tarragon, a little chopped garlic or shallot and some black pepper. Spread this mixture underneath the skin of the bird before roasting, placing any left over in the body cavity. Rosemary is also good with chicken but because whole bits of rosemary are unpleasant to eat, restrict the rosemary to a few sprigs around or inside the chicken. A few whole cloves of garlic, cooked inside the body cavity, will perfume the chicken (and the kitchen) and can then be mashed into the chicken juices to flavour the gravy when the chicken is cooked. Other delicious things to tuck under the skin of a top-quality chicken are a butter flavoured with some reconstituted, chopped dried porcini mushrooms or, if you have the luck to ever get hold of such a thing, a thinly sliced black or white truffle or fresh cep.

POT ROASTING

If you roast a chicken uncovered, basting with the buttery juices, you'll end up with a delicious crisp, golden skin and pan juices which, de-greased with the addition of a little stock, will make a simple gravy. You'll get a slightly different result if you pot-roast the chicken, adding liquid to the baking dish and

Previous page:
baked chicken
breasts with North
African spices and
pickled lemons
(page 81)

covering for part of the cooking. The chicken will be moister, less crisp, more melting in texture and the liquid – wine, vermouth, stock – will form a delicious sauce as it cooks. Try Oriental flavourings for a pot-roasted chicken – ginger, garlic, star-anise. Use some soy sauce and Chinese Shaoxing wine as the basting liquid. Try stuffing a salted black bean butter under the skin of a chicken or use a paste of coconut, fresh coriander, garlic and lemon grass (see the Thai Green Curry Paste on page 132).

PAN-FRYING

One of my favourite methods of cooking chicken breasts is to fry them, very gently, skin-side down, in a mixture of butter and olive oil. Use a heavy saucepan (I use a wide Le Creuset ovenproof pan) and cook partially covered. Add a few sprigs of herb – tarragon, thyme, rosemary,

sage – while it cooks. When the skin is deliciously browned, turn the chicken over and cook until the chicken is done (the juices should run clear rather than pink). Remove the chicken and keep warm while you complete the sauce with all manner of delicious things: a little wine or vermouth, some good vinegar, like balsamic or white tarragon vinegar, a little chopped garlic, shallot or some mushrooms. Bubble for a few minutes and, for a richer sauce, stir in a little thick cream and perhaps a spoonful of sharp fruit jelly – crab apple, rowanberry, redcurrant – to correct the balance of flavours. This produces a very flavourful and moist result and is excellent served with buttered noodles or mashed potato.

ALTERNATIVES TO CHICKEN

Many chicken recipes can be adapted to use guinea fowl or rabbit. Because these are drier meats, with less fat, pot-roasting, sautéeing and marinading are better cooking techniques than plain roasting. Oil-based marinades are good for rabbit or try a yoghurt and tamarind marinade, which cooks down to form a delicious sharp coating to the meat.

If you long for a bird that tastes like chicken used to taste like you'd be better, nine times out of ten, to go for a guinea-fowl or a young, tender pheasant. Both guinea-fowl and pheasant can be dry and usually need some extra fat for lubrication. On the other hand, if your pheasant seems to have a lot of yellow fat on it, this should be removed as it will taste unpleasantly strong.

Small turkeys can also be cooked like chicken. Again a free-range turkey of one of the older breeds, such as the Norfolk Black or the Cambridge Bronze, will have more character and taste than a production-line bird. Certainly the rich, dark meat of the turkey – from the legs and thighs – is delicious casseroled or stewed with ingredients such as red wine, garlic, thyme, pancetta or bacon, prunes and chestnuts. Duck, which has always been slightly less subject to intensive farming, can be delicious. Duck breasts should be cooked skin-side down at first to thoroughly cook and render the layer of fat beneath the skin, but unlike chicken, which should always be fully cooked, duck breasts are good served pink. I like to marinate them to add flavour. Try the dry, spiced salt marinade of Lightly Salted Duck Breasts with Fresh Peas, Summer Turnips and Thyme on page 89.

The rich, fatty meat of duck takes very well to strong flavours and sharp sauces. Thyme and sage are good herbs, spices such as coriander and chilli and sharp flavours like lime, orange and fruit jelly all go well with duck.

BAKED RABBIT AND POTATOES MARINATED IN WALNUT OIL, ROSEMARY AND GARLIC

Rabbit benefits from an oil-based marinade as it is a very low-fat meat and can be quite dry. Use chicken joints, on the bone, for this dish if you prefer. Slash the skin in a few places to allow the flavours to penetrate.

Serves 4–6

1.5kg/3lb rabbit joints
2–3 medium onions, trimmed and cut
* into wedges*
1–1.25kg/2–2½lb small potatoes,
* scrubbed or peeled*

FOR THE MARINADE:
6 tablespoons walnut oil
4 tablespoons olive oil
2 tablespoons sherry vinegar
2 cloves garlic, peeled and finely
* chopped*
salt and freshly ground black pepper
1 tablespoon fresh thyme sprigs, or 1
* teaspoon dried thyme*
a few rosemary sprigs

Prepare the marinade first: mix together all the ingredients and seasoning to taste. Turn into a shallow tray or baking dish and add the rabbit pieces and the onions, turning them over in the marinade; leave to marinate for several hours, stirring occasionally if convenient. Parboil the potatoes in lightly salted water for 5 minutes (do not overcook), cool and cut into halves or wedges, depending on size. Add to the rabbit and the onion and marinate for another hour.

Preheat the oven to 200°C/400°F/ gas 6. Bake the rabbit and vegetables, turning once or twice for about 1¼–1½ hours, until the potatoes are browned and the rabbit well done. Serve with a crisp green salad.

Baked rabbit and
potatoes marinated
in walnut oil,
rosemary and garlic

BAKED CHICKEN BREASTS WITH NORTH AFRICAN SPICES AND PICKLED LEMONS

See photograph on
page 77

The oil from lemons preserved in this way (see page 14) makes a wonderful basis for a marinade for fish, lamb and chicken. Serve this dish with a pilau of rice, couscous or millet.

Serves 4–5

1 teaspoon coriander seeds
1 teaspoon cumin seeds
½ teaspoon cardamom seeds
½ teaspoon paprika
salt and freshly ground black pepper
4 tablespoons oil from pickled lemons
  or olive oil
4–5 chicken portions, skin on
2 medium red onions, cut into wedges
2 medium green peppers, de-seeded
  and thickly sliced
3 fresh bay leaves
8–10 slices pickled lemons
8–10 plump, no-soak prunes
1–2 tablespoons coarsely chopped
  fresh coriander or flat-leaved
  parsley, to garnish

Heat a small, dry frying pan over a low heat until warm. Add the coriander, cumin and cardamom and cook, shaking the pan frequently, for a few minutes until the spices give off their fragrance, then grind in a coffee grinder or pestle and mortar. Mix with the paprika, ½ teaspoon salt and ½ teaspoon ground black pepper. Mix to a paste with the oil. Cut diagonal slashes on the skin side of the chicken and rub in the spice paste.

Place in a baking dish and add the onions, peppers and bay leaves. Turn to cover all the vegetables in the oil. Cover, and leave to stand for at least 4 hours.

Preheat the oven to 190°C/375°F/ gas 5. Uncover the chicken and cook, basting with the juices from time to time, for 20 minutes. Lay the lemon slices over the chicken and tuck in the prunes, then cook for a further 15–20 minutes or until the chicken is fully cooked and the vegetables touched with brown. Serve sprinkled with the chopped herbs.

Sautéed Chicken Breasts with Salsify and Rosemary

Although salsify and scorzonera look unpromising, they have a succulent, waxy texture and a subtle smoky flavour that goes well with other mild flavours such as chicken, rabbit or veal. Either vegetable may be used in this dish. Choose free-range chicken.

Serves 4

450–750g/1–1½lb salsify
salt and freshly ground black pepper
4 free-range chicken breasts, partly or
*   wholly boned*
25g/1oz butter
1 tablespoon olive oil
4 x 5cm/2 inch sprigs fresh rosemary
225g/8oz chestnut cap mushrooms,
wiped and sliced
4 tablespoons white wine or dry
*   vermouth*
4–5 tablespoons double cream
lemon juice (optional)

Scrub and trim the salsify. Bring a large pan of boiling salted water to the boil and cook the salsify, covered, until tender when tested with the tip of a sharp knife (20–30 minutes). Drain, run under the cold tap, then peel. Cut into 5–7.5cm/2–3 inch lengths and set aside.

Season the chicken breasts well with salt and pepper. Heat the butter and oil together in a roomy frying or sauté pan over a medium heat. Add the chicken, skin-side down, and the rosemary. Cook gently for 10 minutes, turn the breasts over and cook for 5 minutes more.

Add the salsify to the pan and cook, turning the salsify in the juices, for 5–15 minutes more. (Cook partly-boned breasts for a little longer than boned chicken.) Remove the chicken and rosemary to a plate and keep warm. Add the mushrooms to the pan and cook, stirring occasionally, for 2–3 minutes. Turn up the heat and add the wine or vermouth. Allow to bubble for a few minutes, then add the cream. Stir and cook to produce a sauce. Taste and correct the seasoning, adding a little lemon juice if you like. Return the chicken to the pan, skin-side up, and cook for a minute more.

Serve immediately with rice (basmati or Thai jasmine), buttered egg noodles or mashed potato.

CHICKEN BAKED WITH SHALLOTS, GARLIC AND THYME

This is a simple supper dish. Use quartered guinea fowl or even young rabbit joints as alternatives. If you have time to let the chicken marinate with the shallots and garlic, it will taste even better.

Serves 4

1 x 1.5–1.75kg/3½–4lb free-range
  chicken, jointed into 4–8 pieces
225–275g/8–10oz shallots, peeled
1 head garlic, separated into cloves
  and peeled
4 tablespoons extra virgin olive oil
3–4 tablespoons balsamic vinegar
salt and freshly ground black pepper
1 tablespoon fresh thyme sprigs
2 sprigs of rosemary
1–2 teaspoons redcurrant (or other
  fruit) jelly
3–4 tablespoons double cream or
  crème fraîche

Place chicken, shallots and whole garlic cloves in a baking dish that just holds them in one layer. Add the oil and 2 tablespoons of vinegar. Turn the joints in the oil and vinegar. Season well and add the thyme and rosemary. Allow to stand (in the fridge if longer than 1 hour), prefer-ably for several hours. Preheat the oven to 190°C/375°F/gas 5. Add a couple of tablespoons of water to the chicken and cook, turning once or twice, for about 40 minutes. Test the chicken for doneness, inserting a skewer into the thickest part of the joint – the juices should run clear rather than pink.

When cooked, remove chicken, garlic and shallots to a serving dish, leaving the juices in the dish. Skim to remove as much fat as possible, then place over a high heat, add 1 tablespoon balsamic vinegar and 1 teaspoon redcurrant jelly. Boil vig-orously, stirring all the time. Add the cream and boil, continuing to scrape all the delicious juices to make the sauce. Taste, adding more vinegar, jelly or cream as required. Season to taste with salt and pepper and pour over the chicken. Serve immediately with boiled potatoes or lightly buttered egg noodles.

Chicken baked with
shallots, garlic and
thyme

STEW OF CHICKEN AND SPRING VEGETABLES WITH GREMOLADA

Although there may seem to be a lot of ingredients in this recipe, it does make a full meal – both vegetables and meat cooked in one pot. Simply serve with bread rather than more potatoes – the Buttermilk and Corn Rolls on page 141 are particularly delicious. Marinate the chicken the day before the meal and try the gremolada – the mixture of chopped herbs, garlic and lemon zest – which adds a real 'lift' in flavour.

Serves 6

6 free-range, corn-fed chicken
    quarters
2 teaspoons fennel seeds, lightly
    crushed
finely shredded zest of 1 lemon
½ teaspoon dried red chilli flakes
salt, black pepper and caster sugar
1 bottle medium white wine
1 large head garlic, separated into
    cloves and peeled
2 tablespoons olive oil or chicken fat
175g/6oz piece of pancetta or thick-
    cut streaky bacon
225g/8oz shallots or small onions,
    peeled
350g/12oz young carrots, trimmed
    and scrubbed
350g/12oz young turnips, trimmed
    and scrubbed
2 bulbs Florence fennel, trimmed but
    tops reserved
225g/8oz French beans or sugar snap
    peas, trimmed
1 tablespoon tarragon or Dijon
    mustard
3 tablespoons chopped fresh chervil or
    parsley

Score the skin of the chicken joints a few times with a sharp knife. Place in a non-metallic dish and rub in the crushed fennel seeds, half the lemon zest and the chilli, and grind over plenty of black pepper, then pour over the wine. Reserve the remaining lemon zest, covered. Finely chop 1 of the garlic cloves and add to the chicken, cover and leave to marinate overnight or for several hours.

When you are ready to cook the chicken, set the oven to 190°C/375°F/gas 5. Remove the joints from the marinade, dry on kitchen paper. Heat the oil in a roomy frying pan over a moderate heat and brown the chicken on all sides, then place in a large, preferably cast iron, casserole. Cut the de-rinded pancetta (or bacon) into small strips and add to the same pan and fry until browned, then add to the chicken. Turn down the heat slightly, and brown the shallots and all but 1 of the garlic cloves on all sides and add to the chicken.

Pour the marinade into the pan, and bring to the boil, stirring to dislodge all the crusty bits from the pan. Boil for a few minutes, then pour over the chicken. Season with salt, pepper and a pinch of caster sugar, then cover and cook for 30 minutes in the hot oven.

Depending on their size, either leave the carrots and turnips whole or cut into halves or quarters, and slice each fennel bulb into 6–8 wedges. Add to the casserole, stir and cook, covered, for a further 30–40 minutes or until all the vegetables are tender. Meanwhile, blanch the beans or peas in boiling, salted water for 5 minutes, drain and refresh under the cold water tap, drain again and set aside. (The stew may be prepared a few hours in advance up to this point, cool quickly then reheat before proceeding.) When the casserole is done, remove the chicken and vegetables to a serving dish and keep warm. Bring the juices to the boil and reduce by fast boiling until syrupy, stir in the mustard and adjust the seasoning. Add the beans or peas and cook gently for a few minutes to heat through. Pour over the chicken and vegetables. Finely chop the remaining clove of garlic, the chervil or parsley and the reserved fennel tops. Mix in the reserved lemon zest and strew the mixture over the stew.

CHICKEN COOKED WITH LIME AND GINGER

Serves 4

4 free-range chicken breasts, boned or
   partly-boned
salt and freshly ground black pepper
4cm/1½ inch piece fresh ginger,
   peeled and cut into thin strips
finely shredded zest and juice of 2
   limes
3 teaspoons honey
1 teaspoon coriander seeds, coarsely
   ground
2 tablespoons vegetable oil
250ml/8fl oz medium white wine or
   cider
1 tablespoon dark soy sauce
lime wedges, to garnish

Score the skin of the chicken a few
times with a sharp knife. Season with
salt and pepper. Chop or blend half
the ginger and lime zest and mix with
the juice of 1 lime, the honey and the
coriander seeds. Spread this paste
over the chicken and set aside for 1
hour or more to absorb the flavours.

Heat the oil in a deep frying pan
over a medium heat, dry off the
chicken (reserving the marinade) and
brown on both sides. Remove to a
plate. Add the marinade to the pan
and cook for 1 minute. Add the wine
(or cider) and soy sauce, and
100ml/4fl oz water. Cook for a minute
or two, then return the chicken,

Stew of chicken and
spring vegetables
with gremolada,
served with
buttermilk and corn
rolls (page 141)

85

skin-side up, to the pan. Cook gently for 20 minutes or until the chicken is cooked through, spooning the sauce over the chicken occasionally and adding a little more water if the sauce seems to reduce too much.

Meanwhile, blanch the remaining ginger and lime zest in boiling water for a minute or so. Drain and reserve.

Remove the chicken to the serving plate, add the blanched ginger and lime zest to the pan and let the sauce bubble and reduce for a few minutes. Taste for seasoning, adding more lime juice, honey or soy to taste. Pour over the chicken and serve immediately, garnished with lime wedges. Serve with rice and stir-fried spinach and carrots.

SAFFRONED RICE WITH CHICKEN AND BROAD BEANS

There is a huge range of Spanish and Catalan rice dishes, using the round-grain rice grown in the province of Valencia. These follow the basic *paella* method but vary the ingredients. This recipe uses chicken and broad beans, and enriches the finished dish with a *picada* of garlic and almonds. You could use rabbit if you prefer. If you cannot find Valencian rice, use an Italian risotto rice, such as *arborio*.

Serves 4–6

salt and freshly ground black pepper
225g/8oz shelled broad beans
generous ¼ teaspoon saffron strands
6 tablespoons olive oil
90g/3½oz blanched almonds
4 cloves garlic, peeled
small bunch (about 1oz) of parsley,
  chopped
1 x 1.5–1.75kg/3–4lb chicken, cut into
  small joints
1 large onion, peeled and chopped
2 red or yellow peppers, de-seeded
  and sliced
½ teaspoon dried red chilli flakes
  (optional)
450g/1lb Valencian or arborio rice
900ml/1½ pints chicken stock

Bring 1.2 litres/2 pints of lightly salted water to the boil and blanch the beans for 2–3 minutes until tender. Drain, reserving 600ml/1 pint of the water, and refresh the beans under cold water. Remove the tough outer skin, then set aside. Soak the saffron in two tablespoons of the hot water.

In a large, deep frying pan or *paella* pan, heat half the oil and gently fry the almonds and garlic until lightly browned. Remove to kitchen paper with a slotted spoon. When cooled, pound the garlic, half the almonds and parsley and 2 tablespoons oil in a pestle and mortar or processor to make a paste, then set aside. Reserve the remaining almonds for the garnish.

Add the remaining oil to the pan and brown the chicken pieces (in batches if necessary), over a medium to high heat. Remove to a plate, add the onion, peppers and chilli, if using, to the pan and cook gently for 10–15 minutes to soften. Return the chicken to the pan. Add the rice and stir around for a few minutes until it begins to go translucent. Add the chicken stock, 300ml/10fl oz of the reserved water, the saffron and its liquid, and 1 teaspoon salt. Let the rice cook fairly briskly for about 10 minutes, reduce the heat and cook for a further 8–10 minutes until the rice is almost cooked and the liquid almost absorbed. Add more water if too dry, but do not stir the rice too much while it is cooking. When the rice is almost cooked, stir in the beans and the garlic/almond paste and cook for a few minutes. Check for seasoning. Turn off the heat. Cover the rice with a clean tea-towel, then either the lid of the pot or foil. Leave, covered, for 5–10 minutes. Garnish with the reserved almonds before serving.

Saffroned rice with
chicken and broad
beans

CHICKEN OR RABBIT STEW WITH FENNEL AND SAFFRON

This delicious, Provençal-style stew is based on a recipe in Patricia Wells' *Bistro Cooking*.

Serves 4–5

*225g/½lb tomatoes, peeled, seeded
    and chopped
2 red onions, peeled and cut into thin
    wedges
2 cloves garlic, finely chopped
2 large Florence fennel bulbs,
    trimmed and cut into wedges
    (reserve the feathery tops)
4 tablespoons extra virgin olive oil
large pinch (¼ teaspoon) saffron
finely shredded zest and juice of
    ½ orange
4 bay leaves
2 dessertspoons fresh thyme sprigs
1.5kg/3lb rabbit or chicken joints
    (bone in)
salt and freshly ground black pepper
300ml/½ pint dry white wine
450g/1lb waxy-fleshed potatoes,
    peeled
300ml/½ pint chicken stock
    (optional)*

Mix the tomatoes, onions, garlic, fennel, half the oil, orange zest and juice, and herbs in a large bowl. Add the chicken or rabbit joints and mix well. Season with black pepper and pour in the wine. Marinate for several hours or overnight, covered, in the fridge. When you are ready to cook the stew, remove the rabbit or chicken and onion from the marinade and dry slightly on kitchen paper. Reserve the remaining marinade.

Heat the oven to 180°C/350°F/gas 4. Heat the remaining oil in a frying pan and brown the rabbit or chicken on all sides, and place in a casserole. (Do the browning in batches if you haven't got a large enough frying pan – be prepared to use a little extra oil if necessary.) Add the onions to the pan and cook them until browned (about 5 minutes). Add to the rabbit or chicken. Season the meat and onions well with salt. Pour the marinade into the frying pan and bring to the boil, stirring to incorporate the meat and onion juices.

Simmer for a few minutes, then pour over the meat and onions.

Cover, then cook in the preheated oven for 30 minutes. Cut the potatoes into equal-sized chunks, stir into the stew and add the chicken stock (or use water). Cover again and cook for another 40–50 minutes until the potatoes are fully cooked. Correct the seasoning. If the sauce is too thin, remove the meat and vegetables to a plate, and reduce the sauce by fast boiling, then return the other ingredients to the sauce. Serve sprinkled with the reserved, chopped fennel tops, with slices of country bread, grilled and spread with Rouille (see page 185).

Chicken or rabbit
stew with fennel and
saffron, served here
with rouille (page
185)

LIGHTLY SALTED DUCK BREASTS WITH FRESH PEAS, SUMMER TURNIPS AND THYME

The light salting in this recipe is really no more than a spiced, dry marinade. It adds flavour and savour to the meat and the slight saltiness goes well with the sweetness of the fresh peas and turnips, both traditional partners to summer duckling.

Serves 4

1½ tablespoons coarse sea salt
2 teaspoons Szechuan peppercorns
1 teaspoon whole coriander seeds
1 teaspoon chopped fresh thyme
salt and freshly ground black pepper
4 duck breasts
40g/1½oz butter
450g/1lb young white turnips
1 teaspoon sugar
225–350g/8–12oz shelled fresh peas
8–12 spring onions, trimmed
a few sprigs of fresh thyme
sprigs of fresh thyme, to garnish

Heat the salt and spices in a small frying pan over a medium heat until fragrant (do not allow to darken too much). Cool, then grind coarsely in a mill or mortar. Add the chopped thyme and a few twists of the pepper mill. Cut a few diagonal slashes in the skin of the duck breasts and rub the salt/spice mixture all over the duck. Leave overnight or for at least 8 hours, rubbing the mixture into the breasts once.

When you are ready to cook, heat 25g/1oz butter in a heavy-based saucepan over a medium heat. Add the trimmed turnips, peeled and halved if larger than a golf ball. Cook for a few minutes, then add the sugar and cook for 2 minutes more. Add 3 tablespoons water, cover and cook for 5 minutes. Add the peas, onions and thyme sprigs, stir to mix, then cover and continue cooking until the peas and turnips are very tender. There should be a few tablespoons of liquid in the pan; if it is too liquid, evaporate by rapid boiling. Stir in the remaining butter. Season to taste.

Meanwhile, cook the duck. Brush the marinade from the breasts. Heat a heavy, preferably cast-iron or non-stick frying pan over a medium to high heat until hot. Slap the duck breasts, skin-side down, into the pan and cook for 5 minutes or until the skin is well-browned and crisp in places. Turn and cook for a further 5 minutes on the other side. Remove to a plate and allow to 'rest' in a warm oven for 10 minutes before serving. Serve the duck, sliced if liked, on a bed of the peas and turnips and garnished with fresh thyme sprigs.

Lightly salted duck breasts with fresh peas, summer turnips and thyme

89

BALLOTINE OF DUCK WITH PRUNES

This is an adapted version of a recipe from Joyce Molyneux's delightful *Carved Angel Cookery Book*. It is a splendid dish as a centrepiece for a celebratory buffet. It should be made at least 1 day in advance.

Serves 10–12

1 x 1.75–2.25kg/4–5lb duck, boned (bones and giblets retained)

FOR THE STOCK:
2 pig's trotters
bouquet garni *of parsley, thyme and bay*
1 carrot, peeled and sliced
1 large leek, cleaned and halved
2 sticks celery or a piece of celeriac, chopped

FOR THE STUFFING:
1 tablespoon Earl Grey tea
7 plump pitted prunes
225g/8oz duck or chicken livers
450g/1lb fat, boned belly pork
2 tablespoons madeira or port
2 tablespoons cognac
2 teaspoons coarsely ground coriander seeds
4 tablespoons chopped fresh parsley
50g/2oz de-rinded streaky bacon
1 clove of garlic, peeled and finely chopped
1 teaspoon chopped fresh thyme or ½ teaspoon dried thyme
salt and freshly ground black pepper
5 tablespoons white wine
50g/2 oz shelled pistachio nuts
1 tablespoon butter and 1 tablespoon olive oil
1 egg white
fresh thyme, to garnish

Put the chopped duck bones and giblets into a large saucepan with the rest of the stock ingredients. Add 1.75 litres/3 pints water, bring to the boil, skim, and simmer gently, covered, for 2 hours. Strain into a clean pan and reduce by fast boiling until about 600ml/1 pint remains. Set aside. Pour 300ml/½ pint boiling water over the tea, allow to brew for 5 minutes, then strain over the prunes and leave to soak for 2 hours.

Lay the boned duck skin-side down on a shallow tray. Remove half the leg and breast meat from the skin. Cut the removed breast meat into thin strips, cut half the livers and half the pork into thin strips also. Place all these strips in a bowl and add the alcohol, half the coriander and half the parsley. Strain the liquid from the prunes and cut into halves, add to the meat and tip the contents of the bowl over the boned duck. Cover and marinate for at least 3 hours or overnight.

Mince or chop the remaining pork, livers, duck-leg flesh and bacon, place in a bowl and mix in the remaining parsley, coriander, garlic and thyme. Season with 1½ teaspoons salt and 1 teaspoon of ground black pepper. Mix in the wine. Set this forcemeat aside, covered. Skin the pistachios by pouring boiling water over them in a small bowl, leave for 10 minutes, drain and slip off the skins. Mix into the pork forcemeat.

Now assemble the ballotine. Set the oven at 150°C/300°F/gas 2. Uncover the duck and remove the strips of meat and set these aside. Mix the marinade juices into the forcemeat. Place half the pork forcemeat over the duck, leaving a 4cm/1½ inch border all the way round. Cover this with the marinated strips of pork, duck and liver and also the prunes, then season this layer with salt and pepper. Cover the strips with the remaining forcemeat. Now roll up the duck widthways, folding in the ends first, sew up the edges with strong thread and a darning needle. Heat the butter and oil in a large, deep heat-proof casserole. Add the duck and brown it all over, pricking the skin all over with the darning needle to release the fat. Pour over the stock and bring to the boil, cover and cook in the preheated oven for 2 hours. Turn the ballotine halfway through cooking. Leave to cool in the stock for 5–6 hours or overnight.

Next day, remove all the fat from the jellied stock and lift out the duck. Remove all the thread, wrap in foil and refrigerate. Heat the stock until it liquefies, lightly whisk the egg white, add to the stock and bring to a simmer. Remove from the heat and pour immediately through a muslin-lined sieve (or use a coffee filter paper). Adjust the seasonings and allow to set.

Serve the duck in thin slices with a little of the chopped, jellied stock. Garnish with fresh thyme.

Ballotine of duck
with prunes

SPICED DUCK SALAD

This elegant starter is inspired by a Thai beef salad, *Yam Neua*. The main ingredients may be prepared in advance and the salad dressed at the last moment.

Serves 8

4 duck breasts, skin removed
3 teaspoons coriander seeds, coarsely
   ground
salt and freshly ground black pepper
2–3 tablespoons groundnut oil

FOR THE DRESSING:
10cm/4 inch length of lemon grass,
   finely chopped or minced
1 clove garlic, finely chopped
½–1 green chilli, seeded and finely
   chopped (optional)
4 tablespoons coconut milk
1 tablespoon fish sauce (nam pla)
2 tablespoons lime juice
finely grated zest of 1 lime or 2
   kaffir lime leaves, shredded
1–1½ teaspoons caster sugar

FOR THE SALAD:
2 handfuls (approximately 225g/8oz)
   assorted salad leaves – young
   spinach, lettuces, rocket, endive
4 tablespoons crispy fried onion slices
½–1 teaspoon dried red chilli flakes
½ teaspoon caster sugar
sprigs of coriander, basil and red
   chillies, to garnish

Wash and dry the duck breasts. Season well and rub all over with the coriander. Set aside in a cool place for at least 1 hour. Set oven at 220°C/425°F/gas 7. Heat the oil in a heavy, preferably non-stick frying pan until hot. Add the duck breasts and quickly sear on all sides. Transfer to a baking sheet, and cook in the oven for 7–8 minutes. Remove to a plate, cover and set aside.

Mix together all the ingredients for the dressing, seasoning to taste with caster sugar. Arrange the salad leaves on serving plates, slice the duck breasts thinly across the width at a slight angle and arrange on the salad leaves.

Spoon over the dressing, then top with the fried onion slices. Mix together the chilli flakes and sugar, and sprinkle over the salad. Garnish with herb sprigs and chillies.

Spiced duck salad

TERRINE OF RABBIT WITH GARLIC AND PARSLEY

A terrine such as this makes a good choice for a dinner party as it can be prepared well in advance. In fact, it is best made 1 day in advance. Young radishes, small pickled gherkins or other pickles, and perhaps a few slightly bitter salad leaves also make good accompaniments. Accompany the terrine with some good, country-style bread, toasted or not, as you prefer.

Serves 8

1.25kg/2½lb rabbit joints
450g/1lb belly pork
salt and freshly ground black pepper
2 fat cloves garlic, peeled and
    chopped
1½ teaspoons coarsely ground
    coriander seed
300ml/½ pint white wine
1 teaspoon chopped fresh thyme
225g/8oz streaky bacon rashers,
    de-rinded
1 onion, peeled
2 carrots, peeled
1 envelope powdered gelatine
small bunch (15g/½oz) parsley,
    finely chopped

Take the rabbit meat off the bone, cutting it into 2cm/¾ inch pieces. Remove any skin and bone from the pork and cut it into similar-sized pieces. Put the rabbit and pork into a dish, season well and mix in the garlic, the coriander and the thyme. Pour over the wine, cover and marinate in the fridge for several hours.

Meanwhile, put the rabbit bones, pork skin and bones, the roughly chopped onion and carrots into a large saucepan. Cover with water, bring to the boil, skim and then simmer gently, covered, for 2 hours. Skim from time to time. Strain and, if you have time, cool and chill, then remove the fat; otherwise try to remove as much fat as you can by skimming, then return the stock to the cleaned pan. When the rabbit and pork have marinated, strain, discard the bones and debris, add the marinade to the stock and reduce by fast boiling to about 600ml/1 pint, skim well and taste for seasoning. Take off the heat, sprinkle in the gelatine and stir until dissolved, then stir in the chopped parsley.

Set the oven to 150°C/300°F/gas 2. Use the bacon to line the base and sides of a 1.2–1.5 litres/2–2½ pint loaf tin or soufflé dish, letting the ends of the rashers hang over the edge of the dish. Loosely pack the rabbit and pork pieces into the lined dish. Pour in as much of the stock as possible – you may not need it all.

Fold over the ends of the bacon strips and cover the dish tightly with foil. Set the dish in a roasting tin and pour in hot water to come 2.5cm/ 1 inch up the side of the dish, set the whole thing in the oven and cook for 3 hours. Cool a little, then place some heavy weights on the terrine and refrigerate, still weighted, until the jelly has fully set. Either turn out to serve (dip the bottom of the dish in hot water to loosen), or cut wedges or slices directly from the dish.

GUINEA FOWL ROASTED WITH LEMON AND ROSEMARY

Serves 6–8

5 sprigs of fresh rosemary
2 lemons, well scrubbed
175g/6oz unsalted butter
2 cloves garlic, peeled and finely
    chopped
4 shallots, peeled
salt and freshly ground black pepper
3 x 1.5kg/3–3½lb guinea fowl
3 fresh bay leaves
3 tablespoons extra virgin olive oil

FOR THE SAUCE:
2 shallots or small onions, peeled
    and finely chopped
450ml/15fl oz chicken, guinea fowl or
    giblet stock
2 small sprigs fresh rosemary
2 fresh bay leaves
150ml/5fl oz red wine
2 tablespoons balsamic vinegar
120ml/4fl oz double cream
finely grated zest of ½ lemon
salt, freshly ground black pepper and
    caster sugar
25g/1oz chilled butter, cut into
    4 pieces
branches of fresh rosemary and bay
    leaves, to garnish

Set the oven to 200°C/400°F/gas 6. Strip the leaves off 2 sprigs of rosemary and chop finely. Finely grate the zest from the lemons. Cream the butter with the chopped rosemary, lemon zest, garlic and 1 of the finely chopped shallots. Season well with salt and black pepper. Wash and dry the guinea fowl. Gently lift the skin of the birds away from the breast meat and spread the flavoured butter underneath the skin – you may not use all the butter. Place the birds in a large roasting tin, insert a sprig of rosemary, a bay leaf and a shallot inside the cavity of each fowl. Cut 1 lemon into 6 and place 2 pieces inside each guinea fowl. Distribute any remaining butter between the birds. Pour a tablespoon of oil over each bird, season well and cover loosely with foil.

Roast for 20 minutes, then turn down the heat to 170°C/325°F/gas 3 and roast for 1 hour. Remove the foil, squeeze over the juice of the remaining lemon and roast for a further 15–30 minutes, basting regularly. When done, the juices should run clear when a skewer is pushed into the thickest part of the leg. Remove the birds to a large serving dish, cover loosely with foil and rest in a warm place for 20–35 minutes.

To make the sauce: spoon out 2 tablespoons of the fat from the roasting tray into a medium-sized saucepan. Fry the shallot (or onion) for 5 minutes over a low heat until soft. Add the stock, rosemary and bay leaves. Reduce the liquid by half by fast boiling. Remove the rosemary and bay leaves when the flavour is strong enough (after about 5 minutes). Add the wine and reduce again until the sauce looks syrupy (about 5 minutes fast boiling). Discard as much fat as you can from the roasting juices and add them to the sauce, then simmer for 5 minutes. Add the vinegar, cook for a few minutes, then add the cream and lemon zest, and bubble the sauce until it thickens. Taste for seasoning and add salt, black pepper and a pinch of sugar, if necessary. Turn off the heat and swirl in the butter, a little at a time. Serve with the guinea fowl, garnished with branches of rosemary and bay.

It is unlikely that I should ever give up eating meat, yet I certainly eat less red meat than I did, say, five years ago. I suspect that this is the case for many people. As we learn about the dangers of excess saturated fats in our diet, as we eat more fish and chicken and as we base our meals more on carbohydrates such as pasta, rice, bread and potatoes, so we are less likely to centre our meals around large pieces of animal protein. Now when I do eat meat, I tend to use it as an almost subsidiary ingredient in a meal rather than as the main event – tossed into a warm salad or in a sauce for pasta or rice, for instance.

You will gather from this that I rarely eat steak but when I do I now want a really good steak, from a pasture-grazed animal that has been properly aged. As we eat less meat, more and more people are prepared to pay the extra money for high-quality meat which is worth eating. Organic meat should mean that the animals have been reared without the use of drugs, hormones and chemically derived foodstuffs. It should mean that the pasture the animals have grazed on does not contain herbicidal residues. More importantly, meat should have been reared in genuinely free-range conditions and killed with the minimum of stress to the animal. I am beginning to see these qualities as basic requirements for the meat I choose to eat.

BEEF

Good beef, cared for in this way and properly aged (Anne Petch of Heal Farm Meats in Devon, who specializes in old-fashioned breeds and non-intensive rearing methods, ages her beef for three weeks), deserves only the simplest cooking and treatment. Properly aged beef is more tender and has far more flavour. Searing or roasting beef at high temperatures gives a delicious contrast between the crusty, well-cooked exterior and the meltingly pink inside.

GOOD FLAVOURS WITH BEEF

Traditionally beef is matched with hot flavours – mustard, horseradish, chilli, black pepper. Other good flavours with beef are tarragon – a classic *sauce béarnaise* flavoured with chopped tarragon can't be beaten – cumin, shallots (try some chopped shallot scattered over a grilled steak or serve with a shallot butter) and Chinese salted black beans.

Many vegetables are delicious with beef. Try old-fashioned cauliflower in cheese sauce with roast beef or partner a seared steak with grilled parsnips or grilled potatoes. Braised celery or a mash of celeriac, potato and garlic are also good things to eat with beef. Mushrooms make a traditional partner to beef and fried onion rings are delicious too. Forget the reconstituted travesties put out by the frozen food companies under the name of onion rings. Soak some red or yellow onions, sliced into rings, in milk. Heat some oil for deep frying, then toss the drained onions with seasoned flour and deep-fry until crisp and golden. Or try tossing the onions in yellow corn (maize) meal seasoned with some flaked, dried red chilli and some ground toasted cumin. If you want a proper batter, try the beer one on page 133.

LAMB

Lamb is probably my favourite red meat and is the one least susceptible to the depredations of intensive farming. Roast leg of lamb studded with garlic and rosemary is my favourite Sunday lunch, especially if served with a *gratin dauphinois* of potatoes cooked in cream and garlic. Lamb is especially

Previous page: oxtail
hotpot (page 101)

delicious cooked with potatoes or pulses. The fat from the lamb flavours these vegetables in the most delicious way. Try a casserole of shoulder of lamb cooked with flageolet beans, onions, garlic and thyme. Lamb is also good marinated and grilled. The contrast between the seared exterior and the pink, tender interior makes lamb cooked on (or under) the grill a special treat.

GOOD FLAVOURS WITH LAMB

Flavours that go well with lamb are coriander seed, garlic, rosemary, thyme, orange, apricots, olive oil and balsamic vinegar. Apart from potatoes and dried beans, other vegetables that go well with lamb are aubergines, courgettes and young summer turnips. Try serving lamb with a purée of roasted aubergine mixed with some deliciously toasty, roasted garlic. Or make a gratin of young summer turnips baked in cream scented with fresh rosemary and a touch of garlic.

Fresh peas and broad beans are also good with lamb, and lamb goes excellently with grains such as bulgar wheat or couscous. A sauce of yoghurt with chopped mint and cucumber is delicious with grilled or seared lamb.

PORK

Pork has suffered more than any other meat from the effects of modern breeding and intensive farming. Modern breeds of pork are bred to have less fat, which makes for healthier but uninteresting eating. Pork needs its fat for flavour. Old-fashioned breeds with hilarious names such as Gloucestershire Old Spots, Tamworths and British Lops, reared in the traditional way (i.e. allowed to graze outside in summer and fed without growth additives), produce pork that is full-flavoured and not dry. I love roast loin of pork with a crisp crackling (to get the best crackling, pour a kettle of boiling water over the scored skin then leave to dry thoroughly before roasting).

GOOD FLAVOURS WITH PORK

Serve roast pork with a spiced apple sauce or an apricot or sage and onion stuffing. Fruity flavours go well with a fatty meat like pork. Apples, pears, dried fruit (apricots, prunes, dried cherries), ginger, sage, citrus fruits all go well with pork. Leeks, carrots, braised red cabbage and all the pulses are good with pork, and pork fat makes some of the very best roast potatoes.

Most of the recipes in this section are for tender, prime cuts of meat which cook quickly. But we shouldn't forget the pleasures of slow-cooked dishes made from much cheaper cuts. Oxtail is one of the great underrated cuts of beef and is delicious slowly casseroled with wine or beer, onions, carrots and celery. It is one of the best candidates for cooking the day before and reheating – allowing you to remove any excess fat. Lamb shanks cooked slowly become lip-smackingly sticky and delicious, as does belly pork or pork hocks. Try the recipe for Braised Lamb Shanks on page 106.

SEARED BEEF WITH SALSA VERDE AND PARSNIP CHIPS

The idea for grilling parsnips came from Lynda Brown's *The Cook's Garden*. Sweet potatoes are delicious cooked in the same way. Choose your steak with care – a thick piece of rump or, even better, fillet is called for. If you are well organized, pepper the beef before going out for the day and leave the meat to absorb the flavour in the fridge.

Serves 4

4 thick steaks, weighing 100–150g/
  4–5oz each
2 tablespoons black peppercorns
2 tablespoons coriander seeds
3 tablespoons extra virgin olive oil
6 small parsnips, peeled
salt and freshly ground black pepper

FOR THE SALSA VERDE:
1–2 cloves garlic, peeled and finely
  chopped
25g/1oz flat leaf parsley
15g/½oz basil, mint or fresh coriander
1 tablespoon capers, rinsed
4 fillets canned anchovy, rinsed
1 tablespoon tarragon mustard
1 tablespoon tarragon vinegar
5–6 tablespoons extra virgin olive oil

Wash and dry the steaks. Coarsely crush the peppercorns and coriander seeds in a mortar or give them a short burst in a coffee grinder. Press the crushed spice over the meat. Set aside.

Make the salsa verde: place all the ingredients except the oil in a processor and blend until evenly chopped. Gradually add the oil but do not process to a smooth paste – it should retain some texture. Correct seasoning to taste.

Preheat the grill, place 2 tablespoons of oil on a heavy baking sheet, cut the parsnips into chip-sized wedges and turn in the oil, set under the grill and cook, turning once or twice, for 5–7 minutes until cooked.

Meanwhile, heat a large heavy frying pan over a medium heat, season the steaks with salt, add the oil to the pan then fry the steaks to taste (about 4–5 minutes each side). Serve the steaks, sliced if liked, on heated plates with the parsnip chips and the salsa verde. Serve with a green salad.

Seared beef with
salsa verde and
parsnip chips

PEPPERED BEEF SALAD WITH BLACK BEAN DRESSING AND PICKLED WHITE RADISH

Serves 4

450g/1lb fillet or rump of beef
1 tablespoon black peppercorns
2 tablespoons sunflower oil
about 75g/3oz peppery salad leaves
*   (watercress, mustard leaves, rocket)*
15cm/6 inch length of white radish
*   (mooli), peeled*
salt and black pepper
2 teaspoons sugar
large pinch dried chilli flakes
1 tablespoon light rice vinegar
1 heaped teaspoon salted black beans
1 tablespoon rice wine or dry sherry
4 spring onions, finely sliced
1 red or green chilli, de-seeded and
*   finely sliced*
1 tablespoon coriander sprigs

Trim any fat from the beef. Crush the peppercorns coarsely and roll the beef in them. Set aside for up to 4 hours. Preheat the oven to 220°C/425°F/gas 7. Heat 1 tablespoon of sunflower oil in a stout frying pan until very hot. Brown the beef in the hot pan on all sides. Place on a baking tray and cook in the oven for 15–20 minutes. Allow to 'rest' for 15 minutes, covered with foil. While the beef is cooking, wash and dry the salad leaves and chill until ready to serve. Finely shred the white radish to produce long, thin shreds (a food processor is good for this). Toss with 1 teaspoon salt and leave to drain in a colander for 30 minutes. Rinse, then squeeze dry, toss with 1 teaspoon of the sugar, the dried chilli and rice vinegar. Set aside.

Lightly mash the black beans with the remaining sugar. Stir in the rice wine (or sherry). Set aside. Heat the remaining 1 tablespoon of sunflower oil in a small frying pan or wok until hot, then stir-fry the spring onions and chilli for 1 minute. Add the black bean mixture and 2 tablespoons water, and bubble for a few seconds. Turn off the heat.

Slice the beef and arrange the salad leaves on a serving platter. Toss the beef with the black bean mixture and arrange on top of the salad leaves. Scatter over the coriander, then heap on the pickled radish, drained of excess moisture. Serve the salad immediately.

Peppered beef salad
with black bean
dressing and pickled
white radish

BEEF MARINATED WITH CHILLI AND CUMIN

A mixture of cascabel, mulato and smoked chipotles is very good with beef, but taste the finished paste for hotness before using. Chillies (even the same variety) vary in strength. This recipe makes enough for 4–6 steaks, but it keeps well under a little olive oil in the fridge if there are only a couple of you.

Serves 4–6

25g/1oz large dried chillies (see above)
salt and freshly ground black pepper
1 teaspoon ground toasted cumin
4–6 tablespoons olive oil
4–6 x 175–225g/6–8oz beef steaks

Cut off the stalks from the chillies and empty out the seeds. 'Toast' lightly in a dry frying pan over a medium heat, turning once or twice, until they give off their fragrance. Turn into a small bowl, cover with hot water and leave to soak for 20–30 minutes. Drain and blend the chillies with the rest of the ingredients, except the beef, in a liquidizer or food mill. Add a little of the soaking water to make a runny paste.

Wash and dry the steaks. Rub the paste over both sides and set aside in the fridge for several hours. Heat the grill (or barbecue) and cook the steaks on both sides to your liking (about 5 minutes on each side for slightly pink steaks). Serve immediately with a green salad.

VARIATIONS
This is a basic recipe for homemade chilli paste and can be used for many variations. Vary the spice according to what you are cooking – coriander seed for lamb/pork/chicken, fennel seed for pork/fish steaks, Chinese five-spice powder for chicken/pork/fish. Try adding some roasted or blanched garlic cloves or herbs such as thyme, oregano and finely chopped rosemary.

PORK IN A SATAY MARINADE

Serves 4

450g/1lb pork tenderloin, trimmed
  and well chilled
150ml/5fl oz coconut milk (from a
  can)
1 teaspoon ground turmeric
1 teaspoon dark Muscovado sugar
1 large clove garlic, peeled and
  finely chopped
finely grated zest and juice of 1 lime
2 tablespoons Thai fish sauce (nam pla)
2 tablespoons light soy sauce
1 tablespoon groundnut oil
1 stalk lemon grass, finely minced or
  chopped
1–4 fresh green or red chillies,
  de-seeded and finely chopped, or
  1–2 teaspoons chilli paste
freshly ground black pepper
wedges of lime, to garnish

Chilling the pork well makes it easier to slice thinly. Cut the pork into very thin strips no more than 5mm/¼ inch thick. Mix together the coconut milk, turmeric and sugar. Mix in the garlic, lime zest and juice, fish sauce, soy sauce and oil. Then beat in the lemon grass and chilli to taste. Season well with black pepper (there should be enough salt).

Marinate the pork in the coconut mixture for 2 hours or more, then thread the pork on to bamboo skewers which you've soaked in water for 30 minutes. Grill (on the barbecue or under the domestic overhead grill) for 3–5 minutes, turning and brushing with the marinade once. Serve garnished with lime wedges, and a satay sauce.

See photograph on
page 95

OXTAIL HOTPOT

It is best to prepare this dish over two days, cooking the oxtail and allowing it to cool on the first day, then removing the fat before layering with potatoes on the second.

Serves 6

1.5kg/3–3½lb oxtail pieces
3 tablespoons seasoned flour
2 tablespoons vegetable oil
2 large onions, sliced
450g/1lb carrots, peeled
2 sticks celery, chopped
1 bottle good, rich red wine
herb bundle of bay leaf, thyme and a
  piece of orange rind
salt and pepper
1–2 teaspoons redcurrant jelly
  (optional)
1kg/2lb potatoes, peeled and sliced
8–10 prunes
thyme sprigs (optional)

Preheat the oven to 160°C/325°F/gas 3. Toss the oxtail in the seasoned flour, then brown in the vegetable oil in a large frying pan (this will probably need to be done in two batches). Place the oxtail in a large, ovenproof casserole. Fry one of the onions in the fat for five minutes, then add one of the carrots, chopped, and the celery and cook for a further 5–10 minutes until the vegetables are beginning to brown. Add to the casserole, pour a little of the wine into the frying pan and scrape up all the delicious, crusty bits in the pan. Add the rest of the wine, bring to the boil, then simmer over a low to medium heat for 10 minutes. Add 300ml/½ pint water and bring back to the boil. Pour over the oxtail, add the herb bundle and season with a little salt and lots of black pepper.

Cover the casserole tightly, then cook in the preheated oven for 2½–3 hours, or until the meat is meltingly tender. Cool quickly, then chill (covered), preferably overnight. About 3 hours before you want to eat, preheat the oven to 180°C/350°F/gas 4. Remove as much fat as you can from the oxtail (reserving a little) and bone the meat if you prefer (it should slip off the bone very easily). Place the stock in a saucepan and reheat gently, until it liquefies. Press through a sieve, discard the debris in the sieve, then return the stock to the pan and add salt to taste, adding a little redcurrant jelly, if liked. Slice the remaining onion and carrots and fry in a little of the reserved fat for 5–10 minutes, just to brown.

Make a thick layer of potatoes in the casserole, then add layers of oxtail, prunes, carrots and onions. Cover with a thick layer of overlapping potatoes. Pour over the hot stock, adding water if necessary to bring the level of liquid to just below the top layer of potato. Season, then dot the potatoes with a little of the reserved fat. Cover and cook for 1 hour. Raise the temperature to 190°C/375°F/gas 5 and uncover the hotpot. Cook for a further 30–45 minutes until the potatoes are browned and completely cooked. Serve immediately, garnished with thyme, if liked.

MARINATED AND GRILLED LEG OF LAMB STEAKS WITH FLAGEOLET BEANS AND ROOT VEGETABLES

Serves 2

*2 leg of lamb steaks, weighing
  around 225–250g/8–9oz each
1 tablespoon extra virgin olive oil
1 medium red onion, peeled and
  sliced
2 medium carrots, peeled
100g/4oz piece of peeled celeriac
1 medium parsnip, peeled
salt
1 x 450g/1lb tin flageolet beans,
  drained and rinsed (or freshly
  cooked beans)
sprigs of fresh mint, to garnish*

FOR THE MARINADE & DRESSING:
*7 tablespoons extra virgin olive oil
2 dessertspoons balsamic vinegar
1 level teaspoon tarragon mustard
freshly ground black pepper
1 clove garlic, peeled and finely
  chopped
2 tablespoons chopped fresh mint
½ teaspoon ground cumin*

Make the dressing by mixing together 7 tablespoons olive oil with all the other dressing ingredients. Season with black pepper but not salt at this stage. Marinate the lamb steaks in half the dressing for 1–2 hours.

About 20 minutes before you plan to eat, heat the remaining tablespoon of oil in a heavy-based medium-sized saucepan. Fry the onion for 5 minutes until soft but not browned. Cut the root vegetables into slices or strips. Add to the pan and mix to coat in the oil. Cook for another 5 minutes, then add 2 tablespoons of water, salt and pepper, and cook, covered, for 10 minutes, or until the vegetables are just tender.

Meanwhile, preheat the grill, take the steaks out of the marinade and season with a little salt. Grill, brushed with a little more marinade from time to time, for about 5 minutes each side or to taste.

Add the beans to the root vegetables, gently stir to mix and cook for another 2–3 minutes just to heat through. Stir the remaining dressing into the beans and distribute between two warmed plates. Add a steak to each plate and decorate with sprigs of mint. Good with a watercress salad.

Marinated and
grilled leg of lamb
steaks with flageolet
beans and root
vegetables

LAMB AND APRICOT STEW WITH CHICKPEAS

This is good served with couscous or the Bulgar Wheat Pilaf on page 112.

Serves 5–6

1kg/2lb boneless shoulder of lamb
5 tablespoons olive or vegetable oil
1 large onion, peeled and sliced
1 clove garlic, peeled and chopped
1 teaspoon cumin seed, lightly
  crushed
1 teaspoon paprika
7.5cm/3 inch cinnamon stick
3 bay leaves
salt and black pepper
300ml/½ pint passata (crushed,
  sieved tomato)
150g/5oz dried apricots
225–350g/8–12oz cooked chickpeas
1 medium-sized potato, peeled
2 tablespoons chopped fresh coriander

Cut the lamb into 4cm/1½ inch cubes, trimming off any excess fat. Heat 1 tablespoon oil in a large heavy pan and brown the lamb, in batches if necessary, on all sides. Set aside, lower the heat, and cook the onion in the same pan for 5 minutes, add the garlic, spices and bay leaves, and cook for 5–8 minutes more until the onions are lightly browned. Return the meat to the pan, season well, then add the passata and 300ml/10fl oz water. Bring to a boil, reduce the heat and simmer slowly for 1 hour.

Add the apricots and the chickpeas and cook for a further 30 minutes. Add a little more water if the stew seems too dry. Adjust the seasoning and cook for another 10–15 minutes or until the meat is perfectly tender. Meanwhile, cut the potato into fine, matchstick strips and fry until crisp and browned in the remaining oil. Drain on kitchen paper.

Serve the lamb stew scattered with the fresh coriander and the potato shreds.

LAMB KEBABS MARINATED WITH YOGHURT, CHILLI AND MINT

Kebabs are everybody's favourite, especially for barbecues, as they cook quickly and are easy to eat. Yoghurt marinades cook to form a delicious, sharp crust sealing in the juices of the meat.

Serves 4–6

1kg/2lb lean lamb (shoulder or leg)
2 red or yellow sweet peppers
fresh bay leaves

FOR THE MARINADE:
250ml/8fl oz plain, unsweetened
  yoghurt
1–2 fresh green chillies, de-seeded
  and finely chopped
2.5cm/1 inch piece of fresh ginger,
  finely chopped
2 cloves garlic, peeled and finely
  chopped
2–3 tablespooons chopped fresh mint
2 teaspoons ground cumin
salt and freshly ground black pepper

Cut the meat into 2.5–4cm/1–1½ inch pieces. Cut the peppers into similar sized squares. Mix all the ingredients for the marinade, seasoning to taste with pepper. Mix the meat and peppers with the marinade, turn into a polythene box, cover and refrigerate for 1–2 days. Season with salt, then thread the ingredients on to skewers with the bay leaves and grill, turning a few times, for about 10–15 minutes or until cooked to your liking.

VARIATIONS
Other spices and herbs can be used. Try garam masala, ground coriander and fresh coriander. For vegetable kebabs substitute mushrooms and small parboiled potatoes or thick slices of courgette for the lamb. Vegetables will need less time in the marinade.

ROASTED LAMB FILLET ON A YOUNG SPINACH SALAD WITH A PINE NUT AND GARLIC DRESSING

Lean, tender lamb fillet is well suited to searing in a hot pan, then roasting briefly for a short time. The meat will be quite pink in the centre. Allow the meat to 'rest' for 10–15 minutes after cooking so that the tissues relax and the meat becomes even more tender.

Serves 2–3

275–350g/10–12oz trimmed lamb fillet
½ teaspoon whole cumin seeds
½ teaspoon coriander seeds
salt and freshly ground black pepper
1 tablespoon extra virgin olive oil

FOR THE SALAD AND DRESSING:
150g/5oz young spinach leaves
2–3 tablespoons herb sprigs (parsley,
  chervil, coriander, sorrel, etc)
6 plump cloves garlic
3 tablespoons extra virgin olive oil
1 teaspoon French mustard (tarragon
  mustard is good)
1 tablespoon balsamic vinegar
1–2 tablespoons single cream or
  yoghurt
salt and freshly ground black pepper
2 tablespoons toasted pine nuts

Wash and dry the fillet. Preheat the oven to 200°C/400°F/gas 6. Toast the cumin and coriander in a small pan over a low heat for a few minutes, then grind coarsely. Roll the fillet in the spices. Grind over some pepper (you may set the fillet aside to absorb the flavour for a few hours if you like). Heat the oil in a large frying pan until hot, then brown the fillet on all sides. Place on a baking dish, season with salt, and cook for 10–15 minutes in the oven. Leave the meat to rest, covered with foil, for at least 10 minutes before serving, cut into thin slices.

Wash and dry the spinach and herb sprigs, keep refrigerated until ready to serve. Preheat the oven to 190°C/375°F/gas 5. Wrap the unpeeled garlic in a small piece of foil,

Roasted lamb fillet
on a young spinach
salad with a pine nut
and garlic dressing

104

adding 1 tablespoon oil. Cook for 25–30 minutes until the garlic is soft. Cool then purée the garlic and its oil. Discard the skins. Place the purée in a small bowl and gradually beat in the remaining oil, mustard and vinegar.

Then gradually beat in the cream or yoghurt. Taste for seasoning.

Serve the lamb on a bed of salad leaves, drizzle over the garlic dressing and scatter over the toasted pine nuts.

PORK CHOPS IN MUSTARD SAUCE WITH A PURÉE OF DRIED PEAS

Pork, fresh and cured, is traditionally partnered by dried peas, as the fattiness of the meat is complemented by the mealiness of the pulses. Serve with a green vegetable.

Serves 4

350g/12oz dried, green split peas
1 medium onion, peeled and thickly
    sliced
2 small sticks celery, sliced
herb bundle of bay, thyme and
    parsley stalks
25g/1oz butter or 2 tablespoons extra
    virgin olive oil
1–2 teaspoons lemon juice or wine
    vinegar
salt, plenty of freshly ground black
    pepper and caster sugar
1 tablespoon olive or sunflower oil
4 pork chops
1 large shallot, peeled and finely
    chopped
½ tablespoon chopped fresh thyme
150ml/5fl oz white wine or cider
1 teaspoon crab apple or redcurrant
    jelly
3–4 tablespoons double cream or
    crème fraîche
1–2 teaspoons French mustard (a
    herbes de Provence or green
    peppercorn mustard is good)
salt and freshly ground black pepper
a few sprigs of fresh thyme, to
    garnish

Start the purée first. Soak the peas in cold water to cover for 2 hours, then drain and place in a pan with the vegetables and the herb bundle and water to cover. Bring to the boil and

simmer until cooked (about 1 hour but maybe less if the peas are fairly fresh). Drain the peas, remove the herbs, and purée either through a mouli légumes or in a food processor. The peas may be prepared in advance up to this point.

To serve: reheat the purée over a low heat, beating in the butter or oil and the vinegar or lemon juice. Season to taste with salt, lots of freshly ground pepper and perhaps a large pinch of sugar.

For the pork: heat the oil in a medium-sized frying pan over a medium heat and brown the chops on each side. Set the chops aside. Lower the heat and cook the shallot for 2 minutes. Add the thyme and return the chops (and juices) to the pan. Moisten with a few tablespoons of the wine (or cider) and cook very gently, half-covered, for about 15 minutes until the chops are cooked through.

Remove the chops from the pan and keep warm. Raise the heat and add the rest of the wine or cider to the pan. Reduce by rapid boiling, stirring frequently, until the sauce is thick and sticky. Stir in the fruit jelly and the cream and bubble for a few minutes to make a sauce. Stir in mustard to taste, then season with salt and pepper. Pour over the chops and serve immediately, garnished with thyme sprigs.

BRAISED LAMB SHANKS WITH GARLIC, SHALLOTS AND POTATOES

Serves 6–8

25g/1oz butter
1 tablespoon vegetable oil
6–8 lamb shanks
1 large onion, chopped
1 teaspoon caster sugar
1 head of garlic, separated into
  cloves and peeled
450g/1lb shallots, peeled
3 tablespoons cognac
600ml/1 pint of beef or lamb stock
  (use a good-quality stock cube)
salt and pepper
a few sprigs of fresh thyme
2–3 fresh bay leaves
450g/1lb carrots, peeled and cut into
  chunks
750g–1kg/1½–2lb small potatoes,
  peeled
chopped fresh parsley (optional)

Preheat the oven to 160°C/325°F/gas 3. Melt the butter and oil in a large, deep frying pan over a medium to high heat and brown the lamb on all sides (do this in batches if necessary). Place the lamb in a large, deep baking dish. In the fat fry the onion over a medium heat for 5–8 minutes until browned, then add the sugar and cook for 2 minutes more. Add the onions to the lamb.

Add a little more oil to the pan and fry the garlic and shallots until browned (about 5 minutes), then set aside on a plate. Add the cognac to the pan, bubble for 1 minute, then add the stock. Scrape all the juices from the bottom of the pan, bring the stock to the boil, then pour over the lamb. Season well. Add the herbs, cover the lamb tightly and cook for 1½ hours. Remove from the oven, check the seasoning, then add the garlic, shallots, carrots and potatoes. Re-cover and cook for a further 1½–2 hours, stirring occasionally (add extra stock or a little water if the braise seems too dry). Serve sprinkled with parsley, if liked.

Braised lamb shanks
with garlic, shallots
and potatoes

For too long grains and pulses have hidden their culinary lights under the bushel of worthy eating. The sort of food we know is good for us, but which we hardly ever bother cooking. But times change and people have realized that grains and pulses are not only good for you but they also form the basis of some of the most delicious food around. The modern emphasis on healthy eating and the growing popularity of 'peasant' cuisines, which value grains and pulses more than we affluent Britons ever have, means that we now eat far more of these nutritious and delicious foods than ever before.

GRAINS

The choice of grains grows all the time. Bulgar wheat (also known as *burghul* or cracked wheat), millet and quinoa all make delicious pilaf-type dishes. Couscous could be more accurately described as a tiny pasta but it cooks and eats as a grain. Pre-cooked couscous (the only type generally available in Britain) needs little extra cooking. Simply cover it with just under double its volume of hot water or stock and allow to stand until the liquid is absorbed. Fluff with a fork, stirring in spices, herbs, cooked vegetables or dried fruit and nuts, and reheat either by steaming or in a covered dish in the oven. Pearl barley is delicious in pilaf or 'risotto'-like dishes, as well as in stews, which it thickens slightly. I like its chewy texture and earthy taste. But I have not acquired a taste for buckwheat grain – *kasha* – though I like it ground into a flour and used in pasta and *blini*.

Maize or corn is used in many dishes from the northern Italian polenta through Mexican *tortillas* and *tamales* (a polenta-like mixture filled with vegetables or meat, wrapped in dried corn-husks and steamed) to the corn-

Previous page: three rice salad with carrot and orange (page 117); and fragrant rice pilaf with papaya and spring onions (top, page 117) This page: pasta with scallops and saffron and orange butter (page 118)

breads of southern-state American cooking. I love polenta when cooled, sliced and grilled, brushed with olive oil. Serve it with powerfully flavoured salsas of chopped herbs, garlic and salty items like capers, anchovies and olives, or top it with *tapenade* and goat's cheese and flash under a fierce grill. (See recipe for Sage Polenta with Cheese and Caramelized Onions on page 127.)

RICE

Rice is the staple grain of over half the world's population and is eaten two or three times a day in India, South East Asia, Japan and much of China. There are many thousands of varieties of rice of which two, the long-grained *indica* and the stubbier, starchier *japonica* or *sinica*, are the principal kinds. In Japan, sticky *japonica* rice is used in the many exquisite kinds of *sushi* in which vinegared and fanned rice is rolled in sheets of *nori* seaweed. In other parts of Asia the various types of sticky glutinous rice are used to make dishes as diverse as sweet coconut rice puddings, stuffings for *dim sum*, and the Chinese breakfast dish of *congee* or rice porridge.

Europe has its own traditions of rice cookery in those areas where rice is locally grown: the Po valley in northern Italy, parts of southern France and the region of Valencia in Spain. Authentic Piedmontese or Venetian risotti should only be made with one of the *superfino* grades of Italian, short-grained rice – of which *arborio*, *Vialone nano* and *carnaroli* are the best varieties. The grains of rice should remain slightly *al dente* in the centre but be soft enough on the outside to lend a creamy quality to the finished risotto. Spanish rice dishes – including the many versions of *paella* – use the locally grown, short-grained Valencia rice. Italian short-grained rice makes the best substitute. In the Camargue region of southern France they have grown a stubby grained 'red' rice for centuries and it is now available in Britain. Camarguaise rice is chewy with a delicious wheaten taste. It is good in mixed grain salads and pilafs.

Today, the USA is the largest exporter of rice, even selling *japonica* rice to Japan. The most common type of American long-grained rice is the Carolina, which has been bred to ensure that each grain remains separate when

cooked. Indian Patna rice is also a good, non-sticky long-grained rice. It is generally agreed, though, that the finest type of long-grained rice is basmati grown in the Punjab of India and Pakistan (there is an American version of this rice, known as Texmati, grown, as its name implies, in Texas). This delicately flavoured rice is excellent for the pilafs of Indian and Middle-Eastern cookery. Another variety of long-grained rice from Thailand is called either fragrant or jasmine rice. It has a fine, lemony-floral fragrance and goes well with all South East Asian food.

Brown rice has only been partially refined, leaving the nutritious inner husk on the grain. People can be very rude about brown rice, principally, I suspect, because of its solid vegetarian associations. But chewy, nutty-flavoured brown rice is delicious in salads and stuffings. Brown rice takes longer to cook than fully milled rice and, for eating straight, I prefer brown basmati over other long-grained brown rices.

And then there is wild rice, indigenous to North America, which isn't a rice at all, but an aquatic grass (*Zizania aquatica*), though it looks and cooks like a long-grained black rice. Wild rice takes from 30–45 minutes to cook and is delicious in salads, stuffings and

mixed rice dishes. It has a chewy texture and a wonderful earthy flavour, which goes well with other wild foods such as game and fungi. Anyone who likes rice and wants to know more about it and how to cook it should read Sri Owen's marvellous book on the subject, *The Rice Book*.

PULSES AND BEANS

There is a huge range of pulses available – from the gloriously red aduki and kidney beans to the prettily speckled pinto and borlotti beans.

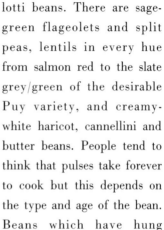

There are sage-green flageolets and split peas, lentils in every hue from salmon red to the slate grey/green of the desirable Puy variety, and creamy-white haricot, cannellini and butter beans. People tend to think that pulses take forever to cook but this depends on the type and age of the bean. Beans which have hung around at the back of the storecupboard since the last spring clean will very probably resist all attempts to soften them. But young, freshly dried haricot or flageolet will need hardly any pre-soaking and will cook very quickly. Lentils of all kinds and colours also cook quite quickly.

Older beans do need soaking. You can speed things up by bringing them to the boil and leaving them to soak in the hot water for 1–1½ hours before draining and cooking in fresh water. Remember that red and black kidney beans should be boiled vigorously for 10–15 minutes after soaking to destroy any toxins they contain. Canned pulses can be good too, especially when you're in a hurry, though when a dish's deliciousness depends largely on the quality of the pulse used – like a chickpea *hummous bi tahina* or an Italian bean salad or soup – I prefer to use the best quality I can find and cook them myself. Some of the finest pulses we can get are the

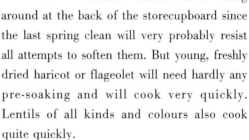

Tormesina beans and peas grown in the Avila region of western Spain. Their *garbanzo pedrosillano* (little chickpeas) and *arrocina* (tiny white haricot beans) soften quickly and are full-flavoured. They are delicious in salads and soups.

Many grain and pulse dishes seem to have an almost mystical affinity with yoghurt or sour cream. Certainly dishes made with bulgar wheat, couscous, millet, quinoa, brown rice, lentils and chickpeas are especially good with yoghurt-based sauces, a Turkish cucumber and mint salad (*caçik*) or just a big bowl of creamy, natural yoghurt.

PASTA AND NOODLES

There are countless varieties and shapes of pasta and noodles. Most are made from wheat flour but there are Italian buckwheat pastas and Asian noodles made from buckwheat, rice and moong beans. I try to keep a stock of these in my storecupboard. Wholemeal spaghetti is a personal favourite, especially in winter. In my experience, unless you get it from a good Italian delicatessen, most fresh egg pastas are not worth buying. They have a curiously tough and slimy texture when cooked. You will get better results from a good Italian dried pasta (Cipriani is a good brand), even if it does take marginally longer to cook. Homemade fresh pasta is a different kettle of fish and is great fun to put together if you invest in one of those hand-cranked pasta machines. You should use Italian grade 00 flour for pasta making if you can find it – it is available in good Italian delicatessens and large supermarkets. Homemade pasta cooks in a few minutes and needs only simple sauces to show off its fresh flavour and tender texture.

There are very few recipes for pasta in this chapter, yet I eat pasta all the time. This seems like a contradiction, but when I thought about it the reason is simple. I rarely follow 'recipes' for pasta sauces. I tend to sauce my pasta with spur-of-the-moment mixtures made from what I have in the storecupboard and fridge. Here are a few ideas.

– Cook diced courgettes in a little butter or olive oil until tender but not browned. Add some skinned, de-seeded and diced tomato and cook for a few minutes. Season with salt and freshly ground black pepper and toss in some fresh, snipped chives. A delicious sauce for summer pasta.

– Fry diced courgettes and sweet red peppers in olive oil with a sprig of fresh rosemary until tender. Raise the heat a little, remove the rosemary and stir in a little double cream or *crème fraîche*. Season well with black pepper and add a little chilli paste if you like.

– Cook some fresh peas with the pasta. Then melt some butter in a pan until foaming, add some thick cream and a little grated lemon zest. Bubble for a few minutes, then stir in some chopped fresh mint or basil. Season with black pepper and a little nutmeg. Toss the drained pasta and peas with this sauce.

– Fry some finely sliced sweet pepper and fennel in a little olive oil with a little garlic and chilli, add some torn spinach and cook until it wilts. Season well, then toss with wholemeal spaghetti, some toasted pine nuts and grated Parmesan cheese.

– Cubes of winter squash or pumpkin, pan-fried in olive oil with a few sage leaves, then tossed with goat's cheese and chopped walnuts are delicious on wholemeal pasta with a little *crème fraîche*.

– I love Asian rice or egg noodles tossed with a peanut satay sauce. Try cold rice noodles tossed with vegetables and the Thai-style dressing on page 18.

RED RICE SALAD

Red rice, grown in the Camargue region of southern France for centuries, is a short-grain rice with a reddish brown husk and a distinctive nutty, almost wheaten, taste. If you cannot find it use a short-grained brown rice (do not use brown basmati which is too delicate for this salad), cooking it for less time.

Serves 8

FOR THE DRESSING:
5 tablespoons olive oil
1–2 tablespoons lemon juice
½ teaspoon Dijon mustard
1 heaped teaspoon sun-dried tomato paste
salt, freshly ground black pepper and caster sugar

FOR THE SALAD:
350g/12oz Camarguais red rice (or short-grained brown rice)
1 large (or 2 small) ripe, red peppers, halved and de-seeded
100g/4oz ripe, cherry tomatoes, halved
½ cucumber, halved lengthways and thinly sliced
5–6 spring onions, trimmed and sliced
2 tablespoons chopped flat-leaved parsley
2 tablespoons torn fresh basil
1 tablespoon chopped fresh mint
sprigs of fresh flat-leaved parsley and basil to garnish

Make the dressing by whisking all the ingredients together, adding lemon juice and seasoning to taste. Rinse the rice and cook in lightly salted boiling water for 30–35 minutes, when the rice will still be fairly nutty; for softer rice, cover the pan and leave the rice to stand in the hot water for up to 15 minutes more. Drain and dress while still warm with almost all the dressing.

Grill the peppers, skin-side uppermost, until the skin blackens and blisters. Set aside in a closed paper bag or a covered bowl for 10 minutes so that the steam softens the skin. Peel and cut into strips or dice. Add the peppers (and any juices they have given off) to the rice. (The salad can be made well in advance to this point – keep refrigerated and covered, then bring back to room temperature before proceeding.)

Stir in the rest of the ingredients, including the remaining dressing, and adjust the seasoning. Garnish with parsley and basil.

Top: potato salad with rocket and anchovy (page 45); and, centre, red rice salad

SALMON AND COUSCOUS CAKES WITH LIME AND CORIANDER

Serves 6

175g/6oz couscous
225g/8oz skinned and boned salmon
  fillet
3 tablespoons olive or vegetable oil
5 spring onions, chopped
1–1½ teaspoons ground, toasted cumin
finely grated zest of ½ lime
1 egg, size 2, beaten
2 tablespoons chopped fresh coriander
2–3 tablespoons fromage frais *or*
  crème fraîche
salt and freshly ground black pepper

Soak the couscous in 300ml/10fl oz hot water for 10–15 minutes, until it has absorbed the water. Rub the salmon with ½ teaspoon oil and grill for 2–3 minutes on each side until just cooked. Cool the fish, then flake with a fork. Mix the salmon into the couscous. Heat half the remaining oil in a small frying pan and cook the spring onions for a few minutes until soft, add the cumin and lime zest, and cook for another few minutes. Stir into the couscous and salmon mixture with the rest of the ingredients, adding sufficient *fromage frais* (or *crème fraîche*) to bind the mixture. Season generously with salt and pepper. Form into 6–12 flattish cakes and refrigerate until ready to cook.

To cook: heat the remaining oil in a large, non-stick frying pan over a medium heat and cook fairly gently until brown on each side (about 5–6 minutes each side). You may need a little extra oil. Serve with a tomato salad and some natural yoghurt stirred through with diced, salted cucumber, chopped mint and ground, toasted cumin.

Ⓥ BULGAR WHEAT PILAF

The same basic method may be used for millet and quinoa. It is best to 'toast' both of these grains in a little oil before adding the liquid to bring out their nutty flavours. Also both millet and quinoa will take longer to cook than bulgar wheat, and you should be prepared to add extra water or stock if the pilaf seems too dry. Good with the Lamb and Apricot Stew with Chickpeas on page 103.

Serves 5–6 as an accompaniment

3 tablespoons olive oil
2 medium onions, peeled and thinly
  sliced
1–2 teaspoons ground coriander seeds
2 cloves garlic, peeled and finely
  chopped
350g/12oz bulgar wheat
350–600ml/12fl oz–1 pint water or
  chicken or vegetable stock
salt and freshly ground black pepper
2 tablespoons chopped fresh coriander
  or mint (optional)

Heat the oil in a deep frying pan and cook the onion for about 10 minutes until browned. Set half the onion aside. Add the coriander seed and garlic to the remaining onion in the pan and cook for 2 minutes more. Add the bulgar wheat and cook, stirring to coat the wheat in the oil, for a few minutes. Add 350ml/12fl oz water (or stock), season, cover and cook at a very low simmer for about 20 minutes or until the liquid is absorbed. Add more liquid if too dry. Just before serving, stir in the remaining onion and the chopped herbs, if using, and correct the seasoning.

'RISOTTO' OF BARLEY WITH ROASTED SQUASH, CARROT AND CELERY

Serves 4

150g/5oz pearl barley
salt and freshly ground black pepper
*1 small butternut squash, peeled,
    seeded and cut into chunks*
4 tablespoons olive oil
1 medium onion, peeled and chopped
100g/4oz celery, finely sliced
*175g/6oz carrots, peeled and coarsely
    grated*
*4–8 tablespoons vegetable or chicken
    stock*
25g/1oz unsalted butter
*1–2 tablespoons chopped, fresh,
    flat-leaved parsley*
*40g/1½oz Parmesan or Pecorino
    cheese, grated or shaved*
*1½ tablespoons toasted pumpkin (or
    sunflower) seeds*

Rinse the barley well. Throw into a saucepan of water, bring to the boil, then drain and rinse again. Return to the rinsed-out saucepan, cover well with water and bring to the boil. Simmer, half covered, for 40–60 minutes until the barley is tender, season with a teaspoon of salt and cook for a little longer. Drain.

Set the oven to 200°C/400°F/gas 6. Toss the squash in half the oil, season and turn on to a baking tray. Roast, uncovered, for 20–30 minutes until golden and tender. Turn the squash once or twice during cooking. Meanwhile, heat the remaining oil in a roomy, deep frying pan over a moderate heat. Cook the onion slowly until translucent and golden yellow but do not brown (about 10 minutes). Add the celery and cook gently for another 5 minutes, then add the carrots. Cook for 1–2 minutes, then season with salt and pepper. Stir in the drained barley and 4 tablespoons stock. Cook for about 5–10 minutes, stirring frequently, adding more stock to keep the mixture moist. Stir in the butter and parsley, followed by the roasted squash. Stir in half the grated or shaved cheese and serve immediately, scattered with the toasted pumpkin (or sunflower) seeds and accompanied by the remaining cheese.

VARIATION
Substitute Florence fennel for the celery and cook 1 teaspoon fennel seeds with the onion. Substitute the chopped, feathery top of the fennel for the chopped parsley in the above recipe. 175g/6oz sliced chestnut cap mushrooms make a good addition to either version.

'Risotto' of barley
with roasted squash,
carrot and celery

Risotto Primavera
(Risotto of Spring Vegetables)

In a classic risotto, the hot liquid is added gradually to the rice so that the rice releases enough starch to make the finished dish creamy but with every grain *al dente* at its centre. This risotto is very much a celebration of late spring, when young vegetables are at their best. The vegetables can be varied according to what is available.

Serves 6

*1 bunch of asparagus (usually about
    225g/8oz)*
salt and freshly ground pepper
225g/8oz young carrots, trimmed
225g/8oz young turnips, trimmed
*175g/6oz sugar snap peas or young,
    shelled peas*
90g/3½oz unsalted butter
*1 large onion, peeled and finely
    chopped*
400g/14oz arborio or other risotto rice
*100–175g/4–6oz young spinach,
    washed and trimmed*
75g/3oz freshly grated Parmesan
*2–3 tablespoons chopped fresh chervil
    or parsley*
sprigs of fresh chervil, to garnish

First prepare the vegetables. Trim the woody, lower part of the asparagus stems and set aside. Cut off the asparagus tips with about 4cm/1½ inches of stem, also set aside. Bring 1.5 litre/2½ pints of water to the boil and add ½ teaspoon salt. Cook the woody parts of the asparagus in the water for 15 minutes, remove them and discard. Then cook the tips in the same water for 3–4 minutes until just tender, remove with a slotted spoon, refresh under cold water and set aside. Then cook the remaining asparagus stalks in the same water until tender (6–10 minutes), remove, roughly chop and set aside. Depending upon size, leave the carrots and turnips whole or cut into halves or quarters. Blanch the carrots and turnips in the same water until just tender (4–6 minutes), remove with a slotted spoon and refresh under cold water, then set aside. Blanch and refresh the sugar snap peas in the same water for about 3 minutes. Reserve the vegetable stock and keep warm.

Melt 50g/2oz of butter in a shallow, wide pan over a low heat. Gently fry the onion in the butter with a pinch of salt for 10–15 minutes until golden and translucent. Then add the rice, turn the heat up to medium and stir the rice until each grain is thoroughly coated with butter. Bring the reserved vegetable stock to the boil and add a couple of ladlefuls to the rice, stirring the rice constantly. Cook until the liquid has been absorbed, then add more liquid, a couple of ladlefuls at a time. Add the reserved, chopped asparagus (not the tips) after 8 minutes of cooking. Use hot water if you run out of vegetable stock. The risotto should be moist but not too soupy. Stir in the spinach and cook for 1 minute, then gently stir in all the blanched vegetables and cook for a few minutes to reheat.

Stir in the chopped chervil (or parsley), the remaining butter and the grated Parmesan. Correct the seasoning with salt and a good grinding of black pepper, if necessary. Garnish with sprigs of chervil.

Risotto primavera;
and Persian chilau
rice with fresh herbs
(page 116)

PERSIAN CHILAU RICE WITH FRESH HERBS

This is one of the most delicious ways to serve rice. Because of its wonderful buttery flavour, it is best served with simply cooked meat or fish. The rice on the bottom of the pan forms a rich, golden brown crust known as *dig*. As Claudia Roden points out, this is the best, most delicious bit of the dish – the part that is offered first to guests.

Serves 5–6

350g/12oz basmati rice
salt
75g/3oz unsalted butter
4–5 tablespoons finely chopped fresh herbs (use a mixture of any of the following – dill, tarragon, parsley, chervil, chives – but the mixture <u>must</u> include some dill)
sprigs of fresh dill, to garnish

Rinse the rice thoroughly and place in a large bowl, add 1 tablespoon salt and sufficient water to cover. Leave to soak overnight or for several hours. Drain. Bring plenty of fresh, lightly salted water to the boil in a large pan, throw in the rice and boil for 2–6 minutes until the rice is just tender – this will depend on the age of the rice and the amount of soaking time. Drain.

In a medium-sized, heavy-bottomed, saucepan over a medium heat melt half the butter. Cover the base of the pan with a 2.5cm/1 inch layer of rice, then mix the rest of the rice with the chopped herbs. Add this rice to the pan, shaping it to make a pyramid. Make a slight hollow at the top of this heap of rice and pour in the rest of the butter, melted. Cover the pan with a clean tea-towel, then jam on the lid of the pan, and fold the edges of the towel over to keep them away from the flame. Cook over a medium heat for 15 minutes, then reduce the heat to low and cook for a further 30 minutes.

Plunge the base of the pan into 2.5cm/1 inch of cold water in the sink and leave to stand for 2 minutes. To serve, spoon the rice on to a serving dish, scrape out the golden crust of rice (the *dig*) from the bottom of the pan (it should have been loosened by plunging the pan into the cold water) and place on top of the rice. Garnish with fresh herbs.

See photograph on
page 107

FRAGRANT RICE PILAF WITH PAPAYA AND SPRING ONIONS

Serves 6

*350g/12oz fragrant 'jasmine' rice, or
use basmati*
*750ml/1¼ pints chicken or vegetable
stock or half stock, half water*
salt and freshly ground black pepper
*1 stalk fresh lemon grass, split in
half*
*2 kaffir lime leaves, or use strips of
lime zest*
1 papaya, ripe but firm
*50g/2oz butter or 2½ tablespoons
sunflower oil*
*1 bunch spring onions, trimmed and
chopped*
*1 green chilli, de-seeded and finely
sliced*
*2–3 tablespoons chopped fresh
coriander*
*sprigs of fresh coriander and red
chillies, to garnish (optional)*

Rinse the rice and put it into a medium-sized saucepan with the stock, 1 teaspoon of salt, the lemon grass and 1 of the lime leaves or pieces of lime zest. Bring to the boil, stir, then cover and turn heat to low. Cook for 12 minutes or until the liquid has been absorbed. Cover the rice with a clean cloth, jam on the lid of the pan and set aside.

Finely shred the remaining lime leaf or lime zest, and then peel, de-seed and slice the papaya. Heat the butter (or oil) in a frying pan and cook the spring onions and chilli for a few minutes to soften, then add the papaya and cook for 1–2 minutes. Stir the onions and papaya into the rice along with the shredded lime leaf and the coriander. Mix gently. Serve garnished with fresh coriander and red chillies, if liked.

THREE RICE SALAD WITH CARROT AND ORANGE

See photograph on
page 107

Serves 6

50g/2oz wild rice
50g/2oz brown basmati rice
50g/2oz long-grain American rice
salt and freshly ground black pepper
3 tablespoons olive oil
*the thinly pared zest of 1 unwaxed or
well-scrubbed orange*
2 teaspoons caster sugar
*2 medium-sized carrots, peeled and
trimmed*
*1 teaspoon coarsely ground coriander
seeds*
50g/2oz currants or raisins
*65g/2½oz pine nuts or slivered
almonds, toasted*
3–4 tablespoons chopped parsley
*2 tablespoons rice or cider vinegar,
plus more to taste*

Cook each of the rices separately in lightly salted boiling water: the white rice for 15–20 minutes, the basmati rice for 20–30 minutes, the wild rice for 40–50 minutes. Drain and mix together in a large bowl with 1 tablespoon of the oil.

Cut the zest into fine julienne strips. Blanch the orange zest in plenty of boiling water for 1 minute, drain and rinse under cold water, repeat the blanching and rinsing process, then return the zest to a small pan with 5 tablespoons of water and the sugar. Cook the zest until the water has almost evaporated, making sure that it does not burn, then set aside.

Cut the carrots into thin julienne strips about 4cm/2 inches long. Heat the remaining oil in a frying pan and cook the carrots and ground coriander for 3–4 minutes until the carrots are just tender and slightly browned. Mix the carrots, orange rind and all the other ingredients into the rice, seasoning to taste with salt, pepper and more vinegar, if liked. Leave to stand for 2 hours before serving at room temperature.

WARM PIGEON AND LENTIL SALAD WITH DEEP-FRIED ROOTS

All kinds of root vegetables may be finely sliced and deep-fried to produce flavourful 'crisps'. They make a great addition to salads of all kinds and are addictive just as themselves. Root vegetable crisps are now sold in packets (at a price) in good delicatessens.

Serves 4

175g/6oz green, preferably Puy
*   lentils*
1 small onion, peeled and halved
2 carrots, peeled
bouquet garni *of bay, thyme and*
*   celery stalk*
5 tablespoons extra virgin olive oil
1 teaspoon mustard
1 clove garlic, peeled and finely
*   chopped*
1 dessertspoon sherry vinegar
2 tablespoons chopped fresh parsley
coarse sea salt and freshly ground
*   black pepper*
sunflower oil for deep-frying
2 medium-sized parsnips, peeled
1 medium-sized beetroot, peeled
8 pigeon breasts
sprigs of parsley, to garnish

Pick over the lentils for stones, rinse, place in a pan and put into a medium-sized saucepan with the halved onion, one carrot and the *bouquet garni*. Cover with water, bring to the boil and simmer, covered, for 30–40 minutes until the lentils are cooked.

Mix together all but one tablespoon of oil, the mustard, garlic, vinegar and parsley. Drain the lentils and dress while hot with the oil mixture. Season to taste with salt (about ½ teaspoon) and black pepper. Set aside. While the lentils are cooking heat 5cm/ 2 inches sunflower oil in a deep saucepan, wok or deep-fat fryer to a temperature of 160°C/325°F. Slice the remaining carrot, parsnip and beetroot into long, thin slices approximately 2mm/1/16 inch thick. Fry for 2–3 minutes until golden and crisp, do not crowd the pan and cook in several batches. Drain on kitchen paper and sprinkle with a little salt.

To serve: heat the remaining olive oil in a non-stick frying pan over a medium-high heat until hot. Fry the pigeon breasts for 3 minutes on the skin side, then turn over and fry for another 3 minutes. Place on a plate and rest in a warm oven for 5 minutes. Distribute the lentils between 4 warm plates, slice the pigeon breasts and arrange them alongside. Arrange some crisps on each plate and garnish with some parsley sprigs.

PASTA WITH SCALLOPS AND SAFFRON AND ORANGE BUTTER

Serves 4

8–12 fresh scallops, shelled and
*   cleaned*
extra virgin olive oil
salt and black pepper
2 large yellow or red peppers
50g/2oz butter
1 large shallot or small onion,
*   chopped*
1 clove garlic, finely chopped
150ml/¼ pint Noilly Prat or other
*   vermouth*

550g/1¼ lb fresh taglierini or
*   tagliatelle, or 350–400g/12–14 oz*
*   dried pasta*
25g/1oz fresh white breadcrumbs
fresh coriander or parsley, to garnish

FOR THE BUTTER:
large pinch of saffron strands
100g/4oz unsalted butter, softened
1 shallot, finely chopped
1 tablespoon chopped fresh coriander
1 tablespoon chopped fresh parsley
finely grated peel of ½ orange

½ *teaspoon ground coriander*
salt and black pepper

First make the butter: soak the saffron in 1 tablespoon hot water for 10 minutes. Cream the butter with all the remaining ingredients, then beat in the saffron strands and liquid. Cover and chill until needed.

Remove the corals from the scallops and cut the white part across into 2 or 3 slices, depending on size. Put these and the corals into a dish or tray, drizzle with 2 tablespoons of oil and season with salt and pepper. Cover and chill for at least 30 minutes.

Halve and seed the peppers and cook under a hot grill until the skin completely chars (about 8–10 minutes). Pop into a paper bag and close, allow the peppers to steam for 10 minutes, then remove the charred skin. Cut peppers into strips and set aside.

Melt half the butter in a large, deep frying pan and fry the shallot (or onion) for a few minutes. Add the garlic and fry for 1 minute more, then add the Noilly Prat, turn up the heat, and reduce the liquid by half. Then add the peppers and all but 2 tablespoons of the saffron butter, and cook for a few minutes so that the butter melts to form a sauce. Set aside.

Bring a large pan of boiling slightly salted water to the boil for the pasta, add 1 tablespoon of oil, then cook the pasta for 3–4 minutes if fresh or according to the packet if dried. In a separate frying pan, melt the remaining butter and fry the breadcrumbs until golden brown and crisp. Set aside on a plate and wipe out the pan. Return the pan to the heat, allow to get hot, then add the scallops and cook briefly for 1–2 minutes. Drain the pasta, add to the saffron and pepper sauce and reheat, seasoning to taste. Arrange on heated plates and top with scallops and a knob of the remaining saffron butter. Sprinkle with the breadcrumbs and garnish with coriander (or parsley).

**Warm pigeon and
lentil salad with
deep-fried roots**

119

PASTA WITH BROCCOLI AND FENNEL WITH PINE KERNELS, CURRANTS AND CAPERS

Serves 3–4

225g/8oz broccoli
1 head Florence fennel
salt and freshly ground black pepper
350g/12oz wholemeal spaghetti
3–4 tablespoons extra virgin olive oil
2 cloves garlic, peeled and finely
  chopped
1 dried red chilli, halved
2 tablespoons salted capers, rinsed
4 tablespoons finely chopped parsley
2 tablespoons currants
40g/1½oz pine nuts, toasted

Cut the broccoli into florets and cut the stalk into slices. Slice the fennel. Bring a large pan of salted water to the boil, add the broccoli stalks, cook for 1 minute, then add the florets and cook for a further 2 minutes, then add the fennel slices, cook for a further 2 minutes. Remove the vegetables with a slotted spoon and set aside in a colander. Add the pasta to the same boiling water.

While the pasta is cooking, heat the oil in a large frying pan. Gently cook the garlic and chilli for a few minutes. Then add the drained broccoli and fennel. Cook for 5 minutes, then discard the chilli. Chop the capers, parsley and currants together, add to the pan with the pine nuts. When the pasta is cooked, drain, then toss with the broccoli and fennel mixture. Season with lots of black pepper.

VARIATION
Salsa di noci makes a delicious sauce for tagliatelle, for fish or grilled chicken and for boiled or steamed cauliflower or broccoli. Bottled versions can be bought but it takes only a moment in a food processor. Process together 75g/3oz walnuts (blanched and skinned if you have time) with 1 peeled clove of garlic, 15g/½oz flat-leaved parsley, 1 slice white bread (crusts removed), and 5–6 tablespoons fruity olive oil. Add sufficient milk or thin cream to produce a spoonable consistency. Season with salt, pepper and lemon juice. Serves 3–4.

To some extent, this chapter is based on a false distinction or at least a distinction which is fast breaking down. Many committed meat eaters now choose to eat vegetarian food for part of the time or, more likely, they choose dishes without even thinking about the fact that they do not contain meat or fish. The old, rigid barriers between mainstream and vegetarian eating are tumbling down. Many of my friends choose not to eat meat or fish, or the food that they eat could be described, in that rather clumsy phrase, as 'demi-veg' – that is, they eat fish and shellfish but not meat. This blurring of categories is mirrored in this book, too, as there are many vegetarian recipes throughout the various sections.

So why a separate section on meat- and fish-free main courses? Firstly because when I was selecting the recipes for this book many of my favourites happened to be vegetarian dishes, which I would serve either as a complete weekday meal or as a main course when entertaining friends. It then occurred to me that it is the main course that people often have a problem with when choosing to serve a vegetarian meal. Meat eaters are so accustomed to organizing their meals around a lump of animal protein – enshrined in the idea of 'meat and two veg' – that they find themselves nonplussed when faced with cooking a meal for non meat- or fish-eating friends or relatives.

One way round the problem is to abandon the idea of the 'main course' completely and serve a collection of little dishes, a sort of *mezze*, from which people can just help themselves. Start off with vegetable- and pulse-based dips, such as a delicious purée of roasted aubergine with garlic, tahini, lemon juice and parsley, then move on to a

collection of hot and cold vegetable dishes – salads of cooked vegetables, little pastries stuffed with spinach, rice and cheese mixtures, or a collection of stuffed vegetables. Serve plenty of good bread to fill corners and mop plates. This is fine for informal entertaining but can be a bit of a bind on the cook who has to keep the succession of dishes flowing from the kitchen. In this section I hope you'll find lots of ideas for imaginative vegetarian eating, some of which would fit into this idea of the less structured meal, others which would make a fine centrepiece to a traditional three-course dinner, and yet others which make simpler supper or lunch dishes.

HEALTHY OPTIONS?

For a long time, vegetarian food has languished under the label of healthy eating. Vegetarians may well be entitled to a share of the high moral ground but not necessarily on the basis of the healthiness of their diet. Many vegetarians have almost puritanical attitudes to the use of butter and cream in food, but will quite happily consume vast quantities of full-fat cheese or eggs each week. There is healthy and unhealthy vegetarian food, just as meat eaters can have healthy or unhealthy regimes. On balance, though, we know we should eat more vegetables and fruit, more grains and pulses, and less processed food and saturated fat. Good vegetarian food fulfils all of these criteria. But more people will be attracted to a healthier diet if the food they are encouraged to eat is delicious and well cooked. Being a vegetarian or eating healthily does not mean giving up eating or cooking for pleasure.

TEXTURE AND FLAVOUR

I love vegetarian food because of the scope it gives for contrasting textures and flavours

Previous page:
chickpea pancakes
with chilli and spring
onions with an
avocado and
coriander salsa
(page 131)
This page: roasted
peppers stuffed with
black beans, corn
and feta cheese
(page 129)

within a meal. Salads and accompanying vegetables often have an equal status with the main element of the meal. Indeed it challenges our perceptions of the traditional structure of the meal. Rich vegetarian foods, using lots of dairy produce – butter, cheese and cream – or pulses and nuts, are best served in small portions with crisp, green salads or lightly cooked, green vegetables. Or try stir-fries of mixed vegetables. Pilafs of rice, couscous and bulgar wheat are excellent with tomato- or cheese-based dishes or those with creamy sauces.

This chapter includes some of my favourite types of vegetarian food. Savoury tarts and pastry dishes are always popular and make a good choice for either a lunch or dinner party or as part of a buffet served with other dishes. Such savoury tarts are very adaptable – for instance, you could make the Courgette and Basil Tart on page 136 with a coriander and walnut pesto, or a sun-dried tomato red pesto instead of the more usual basil and pine nut *pesto genovese*. Another good, simple idea is to make a savoury upside-down tart. Arrange some roasted or grilled vegetables in a solid-based shallow tin, then top with a layer of pastry and bake. Use shortcrust, flaky or several layers of phyllo pastry. Bake until the pastry is cooked then turn out to serve. Good vegetables to use are chicory, onions, leeks, sweet peppers, aubergines and large mushrooms. Root vegetables like parsnips and sweet potatoes are good treated like this, too. I also like the variety of stuffed vegetables which, though they take a little longer to prepare, are delicious and can be prepared well ahead. Again, you could try adapting the recipes I have given here to use different vegetables. The stuffing in the recipe for Baked Stuffed Onions (page 126) could be used for stuffed

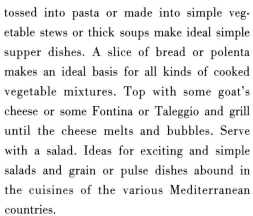

fennel or sweet peppers. And, as well as the ideas here, some of the stuffings in the final chapter can be used to stuff vegetables before baking. Pancakes, too, are often neglected when thinking about vegetarian food but they can be filled with all sorts of vegetable mixtures and then served with a delicious sauce.

SIMPLE VEGETARIAN EATING

The influence of vegetarian ideas on modern cooking is immense. The renewed interest and delight in seasonal vegetables, the growing enjoyment of grain and pulse dishes means that many more of us now eat vegetarian food on a regular basis. Another influence has come from the food and cooking of the Mediterranean region. The cooking of Italy, Greece and the Middle East provides us with many ideas for simple vegetarian dishes. Mixtures of seasonal vegetables tossed into pasta or made into simple vegetable stews or thick soups make ideal simple supper dishes. A slice of bread or polenta makes an ideal basis for all kinds of cooked vegetable mixtures. Top with some goat's cheese or some Fontina or Taleggio and grill until the cheese melts and bubbles. Serve with a salad. Ideas for exciting and simple salads and grain or pulse dishes abound in the cuisines of the various Mediterranean countries.

A combination of pulses and grains provides an ideal dietary mix of complementary proteins, so serving rice or bulgar wheat or pasta or bread with a pulse-based dish tastes good and makes sound nutritional sense. The previous chapter includes many ideas for using pulses and grains which would make an ideal basis for a vegetarian meal, and the earlier sections on salads and vegetable cookery have many recipes which would fit well into a vegetarian meal.

Roasted squash stuffed with rice and mushrooms (page 135)

YEASTED THREE ONION TART WITH GOAT'S CHEESE AND THYME

This tart, a sort of cross between a pizza and a quiche, makes a substantial and delicious supper or lunch dish. It contrasts the gently fried, meltingly-soft red and yellow onions with the fresh, green flavour of spring onions. Goat's cheese and thyme are natural partners to onions, but if you don't like goat's cheese use Gruyère or Emmental.

Serves 4–6

FOR THE PASTRY:
175g/6oz strong, plain flour
½ teaspoon salt
½ sachet easy-blend dried yeast, or
  10g/¼oz fresh yeast
1 egg, size 3, beaten
2 tablespoons olive or vegetable oil

FOR THE FILLING:
50g/2oz butter
450g/1lb yellow onions
225g/½lb small, red onions
salt and black pepper
2 eggs, size 2 or 3
150ml/¼ pint single or whipping
  cream
1½ bunches spring onions, trimmed
150g/5oz goat's cheese
1 tablespoon thyme sprigs

First make the pastry. Warm a bowl, add the flour, salt and easy-blend yeast. Beat the egg with 3 tablespoons warm water. Add the egg to the flour with the oil and mix to make a soft dough. (If using fresh yeast, cream the yeast with 3 tablespoons warm water, then use to bind the flour with the beaten egg and oil.) Using a floured hand, knead the dough lightly in the bowl. Cover the bowl with cling film and leave in a warm place until doubled in size (about 1–1½

hours). Knead again, sprinkling with flour if the dough is very soft. Then press out to roughly line a stout baking tray approximately 25 x 33 x 2.5cm/10 x 13 x 1 inch. Set aside, covered.

Meanwhile, prepare the filling. Melt the butter in one large or two smaller frying pans and cook the sliced yellow and red onions very gently, half-covered, until soft and the yellow onions are golden but not browned. Stir frequently and keep the heat low. This takes about 25–30 minutes. Beat the eggs with the cream and season well with salt and pepper, slice the cheese and chop half of the spring onions. Preheat the oven to 220°C/425°F/gas 7.

Press out the pastry to form a rim approximately 2.5cm/1 inch high to contain the filling. Spread the cooked onions and chopped spring onions over the dough, then add the goat's cheese and lay the whole spring onions over the top (if thicker than a pencil, cut the spring onions in half lengthways). Pour in the cream and egg mixture, then scatter over the thyme. Place the tart in the oven, reduce the heat to 190°C/375°F/gas 5 and bake for 25–35 minutes, until the filling is risen and browned and the pastry firm.

Serve immediately or lukewarm with salad.

Yeasted three onion
tart with goat's
cheese and thyme;
and baked stuffed
onions (page 126)

BAKED STUFFED ONIONS

A dish of baked, stuffed onions, the crisp, roasted exterior contrasting with the soft, tender centres, makes a great supper dish.

Serves 4–6

12 medium-sized, firm round onions,
*   peeled but the root left intact*
salt

FOR THE STUFFING:
4 tablespoons extra virgin olive oil
1 clove garlic, finely chopped
225g/8oz fresh spinach
100g/4oz white breadcrumbs
1 teaspoon finely shredded lemon
*   zest*
2 tablespoons chopped fresh parsley
50g/2oz toasted pine nuts
75–100g/3–4oz feta or Lancashire
*   cheese, crumbled*
salt and freshly grated black pepper
freshly grated nutmeg

Bring a large pan of salted water to the boil and cook the onions, covered, for 10–15 minutes. Drain and cool. Cut off the top layer and, using a small, sharp knife and a pointed teaspoon, remove the centre of the onion, leaving a shell of at least 2 layers. Stand the onion shells on a baking tray or dish.

Chop the removed onion and sauté with the garlic in 2 tablespoons of the oil over a medium heat. Cook for 10–15 minutes, making sure that the mixture doesn't brown too much. Chop the spinach and add to the pan, cook, stirring frequently, until the spinach collapses. Place the rest of the ingredients in a bowl and mix in the onion mixture. Season well with salt, pepper and grated nutmeg.

Stuff the mixture back into the onion shells, scattering any leftover stuffing between the onions. Preheat the oven to 190°C/375°F/gas 5. Sprinkle the remaining olive oil over the onions and cook, uncovered, for 40–45 minutes, basting with a little more oil if necessary, until the onions are browned and tender. Serve immediately with salad. A homemade tomato sauce goes well with the stuffed onions, too.

SAGE POLENTA WITH CHEESE AND CARAMELIZED ONIONS

Serves 4–6

*750g/1½lb red or yellow onions,
   peeled*
3–4 tablespoons extra virgin olive oil
salt and pepper
1 teaspoon caster sugar
a few sprigs of fresh thyme
2 tablespoons sherry vinegar
extra virgin olive oil
*100–175g/4–6oz cheese – try either a
   chèvre goat's cheese or some Italian
   Fontina or Taleggio – sliced*

FOR THE POLENTA:
150g/5oz polenta (maize) meal
salt
*50g/2oz freshly grated Parmesan
   cheese*
*5–6 fresh sage leaves, chopped, plus a
   few whole leaves*

First make the polenta. Bring 900ml/1½pints water to the boil and add 2 teaspoons salt. Turn the heat down to a simmer then, stirring all the time in one direction, add the polenta in a steady stream. Bring to the boil, still stirring, then cook over the lowest heat for 30–40 minutes until very thick and smooth. Stir very frequently as it cooks. When done, stir in the Parmesan and sage, turn on to a tray and allow to cool and set.

Preheat the oven to 200°C/400°F/ gas 6. Slice the onions into thick slices. Set on a stout baking tray, season well with salt, pepper and sugar. Sprinkle with 2 tablespoons oil and add the thyme. Cover with foil and cook for about 25 minutes.

Uncover, turn the onions and sprinkle with the vinegar. Return to the oven and cook for 20–30 minutes, stirring once until caramelized and browned but not charred. Sprinkle with a little more vinegar, if liked, then stir in the chopped parsley.

When the polenta has cooled and set, cut into thick 1cm/½ inch slices. Set on a baking tray, brush with a little oil and grill for about 5 minutes until crisped and browned, turn the slices over, brush with oil and grill for 2–3 minutes. Heap the onions over the polenta and top with the sliced cheese. Grind over some black pepper and top with one or two whole sage leaves. Return to the grill until the cheese is melted. Serve with an undressed salad of peppery rocket and crisp cos lettuce.

TOMATO AND PARMESAN TART

Serves 6

FOR THE PASTRY:
200g/7oz plain, unbleached flour
pinch of salt
75g/3oz butter
40g/1½oz freshly grated Parmesan
  cheese
1 egg yolk

FOR THE FILLING:
1.25kg/2¼lb ripe tomatoes
4 tablespoons extra virgin olive oil
2 medium red onions, thinly sliced
2 cloves garlic, chopped
¼–½ teaspoon dried red chilli flakes
heaped tablespoon fresh thyme sprigs
2 tablespoons balsamic or sherry
  vinegar
salt, pepper and caster sugar
2 tablespoons torn basil leaves

Sift the flour and salt into a bowl, add the butter and cheese and either rub in or process until the mixture forms breadcrumbs. Bind the pastry with the egg yolk and 2–3 tablespoons cold water. Press together to form a ball, wrap in foil and chill for 30 minutes.

Heat the oven to 190°C/375°F/gas 5, then roll out the pastry to line a 25cm/10 inch round tin or an oblong tin 30 x 23cm/12 x 9 inches. Protect the sides with strips of foil, prick the base with a fork, then bake blind for 15–20 minutes until pale brown. Remove the strips of foil after about 10 minutes. Allow to cool a little.

Meanwhile, make the filling. Skin the tomatoes by covering them with boiling water for 30 seconds then set 3–4 aside (depending on size). Halve, de-seed and chop the remainder. Heat half the oil in a non-aluminium pan and cook the onions and garlic over a gentle heat until just beginning to

Tomato and
parmesan tart

brown (about 10–15 minutes). Add the chilli and half the thyme and cook for a little longer. Add the tomatoes and vinegar. Cook for 15–20 minutes, stirring regularly, until the mixture is thick. Season with salt, pepper and a pinch or two of sugar to taste. Cool, then spoon into the prepared flan case. Slice the remaining tomatoes and arrange on the tart, layering them with the basil. Season well with black pepper and a little salt then sprinkle over the remaining thyme and olive oil. Bake at 190°C/375°F/gas 5 for 15–20 minutes and serve hot or warm. A mixture of red and yellow tomatoes looks good for this tart.

See photograph on
page 122

ROASTED PEPPERS STUFFED WITH BLACK BEAN, CORN AND FETA

Serves 6

100g/4oz black beans, cleaned and
  soaked
6 large, squat peppers, red or yellow
2 small onions, peeled
6 tablespoons olive oil
salt and freshly ground black pepper
2 cobs sweetcorn
1 clove garlic
1–2 red or green chillis, de-seeded
  and finely chopped
3 medium, ripe tomatoes, skinned,
  de-seeded and chopped
2 heaped tablespoons sun-dried
  tomato paste
1 tablespoon chopped fresh marjoram
  or oregano
100g/4oz feta cheese or young,
  crumbly Lancashire
sprigs of marjoram and sour cream,
  to serve

Soak the beans overnight (or for several hours) or cover with water, bring to the boil, and leave, covered, for 1–1½ hours. Drain, then proceed with the recipe.

Cut the caps off the peppers and remove the seeds and inner membranes. Bring a large pot of water to the boil, toss in the peppers and blanch for 5 minutes. Drain well. Place the soaked beans, one of the onions, thickly sliced, and 900ml/1½ pints water in a large saucepan and bring to the boil. Boil fiercely for 10 minutes, then simmer gently for about 1 hour, add 2 tablespoons oil and cook until tender, adding more boiling water if necessary. Drain, reserving the cooking liquid.

Heat the grill. Rub the corn with 1 tablespoon oil and place it on a foil-covered tray under the grill. Cook for 5–10 minutes, turning the corn once or twice until the corn is tender and well-browned. Cool, then remove the corn niblets from the cob with a sharp knife.

Heat 2 of the remaining tablespoons of oil in a heavy frying pan and cook the remaining onion, finely chopped, until tender but not too browned. Add the garlic, chilli and cumin. Cook for 3–4 minutes more, then add the beans, tomatoes, tomato paste and marjoram (or oregano). Cook for 5–10 minutes, adding a few spoonfuls of the bean cooking water if the mixture seems too dry. Season to taste (remembering that the cheese is salty), then stir in the corn and the crumbled cheese.

Preheat the oven to 190°C/375°F/gas 5. Spoon the filling into the pepper shells and stand in a baking dish (any remaining filling can be spooned around the peppers). Moisten with a few spoonfuls of bean cooking water and drizzle with the remaining 1 tablespoon of oil. Cook for 35–45 minutes until the peppers are very soft and patched with brown. Serve warm rather than piping hot, with a bowl of soured cream and some warm bread (pitta or *naan* are both good) and a crisp green salad.

BASIC PANCAKE BATTER

Makes about 12 pancakes

175g/6oz unbleached plain flour (or
use half buckwheat flour)
½ teaspoon salt
2 eggs, size 2
400–475ml/14–16fl oz milk (or half
milk, half beer)
40g/1½oz unsalted butter, melted
butter or oil for frying

Sift the flour and salt into a large bowl. Beat the eggs and gradually whisk in 400ml/14fl oz milk. Make a well in the centre of the flour and gradually whisk in the milk and egg mixture. Then whisk until smooth. At this stage the batter may be left, covered, for several hours. The flour grains will swell and the resulting pancake will be slightly more tender. The batter may thicken and need thinning with an extra tablespoon or so of milk, so aim for a batter the consistency of thin cream. Just before cooking, whisk in the melted butter. Pour the batter into a measuring jug for pouring.

Heat an 18–20cm/7–8 inch heavy frying or *crêpe* pan over a medium heat. Lightly grease with butter or oil. Pour in about 4–5 tablespoons of the batter and swirl the pan to cover the base thinly. Cook until the top of the pancake looks set and the underside is golden brown, flick over with a palette knife (or toss with a deft flick of the wrist). Cook for a further minute or two, then remove to a heated plate and keep warm.

A quire of pancakes
with pumpkin and
goat's cheese, and
leek and chicory
fillings

QUIRE OF PANCAKES WITH PUMPKIN AND GOAT'S CHEESE AND LEEK AND CHICORY FILLINGS

A quire of pancakes, so called because the stack of layered pancakes resembles a quire of paper, is an excellent way of serving pancakes as a main course supper dish. All the preparation can be done in advance and the finished dish reheated before serving.

Serves 4–5

*8–9 pancakes (either plain or made
  with half buckwheat flour)*
25g/1oz butter, melted

FOR THE PUMPKIN AND GOAT'S CHEESE
LAYERS:
50g/2oz butter
*1 small onion, peeled and finely
  chopped*
½ teaspoon crushed, dried red chilli
*450g/1lb peeled and seeded pumpkin,
  squash or courgettes, chopped into
  1cm/½ inch cubes*
*100g/4oz well-flavoured goat's
  cheese, cut into 1cm/½ inch cubes*
75g/3oz walnuts, roughly chopped
*2 tablespoons finely chopped fresh
  parsley*
salt and freshly ground black pepper

FOR THE CHICORY AND LEEK LAYERS:
2 tablespoons extra virgin olive oil
3 leeks, trimmed, washed and sliced
3 heads chicory, trimmed and sliced
*50g/2oz roughly grated Parmesan
  cheese*
*1 teaspoon finely chopped fresh
  thyme*
salt and freshly ground black pepper

For the pumpkin and goat's cheese layer: melt the butter in a heavy medium-sized saucepan and cook the onion over a low heat for 10–15 minutes until soft but not browned. Add the chilli and pumpkin, cover and sweat until the pumpkin is tender (about 10–15 minutes). Remove from the heat and allow to cool, stir in the rest of the ingredients and season to taste. Set aside.

For the leek and chicory layer: heat the oil in a medium-sized saucepan and cook the leeks over a low heat for 3–4 minutes, stirring a few times. Add the chicory and cook for 5 minutes more, the chicory should retain some crispness. Cool, add the Parmesan and thyme, and season to taste.

To assemble: set the oven at 190°C/375°F/gas 5. In a buttered, shallow ovenproof dish layer the pancakes with the fillings to make a 'cake'. Brush with melted butter. Cover with foil and reheat in the preheated oven for 35–40 minutes, removing the foil for the last 5 minutes. Cut into wedges to serve.

CHICKPEA PANCAKES WITH CHILLI AND SPRING ONIONS WITH AN AVOCADO AND CORIANDER SALSA

See photograph on
page 121

Chickpea flour, or gram flour as it is sometimes known, is used to make pancakes as diverse as the Niçois *socca*, the eastern Indian *chilla* and the Italian *farinata*. This delicious recipe is useful for people who do not eat dairy products, as the pancakes contain neither eggs nor milk. Chickpea flour may be found in wholefood shops and Asian stores.

Serves 4–5

175g/6oz chickpea flour
7–8 tablespoons sunflower oil
1 teaspoon ground toasted cumin
1 scant teaspoon salt

freshly ground black pepper
1 fresh red chilli, de-seeded
*1 bunch of spring onions, washed
  and trimmed*
*16–20 small sprigs of fresh
  coriander*

FOR THE SALSA:
2 avocados, peeled and diced
½ red onion, peeled and finely diced
2 tomatoes, halved, de-seeded and
*   diced*
1 large kiwi fruit, peeled and diced
1 small fresh red chilli, de-seeded
*   and finely diced*
3 tablespoons finely chopped fresh
*   coriander*
1 teaspoon ground toasted cumin
2½ tablespoons sunflower or
*   grapeseed oil*
finely grated rind and juice of ½ a
*   lime*
rice vinegar, salt and freshly ground
*   black pepper to taste*
coriander sprigs, to garnish (optional)

Place the flour, 450ml/¾ pint warm water, 3 tablespoons of oil, cumin, salt and pepper in a liquidizer or processor and blend until a smooth batter. Finely shred the chilli and cut the spring onions into quarters lengthways.

Heat 1–2 teaspoons of oil in an 18–20cm/7–8 inch frying pan (preferably non-stick) over a medium heat. Add 4 tablespoons batter and quickly swirl the pan so that the batter covers the base. Sprinkle over a few spring onions, a couple of strands of chilli and 1–2 sprigs of coriander. Trickle a further 1 teaspoon of oil around the edge of the pancake as it cooks. Cook for 2–3 minutes, until the underside is golden brown. Turn the pancake and cook for a few minutes before removing to a heated plate. Make all the pancakes in this way and keep warm.

For the salsa, simply mix all the ingredients in a bowl and season to taste with salt, pepper and rice vinegar. Serve the pancakes with the salsa, decorated with coriander sprigs, if liked.

AUBERGINE AND POTATO STEW WITH THAI GREEN CURRY PASTE

You could use some of the ready-made Thai curry pastes you can get in jars but I find them rather acidic and prefer this freshly made version.

Serves 4

450g/1lb waxy variety potatoes
salt and sugar
12 baby aubergines or 2 large
*   aubergines*
2 tablespoons vegetable oil
2 shallots, sliced
1–2 red chillies, de-seeded and finely
*   sliced*
½ teaspoon fennel seeds, crushed
150ml/5fl oz canned coconut milk
200ml/7fl oz vegetable stock (use a
*   good-quality cube)*
1 kaffir lime leaf, shredded
*   (optional)*
2 tablespoons basil leaves

FOR THE GREEN CURRY PASTE:
3 green chillies, chopped (or more to
*   taste)*
1 stalk lemon grass, outer leaves
*   removed, chopped*
1 shallot, chopped
3 cloves garlic, chopped
2.5cm/1 inch piece of fresh ginger
*   (or galangal), peeled and*
*   chopped*
4 tablespoons chopped fresh coriander
*   (including any roots)*
1 teaspoon ground, toasted coriander
*   seed*
½ teaspoon ground, toasted cumin
*   seeds*
½ teaspoon ground pepper
2 kaffir lime leaves or finely grated
*   zest of 1 lime*
1 tablespoon Thai fish sauce (nam
*   pla) or light soy sauce*
3 tablespoons vegetable oil
salt and lime juice to taste

Grind all the curry paste ingredients together in a mill or processor. Season to taste with salt, lime juice and a pinch of sugar. Set aside.

Boil the potatoes in boiling salted water until not quite cooked. Drain, peel and cut into chunks. Cut baby aubergines in half or cut bigger aubergines into 3cm/1¼ inch pieces. Heat half the oil in a deep frying pan or wok and stir-fry the aubergine until brown and almost tender. Scoop out on to a plate. Add the remaining oil to the pan and cook the shallots until soft and browned (about 5 minutes), add half the chilli and the fennel seeds and fry for 1 minute more. Add the coconut milk and cook until it thickens. Add 1 heaped tablespoon of the green curry paste, the stock and potatoes. Simmer for 5 minutes or until the potatoes are tender. Add the aubergine and more curry paste to taste and cook for a few minutes more. Adjust the seasoning, adding salt or sugar to taste, then serve sprinkled with the shredded lime leaf, if using, the remaining shredded chilli and the torn basil leaves. Serve with Thai jasmine rice.

SWEET POTATO, BROCCOLI AND ONION IN A HERB AND BEER BATTER

Serve with soured cream mixed with chopped fresh herbs or with the spiced pepper and hazelnut sauce on page 187.

See photograph
overleaf

Serves 4–5

225g/8oz unbleached plain flour
salt and freshly ground black pepper
2 eggs, size 2, separated
250ml/8fl oz light ale or lager
3 tablespoons finely chopped fresh
  herbs (coriander or chives, for
  example)
450g/1lb sweet potatoes
300g/11oz broccoli, trimmed into
  small florets
1 large onion, peeled
vegetable oil for deep frying
lemon wedges, to garnish

Sift the flour into a bowl and season with salt and pepper. Make a well in the centre, add the egg yolk and a little beer and begin to beat, gradually adding more beer and incorporating the flour to make a thick batter. Add the herbs. Just before cooking, whisk the egg white in a separate bowl until thick, then fold into the batter.

Peel the sweet potato and cut into 5mm/¼ inch slices. Also slice the onion into 5mm/¼ inch slices, and separate into rings.

Heat a 5cm/2 inch depth of oil in a deep-fat fryer or wok to a temperature of 180–185°C/350–360°F. Dip the vegetables into the batter and deep-fry in batches for about 4–5 minutes, turning occasionally with a slotted spoon. Drain carefully on kitchen paper and keep warm while frying the remaining fritters. Garnish with lemon wedges.

VARIATIONS
Other winter vegetables, such as parsnips or Jerusalem artichokes, can be used in this recipe.

GRILLED PARSNIP KEBABS WITH A HONEY, GINGER AND ORANGE GLAZE

Make a supper of these delicious kebabs by serving them with rice and a crisp salad. If you want to add a protein element try using 225g/8oz of firm tofu, cubed and marinated. Use the remaining marinade as a dipping sauce.

Serves 4

3 large parsnips, peeled and trimmed
salt and freshly ground black pepper
2 medium-sized green peppers
1 tablespoon sesame seeds

FOR THE MARINADE:
2 tablespoons clear honey
4 tablespoons soy sauce
4 tablespoons light sesame oil or
*   sunflower oil*
finely grated zest and juice of 1 orange
1 teaspoon ground coriander
2.5cm/1 inch fresh ginger, peeled and
*   finely chopped*
wedges of fresh orange, to garnish

Cook the parsnips in boiling salted water until almost tender. Drain and cool. Cut into 2–2.5cm/¾–1 inch pieces. De-seed the peppers and cut into 4cm/1½ inch square pieces. Mix all the ingredients for the marinade and pour over the vegetables in a shallow dish. Marinate for at least 1 hour, turning the pieces occasionally.

Thread on to skewers and cook under a preheated grill for 10–15 minutes, turning every now and then, until browned and glazed. Brush occasionally with the marinade. When cooked, sprinkle with the sesame seeds and return to the grill for a few moments to brown.

Bring the remaining marinade to the boil in a small pan and let it bubble for a few minutes, then serve in a small bowl with the kebabs, garnished with wedges of orange.

Clockwise from top: sweet potato, broccoli and onion in a herb and beer batter (page 133); spiced pepper and hazelnut sauce (page 187); and grilled parsnip kebabs with a honey, ginger and orange glaze

ROASTED SQUASH STUFFED WITH RICE AND MUSHROOMS

For this dish, an orange-skinned onion squash is good or try a green-skinned hoikoido. Alternatively, you could cook the stuffing in several smaller squash: little gems, acorn squash, butternuts or the charmingly named Jack-be Littles are names to look out for.

Serves 4–6

1 large or 4–6 smaller squash
3½–4½ tablespoons olive oil
salt and freshly ground black pepper
225g/8oz Italian arborio rice
450g/1lb fresh spinach, cleaned,
    trimmed and roughly chopped
nutmeg
1 medium-sized onion, chopped
100g/4oz celery, chopped
225g/8oz mushrooms, chopped
1–2 teaspoons chopped fresh sage or
    thyme
grated zest of ½ lemon
2–3 tablespoons toasted pine nuts
1 large egg, beaten

Preheat the oven to 190°C/375°F/gas 5. Cut a 'lid' off the squash and scoop out all the seeds and membranes. Rub the squash, inside and out, with 1–2 tablespoons oil, season well and stand on a stout baking tray or dish. Roast the squash, uncovered, for 20–30 minutes, until almost tender when tested with a sharp knife.

Meanwhile, make the stuffing: cook the rice in boiling, salted water until just tender (12–15 minutes), drain well and place in a large bowl. Cook the spinach in the same pan, covered, with no extra water for around 5 minutes until it collapses. Turn into a colander and press out as much water as you can. Mix into the rice and season with salt, pepper and a little nutmeg. Heat 1½ tablespoons oil in a frying pan and fry the onion and celery for 10–15 minutes; stir frequently and do not allow to brown. Add the mushrooms, raise the heat, and cook until the mushrooms have collapsed and reabsorbed their juices. Mix into the rice. Add the sage (or thyme), the lemon zest and pine nuts. Correct the seasoning and mix in the egg. Fill the squash with the stuffing (any extra may be cooked in a separate dish), sprinkle with the remaining oil and cook for a further 20–30 minutes in the hot oven. Allow to cool a little before serving. Good with a sharply dressed green salad and perhaps a fresh tomato sauce.

AUBERGINES STUFFED WITH INDIAN SPICED POTATOES

Serves 2–4, depending on accompaniments

2 large aubergines (about 225g/8oz
    each)
salt and freshly ground black pepper
450g/1lb waxy variety potatoes,
    scrubbed
6–7 tablespoons sunflower oil
1 teaspoon black mustard seeds
2 teaspoons cumin seeds
½ teaspoon ground turmeric
1 teaspoon ground coriander
1 teaspoon ground toasted cumin
1 medium onion, peeled and chopped
1 clove garlic, peeled and finely
    chopped
½–¾ teaspoon cayenne pepper
lemon juice
2 tablespoons chopped fresh coriander
    leaves, to garnish

Cut the aubergines in half lengthways and, using a sharp knife, cut out the central portion leaving a shell about 5mm/¼ inch thick. Salt the inside of the shells lightly and leave to drain upside-down in a colander. Cut the rest of the aubergine into 1cm/½ inch pieces and set aside. Cut the unpeeled potatoes into 1cm/½ inch cubes and dry a little on kitchen paper. In a wok or deep frying pan, heat 2 tablespoons of the oil over a medium heat until hot, add first the mustard seeds, then the cumin, and stir once or twice. Then add the potatoes. Cook for 1–2 minutes, then sprinkle in the turmeric. Continue to cook, stirring the potatoes frequently, until they are golden brown and almost cooked (about 10–15 minutes). Remove with a slotted spoon to a plate.

Add another 2 tablespoons of oil to the pan over the heat and then fry the onion and garlic for a few minutes until beginning to brown, then add the aubergine pieces. Cook, stirring frequently, until the aubergine is cooked (about 5–7 minutes), then return the potatoes to the pan and stir in the ground coriander and cumin. Cook for a few minutes, then take off the heat. Season to taste with salt, pepper, cayenne and lemon juice. Set aside while you prepare the aubergine shells.

Preheat the oven to 200°C/400°F/gas 6. Rinse and dry the aubergine shells, brush all sides with the remaining oil and set on a baking tray, cook in the preheated oven for 10–15 minutes until they appear soft and slightly browned. Discard any excess oil and divide the potato mixture between the shells.

Turn down the heat to 190°C/375°F/gas 5 and cook the shells for a further 15–20 minutes. Serve warm, with yoghurt, and sprinkled with the chopped fresh coriander.

Aubergines stuffed
with Indian spiced
potatoes

BREADS, CAKES AND BISCUITS

Of all the branches of cookery, bread-making is perhaps my favourite. The handling of silky flours and live yeast, the processes of kneading, proving and rising, and finally the heavenly smell of baking bread itself make yeast cookery one of the great sensuous pleasures of home cooking.

It is yeast which gives the pulse of life to leavened bread. Because it is a living organism many people prefer to use fresh, as opposed to dried, yeast in their bread-making and claim that fresh yeast produces a better-tasting bread. While I prefer handling fresh yeast, dried yeast is a convenient store-cupboard ingredient. As long as dried yeast is not old and stale (it deteriorates quickly once the tin or packet has been opened), it works every bit as well as the fresh variety. There is also a type of dried yeast that should be added directly to the flour, and not reactivated in liquid first. While these rapid-action yeasts can be real time-savers, working well with simple bread doughs, their growth is inhibited in rich mixtures. Indeed all yeasts, while needing a little sugar to activate, are inhibited by the large quantities of fat and sugar in rich bread doughs. This is why many recipes for rich, sweet breads suggest making a simple batter of flour, liquid and yeast to start the yeast into life before adding the rest of the ingredients.

FLOURS

Bread is only as good as the flour you use to make it. Here are some of the main types of flour used in bread-making.

Strong plain flour includes a proportion of strong Canadian wheat – 'strong' in this context means high in the gluten which is essential for good bread-making. Bread made with

ordinary plain flour will be softer and cakier in texture and will lack a good crust. Many supermarkets now stock unbleached and/or organic strong plain flours, which will produce a loaf with a better flavour and an attractive creamy colour. Wholemeal flour is the flour produced from the whole wheat grain with nothing extracted or added. A stone-ground flour will usually be coarser-grained, with larger pieces of wheat bran. Wheatmeal or 'brown' bread flours have had a proportion of the wheat bran removed (usually they contain 85 per cent of the whole grain). For home cooking purposes, you can create your own wheatmeal flours by mixing wholemeal and strong plain white flours. Granary flour is a flour with a brown, wheatmeal base with added malted grains of wheat and rye and produces a nutty, rich-flavoured loaf.

Rye flour contains a different type of gluten to wheat flour, one which will not rise well, so producing a much denser loaf. Mix wheat and rye flours to produce a lighter loaf which retains the characteristic sour taste of the rye grain. You can also dust wheaten loaves with rye flour to produce a good, sourish crust. Barley flour is very low in gluten, so a 100 per cent barley loaf would be very dense and hard. Mixed with a proportion of wheat flour, barley flour produces a deliciously earthy-flavoured loaf.

Corn or maize meal breads in the States are risen with baking powder rather than yeast but I find that maize, polenta or semolina make delicious additions to yeast breads too. Bread made with a proportion of maize meal has a sandy crispness and rich flavour. A small proportion of fine or medium oatmeal to bread dough produces a fine-tasting bread, especially when toasted. You can also use rolled oats to add a chewy texture to bread.

Previous page: coiled chocolate and walnut bread (page 146)

SWEET BREADS

Before the introduction of baking powders in the 19th century, many cakes were yeast-risen. Simnel cake, for instance, was originally a saffron-flavoured yeast cake with a central marzipan layer. Sweet breads and buns are often less rich and sweet than other cakes and have a pleasant, tender dryness which makes them excellent accompaniments to tea or coffee. Any leftover sweet breads can be used to make delicious puddings, including bread and butter and steamed puddings and baked fruit betties (which have layers of crisp breadcrumbs, spices and sugar over fruits such as apple or rhubarb). For a host of stimulating ideas on what to do with bread, sweet and savoury, take a look at Silvija Davidson's book *Loaf, Crust and Crumb*.

CAKES & BISCUITS

In my experience, cakes and home baking are the most popular of recipes, jealously guarded as family secrets (like my grandmother's chocolate cake) or proudly passed around. And many people who otherwise do very little cooking are prepared to get out a mixing bowl, switch on the oven and have a go at making a cake.

If you are going to the trouble of making your own cakes or biscuits, you should start off with good ingredients. Use good, unsalted butter, unbleached flour and yellow-yolked, free-range eggs. I keep a large jar of caster sugar with 2–3 plump vanilla pods in it and I use this for most of my baking; if you want a stronger vanilla flavour, try to find a genuine vanilla extract, rather than a synthetic flavouring.

If you are making a chocolate cake use good-quality bitter chocolate with a cocoa solids content of at least 70 per cent, or a good cocoa powder – Van Houten is one of my favourite brands.

SUGAR, SYRUPS & SWEETENERS

Sugars and sweeteners are important in cakes. I usually try to reduce the amount of sugar in recipes but this can only go so far with cakes and biscuits. Certain cakes – chocolate brownies come to mind – need a high proportion of sugar for their crisp, sugary crust. Different sugars have varied uses in baking. Caster sugar is usually used for cake making because its finer grains meld more completely with the fat in a recipe. Use light or dark muscovado sugar if you want more flavour; these sugars contain a proportion of natural molasses which gives them their colour and flavour.

Demerera sugar, moist and almost alcoholic, is good for giving a crunchy finish to cakes and biscuits. Use treacle in dark fruit cakes or gingerbread, golden syrup in lighter cakes and for biscuits like flapjacks and brandy-snaps. Honey is delicious in cakes, helping them rise and keeping them moist as well as adding flavour.

DIFFERENT FLOURS

As with breads, you can alter cake recipes by using different flours. A proportion of wholemeal flour can produce delicious cakes but a 100 per cent wholemeal cake will always tend to be very heavy. A little yellow corn (maize) meal is also good in cakes, producing a crumbly texture and a crisp crust, and I like to use a little chestnut flour in chocolate cakes as it adds an indefinable smoky taste. Semolina is used to make those delicious Greek cakes which are soaked in orangey, honey syrups.

I often substitute a few tablespoons of ground almonds or hazelnuts for an equal quantity of flour in cakes. The nuts will produce a moister cake which has better keeping qualities.

SAFFRON AND OLIVE BREAD

Makes 1 loaf

*450g/1lb unbleached strong plain
  flour
1 teaspoon salt
a large pinch of saffron strands
15g/½oz fresh yeast (or 1 heaped
  teaspoon dried yeast)
1 teaspoon caster sugar
4 tablespoons extra virgin olive oil
75g/3oz roughly chopped black olives
2 teaspoons chopped fresh thyme
  (plus a few whole sprigs)
a little more oil and coarse salt
  crystals*

Sift the flour and salt into a warmed mixing bowl and set in a warm place. Infuse the saffron with 2 tablespoons warm water for 10 minutes. Cream the fresh yeast with the sugar and add 150ml/5fl oz lukewarm water. Alternatively, dissolve the sugar in the water then sprinkle over the dried yeast. Either way, allow the yeast to froth for 10 minutes in a warm, not hot, place. Make a well in the centre of the flour and pour in the saffron (and its liquid), the yeast and a further 85ml/3fl oz warm water. Add the extra virgin olive oil and mix to a soft but not sloppy dough, adding a little more water if necessary or a little flour if it's too sloppy. Turn the dough on to a floured work surface and knead until smooth (about 5 minutes). Return the dough to the cleaned, oiled bowl, cover with polythene and a tea cloth and leave in a warm place for 1 hour or until the dough is well risen.

Knock down the dough and knead in the olives and chopped thyme. Press out the dough on an oiled baking tray to make a rough rectangle approximately 30 x 25cm/12 x 10 inches. Slip the whole tray into a polythene bag and allow to rise in a warm place for 30–40 minutes. Preheat the oven to 220°C/425°F/gas 7. Brush the loaf with oil and sprinkle with a few thyme sprigs and about 1 level tablespoon of salt crystals. Bake for 20–30 minutes.

PARMESAN, CORN AND BACON BREAD

Makes 1 large, flat loaf

*300g/11oz unbleached strong plain
  flour
150g/5oz fine, yellow, cornmeal, plus
  a little extra
1 teaspoon salt
15g/½oz fresh yeast or 2 teaspoons
  dried yeast
1 teaspoon muscovado sugar
3 tablespoons extra virgin olive oil,
  plus extra for greasing
75g/3oz thick-cut bacon or pancetta
75g/3oz fresh Parmesan, grated
1 teaspoon fresh thyme, chopped
coarse salt crystals*

Mix the flours and salt in a large warmed bowl. Mix the yeast, sugar and 150ml/5fl oz warm water in a small bowl and set it aside to froth for 10 minutes. Add the yeast to the flour with a further 150ml/5fl oz warm water and 2 tablespoons of the oil and mix to make a dough. Knead the dough for 5 minutes on a floured work surface and return to the clean, lightly oiled bowl. Cover with a polythene bag and leave to prove in a warm place for 1½–2 hours.

Meanwhile, de-rind the bacon or pancetta and cut into thick strips. Fry in a small frying pan until crisp, then drain.

When the dough has doubled its bulk, knock it down and then knead in the bacon, parmesan and thyme. Shape into a flat, round loaf. Brush with the remaining oil and dust with a little cornmeal and salt crystals. Cover and leave to prove for 35–50 minutes or until doubled in bulk.

Meanwhile, preheat the oven to 200°C/400°F/gas 6. Bake the bread in the preheated oven for 35–40 minutes. Cool on a wire rack.

BUTTERMILK AND CORN ROLLS WITH BACON AND CHILLI

See photograph on
page 85

Buttermilk adds a sharp tang to these delicious rolls. You can find it in big supermarkets. If it is not available, use milk soured with a dash of lemon juice or a mixture of milk and *smetana* or soured cream.

Makes 12–14 rolls

250ml/8fl oz buttermilk, plus a little extra
1 teaspoon muscovado sugar
2 teaspoons dried yeast
350g/12oz unbleached strong white flour
100g/4oz maize meal
1 teaspoon salt
½–1 red chilli, de-seeded and finely chopped
1 teaspoon chopped fresh thyme (or ½ teaspoon dried)
1 egg, size 2, beaten
2 tablespoons extra virgin olive oil, plus a little extra for the baking tray
75g/3oz de-rinded bacon
1 tablespoon whole fennel seed
coarse salt

Warm the buttermilk slightly and pour half into a small bowl. Stir in the sugar and yeast, and leave in a warm spot to froth. Sift the flour, maize meal and salt into a large, warmed bowl and stir in the chilli and thyme. When the yeast has become frothy, add to the flour with the rest of the warm buttermilk, the beaten egg and the olive oil. Mix to make a soft dough, adding a splash of warm water if necessary. Knead well for 5 minutes until smooth. Return to the cleaned-out bowl, cover and allow to rise for about 1 hour.

Meanwhile, grill or dry-fry the bacon until just crisp. Cool, then crumble into small pieces. When the dough has risen, knock back and knead in the bacon. Roll out the dough to about 2.5cm/1 inch, then cut out rounds using a medium-sized scone cutter. Place on a lightly oiled tray. Cover and allow to prove in a warm place.

Set oven to 190°C/375°F/gas 5. When the rolls have risen and doubled in height, brush with a little extra buttermilk (or milk) and sprinkle each with a few fennel seeds and some coarse salt. Bake for 20–30 minutes in the hot oven or until the rolls sound hollow when tapped on the base. Serve warm – the rolls reheat well and are delicious toasted.

INDIAN-STYLE BARLEY BREADS WITH CORIANDER AND GARLIC

Serve these delicious *naan*-style breads with Indian meals, with grilled meats or chicken, or with salads.

Makes 10–12 breads

350g/12oz unbleached, strong plain flour
100g/4oz barley flour
1 teaspoon salt
200ml/7 fl oz milk
1 teaspoon caster sugar
2 teaspoons dried yeast
50g/2oz melted butter, plus a little extra for brushing, if liked
2 tablespoons plain yoghurt
4 cloves garlic, peeled and finely chopped
bunch (approximately 25g/1oz) of fresh coriander, finely chopped
2 tablespoons black onion seeds (optional)

Sift the flours and salt into a large bowl. Warm the milk and add the caster sugar, sprinkle the dried yeast into the milk and set aside in a warm place for 10 minutes. Add the yeast, melted butter and yoghurt to the flour and mix to make a dough. Knead for 5 minutes to create a smooth dough. Return to the bowl, cover with a plastic bag and allow to rise for 2–3 hours according to temperature.

Preheat the oven to its highest temperature (usually 250°C/500°F/gas 9), place a large, thick baking sheet in the oven to heat also. Knead the dough for a few minutes then divide into 10–12 portions. Roll each piece of dough into a ball shape, then roll out to form a circle 10–13cm/4–5 inches across. Mix the coriander and garlic and distribute between the circles of dough. Gather up the edges of each circle to enclose the garlic and coriander, and pinch to seal the edges, roll out again to form a thin 15–18cm/6–7 inch circle, then stretch to form a teardrop shape. If using the black onion seeds, brush each shape with a little water and scatter over the seeds. Heat the grill to hot, then working with 3–4 breads at a time, slap the dough shapes on to the hot baking sheet and bake in the hot oven for 3–4 minutes. Immediately remove from the oven and place under the grill; the breads will puff up and brown quite quickly (1–2) minutes, remove to a clean tea-towel to keep warm and repeat the process with the rest of the breads. Brush the breads with a little melted butter, if liked, before serving. The breads may be reheated, wrapped in foil, in a moderate oven for 20–25 minutes.

Indian-style barley breads with coriander and garlic (top); and Parmesan, corn and bacon bread (page 140)

SAFFRON CAKES, BREADS AND BUNS

Makes 2 x 450g/1lb loaves

450g/1lb of unbleached strong plain
*   flour, plus a little extra*
½ teaspoon salt
large pinch saffron strands
15g/½oz fresh yeast or 1 heaped
*   teaspoon dried yeast*
75g/3oz caster sugar
120ml/4fl oz warm milk
150g/5oz unsalted butter, softened
1 egg, size 2, beaten
50g/2oz currants
50g/2oz sultanas
50g/2oz candied peel, chopped
finely grated zest of ½ lemon
butter for greasing the baking tins

Sift the flour and salt into a large
bowl and set in a warm place. Infuse
the saffron in 2 tablespoons hot water.
Either cream the fresh yeast and 1
teaspoon of the sugar, and add the
warm milk, or dissolve 1 teaspoon of
sugar in the warm milk and add the
dried yeast. Either way, allow the
yeast to froth for 10–15 minutes. Add
the remainder of the sugar to the
flour and rub in the butter. Make a
well in the centre and add the yeast
mixture, the egg and the saffron. Mix
thoroughly and start to knead the
mixture together. If the mixture is
very sticky add a little more flour.
Turn the mixture on to a floured
work surface and knead until smooth.
Return the dough to the bowl, cover
and leave in a warm place for 40–60
minutes until the dough is well risen.

Knock down the dough, add the
dried fruit and lemon zest, and knead
to incorporate thoroughly. Divide the
dough into two and place in 2 well-
buttered 450g/1lb loaf tins. Slip into a
plastic bag and allow to rise a second
time, until the dough has reached the
top of the tins (about 40–50 minutes
in a warm place). Bake the cakes at
200°C/400°F/gas 6 for 15 minutes,
then lower the temperature to
190°C/375°F/gas 5 for a further 10–15
minutes. Cool in the tin for 10 minutes
before turning out on to a wire rack.

VARIATION
To make saffron and ginger buns,
make up the basic dough as above
but use only 75g/3 oz of butter and
omit the currants, sultanas and lemon
zest. Add 50g/2oz chopped preserved
ginger in syrup. Shape into 12–15
buns, and arrange on a large baking
tray. Allow to rise, brush with warm
milk and sprinkle with flaked
almonds (allow about 50g/2oz) and a
little caster sugar. Bake for 15–20
minutes at 200°C/400°F/gas 6. These
are delicious with clotted cream and
honey for afternoon tea.

Clockwise from top:
saffron and olive
bread (page 140);
saffron and ginger
buns; saffron cake

SPICED HOT CROSS BUNS

Makes 18–20 buns

450g/1lb unbleached strong plain
*   flour*
25g/1oz fresh yeast, or 2 teaspoons
*   dried yeast*
100g/4oz caster sugar
250ml/8fl oz milk, plus a little more
1 teaspoon each ground cinnamon
*   and cardamom*
finely grated nutmeg
1 teaspoon salt
50g/2oz chopped candied peel
75g/3oz sultanas or raisins
50g/2oz butter, melted
1 egg, size 2, beaten
50g/2oz prepared marzipan

Sift 100g/4oz of the flour into a warmed bowl. Blend the fresh yeast with 1 teaspoon of the sugar and add a little of the warmed milk. Allow the yeast to froth a little. If using dried yeast, dissolve the sugar and yeast in a little of the warmed milk and set aside for 10 minutes until frothy. Add the yeast to the flour in the bowl with the remainder of the 250ml/8fl oz of warmed milk, mix well, then cover and leave to rise for about 30–40 minutes. Sift the remaining flour, 50g/2oz of the sugar, the spices and the salt into a large, warmed mixing bowl. Add the yeast mixture, the butter and almost all the egg. Mix together and knead for about 5 minutes to form a smooth dough. Return to the cleaned, greased bowl, cover with a polythene bag and leave to rise for 1–2 hours. Add the fruit and knead the mixture for 2–3 minutes.

Divide the dough into 18–20 pieces. Shape each piece into a round and place on buttered baking sheets. Add 2 tablespoons of milk to the remaining egg and brush the buns with the mixture. Roll out the marzipan on a floured board until thin. Cut into small strips and use to form a cross on each bun. Cover the buns again and leave to rise for 30–40 minutes. Preheat the oven to 220°C/425°F/ gas 7 and bake the buns for 15–20 minutes until browned. Meanwhile,

dissolve the remaining sugar in 3 tablespoons water in a small saucepan and then boil for 2–3 minutes. Brush this syrup over the hot buns as they come out of the oven. Cool on wire racks.

Shaun Hill's
hazelnut and apricot
bread (top); and
spiced hot cross
buns

SHAUN HILL'S HAZELNUT AND APRICOT BREAD

This bread comes from *Shaun Hill's Cookery Book*. It makes a lovely breakfast bread and is delicious served with English farmhouse cheeses such as Lancashire or Duckett's Caerphilly.

Makes 2 loaves

*15g/½oz fresh yeast or 1 heaped
  teaspoon dried yeast
150ml/5fl oz skimmed milk
1 teaspoon honey or caster sugar
50g/2oz hazelnuts
100g/4oz dried apricots
450g/1lb unbleached strong white
  flour
1 teaspoon salt
1½ tablespoons hazelnut oil
butter for greasing
50g/2oz rye flour*

Mix the yeast with half the warm milk and the honey (or sugar) and leave aside to froth for 10 minutes. Chop the hazelnuts and apricots roughly. In a large bowl mix together the white flour, salt and the apricots and hazelnuts. Add the remaining warm milk, 150ml/5fl oz warm water and the oil to the yeast mixture and stir together. Add to the dry ingredients and mix to make a firm dough. Knead for 4–5 minutes on a floured work surface. Return to the clean, lightly buttered bowl, cover with a polythene bag and leave to rise for 1½–2 hours.

Lightly butter 2 x 450g/1lb loaf tins. Knead the dough for a few minutes, divide the dough into two and shape to fit the tin. Roll each loaf in the rye flour and place into the tins. Leave in a warm place, covered, to prove for 35–50 minutes or until the dough has risen to the top of the tins. Preheat the oven to 200°C/400°F/gas 6. Bake the loaves for 35–40 minutes. Cool on a wire rack. Alternatively, shape the loaves into ovals, roll in the rye flour and allow to rise on a buttered baking sheet. Slash diagonally with a very sharp knife before baking.

TUILES AUX AMANDES

This is a classic recipe (based on the one in Anne Willan's *The Observer French Cookery School*) for thin, crisp biscuits with the crunch of almonds. There are few better accompaniments to ice-creams or sorbets.

Makes about 24 biscuits

*90g/3½oz unsalted butter, plus a
  little extra for greasing
75g/3oz unbleached plain flour, sifted,
  plus a little extra for flouring
2 egg whites, size 2
90g/3½oz icing sugar, sifted
100g/4oz slivered almonds
1 teaspoon brandy or Kirsch
½ teaspoon vanilla extract*

Preheat the oven to 190°C/375°F/gas 5. Butter and flour 2 large stout baking trays. Melt the butter very gently until it is pourable but not oily. In a large bowl break up the egg whites with a fork. Then mix in the sifted sugar, flour and slivered almonds. When the dried ingredients are thoroughly mixed in, add the brandy (or Kirsch) and the vanilla extract. Gently stir in the melted butter. Place teaspoonfuls of the mixture on to the baking sheets, leaving a good distance for the *tuiles* to spead. Spread out each *tuile* with the back of a teaspoon until they are 5–6cm/2–2½ inches across.

Bake for 6–8 minutes or until the edges are browned. Remove from the baking sheets with a palette knife and drape over a rolling pin so that they assume the classic curved shape of a *tuile* (supposedly based on the shape of French roofing tiles). Leave until firm. I find it easiest to cook and shape one trayful at a time.

COILED CHOCOLATE AND WALNUT BREAD

This bread is my version of a recipe for a middle-European cake called *Potize* in Barbara Maher's book *Cakes*. The dough is rolled out, filled with a mixture of chocolate, walnuts and cinnamon and then coiled to fit a round cake tin. The resulting cake is great fun to eat, tastes delicious and keeps for 2 days.

Makes one large loaf, serving 10–12

150ml/5fl oz milk
15g/½oz fresh yeast
50g/2oz caster sugar
275–300g/10–11oz unbleached strong, plain flour, sifted, plus more for dusting
50g/2oz butter, softened, plus a little more for greasing
1 small egg and 1 egg yolk
1 teaspoon salt

FOR THE FILLING:
100g/4oz caster sugar (preferably from the vanilla pod jar)
100g/4oz shelled walnuts, finely chopped
100g/4oz good-quality plain chocolate, grated
1 teaspoon cinnamon
icing sugar for dusting

Warm the milk. Mix the yeast and 1 teaspoon of the sugar in a basin and gradually add the warm milk. Beat in 50g/2oz of the sifted flour, cover and set aside for 15–20 minutes to froth. Beat the softened butter and the remaining sugar together in a large bowl and gradually beat in the egg and egg yolk, then beat in half the flour and the salt. Add the yeast to the butter mixture and mix together, then gradually beat in enough of the remaining flour to make a soft but cohesive dough. Knead for 5–10 min-

utes until the dough is shiny and smooth – the dough will be much softer than regular bread dough. Return the dough to the clean, lightly buttered bowl. Cover with a polythene bag and leave until it has doubled in size (1–1½ hours).

Dissolve the sugar in 120ml/4fl oz water over a low heat in a small pan. Bring to the boil and boil for 4–5 minutes to form a syrup. Take off the heat and stir in the walnuts, chocolate and cinnamon. Set aside. Spread a clean tea towel on the work surface and flour it liberally. Turn the dough on to the cloth and roll out to create a strip approximately 1 metre long by 15cm/3 feet long by 6 inches. Flour the cloth and rolling pin frequently. If the filling has set, reheat slightly over a very low heat, then spread it over the dough. Using the cloth, roll up the dough from the long side as you would a Swiss roll. Butter a 25–28cm/10–11 inch round cake tin, preferably a spring-form tin with a loose base. Then coil the roll into the tin, leaving room for the dough to expand. Cover and leave to rise for about 50–60 minutes until the tin is full.

Preheat the oven to 200°C/400°F/gas 6 and bake the cake for 20–30 minutes until risen and golden brown. Cool in the tin for 10–15 minutes before tranferring to a wire rack. Dust with icing sugar before serving.

LEMON AND SPICE SOUR CREAM CAKE WITH NUT AND CINNAMON TOPPING

Adding sour cream to the mixture results in a moist and crumbly cake, rich in lemon and spices. If you leave out the filling and topping, the cake makes a delicious accompaniment to a fruit compote (see the Spiced Fruit Compote on page 168).

Serves 8–10

175g/6oz lightly salted butter, softened
100g/4oz golden caster sugar
2 eggs, size 2, beaten
225g/8oz plain, unbleached flour
1½ teaspoons baking powder
½ teaspoon bicarbonate of soda
½ teaspoon freshly ground cardamom
1 teaspoon freshy ground mace or grated nutmeg
1 teaspoon ground ginger
175ml/6fl oz sour cream
finely grated zest and juice of 1 lemon

FOR THE FILLING AND TOPPING:
75g/3oz caster sugar
1 teaspoon ground cinnamon
100g/4oz chopped mixed hazelnuts and pecans
25g/1oz plain flour
40g/1½oz butter
icing sugar to dust

Preheat the oven to 180°C/350°F/gas 4. Grease and line a 20–23cm/8–9 inch spring-form cake tin. Using a wooden spoon, cream the butter and sugar together in a large bowl until they are light in colour. Beat in the eggs, a little at a time. Sift together the flour, baking powder, bicarbonate of soda and spices, and alternately fold into the butter mixture with the sour cream. Stir in the lemon zest and juice.

To make the filling and topping: mix together the caster sugar, cinnamon and chopped nuts. Spread half of the prepared cake mixture in the greased tin, then scatter over one half of the nut mixture. Spread the rest of the cake mixture over the nuts. Add the flour and butter to the remaining nut mixture and rub in the butter until the mixture resembles breadcrumbs. Scatter this mixture over the top of the cake, then bake for 50–60 minutes until the cake is well risen and firm to the touch in the centre. Let it cool for 10 minutes in the tin then remove to a wire tray. When completely cool, dust with icing sugar and store in an airtight tin.

Lemon and spice
sour cream cake

CHOCOLATE AND CHESTNUT CAKE

This is my very favourite chocolate cake: moist, wickedly rich and deeply flavoured. It is best served with coffee or tea rather than as a dessert after a full meal. The chestnut flour adds an indefinable smoky, earthy tone to the cake which works as an excellent foil to the sweetness of the chocolate. Chestnut flour is increasingly available: try Italian delicatessens or wholefood stores. This special occasion cake demands the best-quality chocolate, with at least 70 per cent cocoa solids and a good, clean flavour.

Serves 8–10

175g/6oz unsalted butter, softened,
  plus a little extra for greasing
65g/2½oz blanched almonds
175g/6oz best-quality plain chocolate
2 tablespoons Kirsch or brandy
100g/4oz caster sugar
4 eggs, size 2, separated
4 level tablespoons chestnut flour,
  sifted
2 level tablespoons plain flour, sifted
a pinch of salt
½ teaspoon cream of tartar

FOR THE GLAZE AND DECORATION:
3 tablespoons sieved apricot or plum
jam
250g/9oz best-quality plain chocolate
1 tablespoon strong black coffee
50g/2oz icing sugar, sifted, plus an
  extra dessertspoon for dusting
50g/2oz unsalted butter, softened
A selection of well-shaped leaves,
  e.g. rose or bay leaves, all
  thoroughly washed and dried

Grease a 23 x 5cm/9 x 2 inch deep round cake tin with a little butter and line the base with non-stick baking paper. Preheat the oven to 190°C/375°F/gas 5. Toast the almonds under the grill or in the oven until browned, cool, then grind finely. Melt the chocolate with the alcohol in a bowl over a small pan of barely simmering water. Stir until smooth, then set aside. Beat the butter until soft, then add the sugar and beat until the mixture is light and fluffy. Beat the egg yolks into the butter mixture, one at a time. Mix the cooled chocolate into the butter mixture, stir in the ground nuts and the sifted flours and salt. In a large, grease-free bowl whisk the egg whites with the cream of tartar until they stand in stiff peaks. Stir a couple of spoonfuls of egg white into the chocolate mixture to lighten it, then fold the mixture into the remaining egg whites.

Pour the mixture into the prepared cake tin and bake for 10 minutes, turn down the heat to 180°C/350°F/gas 4 and bake for a further 25–30 minutes until the cake is risen and just firm in the centre. Allow to cool in the tin for 10 minutes, then turn out to cool on a greased wire tray.

For the decoration: gently heat the sieved jam and carefully spread a thin layer all over the cooled cake. In a medium-sized bowl over a pan of barely simmering water, melt 150g/5oz of the chocolate with the coffee. Stir until smooth, then mix in the sieved icing sugar. Add the softened butter, a knob at a time, until the icing is smooth, glossy and thickly coats the back of the spoon. If too thin, cool quickly over iced water. Pour the icing over the cake, guiding it down the sides of the cake with a small palette knife. Allow to set, then remove the cake to a serving plate.

Melt the remaining chocolate and cool a little. Coat the back of the leaves with a thin layer of chocolate and set on a tray lined with non-stick baking paper. Allow to set, in the fridge if you like, then peel off the leaves. To serve, arrange the chocolate leaves on the top of the cake, then dust with the extra icing sugar.

Chocolate and
chestnut cake

FRESH GINGER AND COCONUT CAKE

This makes a moist, magically flavoured cake with the warm flavour of fresh ginger. Serve it as a cake with tea or coffee, or make a syrup flavoured with ginger and lime, pour it over the warm cake, and serve as a pudding with some lightly whipped cream.

Serves 8–10

175g/6oz lightly salted butter, softened
150g/5oz caster sugar, preferably
    from the vanilla pod jar
3 eggs, size 2, beaten
100g/4oz unbleached self-raising
    flour
1 teaspoon baking powder
1 teaspoon ground ginger
100g/4oz unsweetened desiccated
    coconut
finely grated zest and juice of 2 limes
5cm/2 inch piece of fresh ginger,
    peeled and very finely chopped
icing sugar to dredge (optional)

Preheat the oven to 180°C/350°F/gas 4. Lightly grease and line a 20cm/8 inch round cake tin. Cream the butter and sugar together until well mixed and light coloured. Gradually beat in the eggs, a little at a time. Sift together the flour, baking powder and ground ginger, and fold into the mixture with the coconut and lime zest. Stir in the lime juice and chopped fresh ginger. Spoon into the prepared cake tin and level down. Bake in the centre of the preheated oven for 15 minutes, then turn down the heat to 170°C/325°F/gas 3 and bake the cake for a further 25–35 minutes until the cake is well risen, browned and firm to a light touch. Cool in the tin for 10 minutes then turn out on to a wire rack to finish cooling. Dredge with icing sugar to serve, if liked.

GINGER AND PECAN BISCUITS

This is based on what the Americans call the 'ice-box cookies' method. The dough is formed into a long roll which is chilled (or frozen), then thin slices are cut off and baked. Many ginger biscuit recipes produce thick, hearty biscuits. This method makes excellent, thin and well-flavoured biscuits. Serve with creamy mousses and puddings (such as the Ginger Syllabub on page 170).

Makes about 36 biscuits

100g/4oz unsalted butter, softened,
    plus a little extra for greasing
100g/4oz soft, light brown sugar
1 egg, beaten
175g/6oz unbleached plain flour
1 teaspoon ground ginger
pinch of salt
90g/3½oz chopped pecans
3 globes stem ginger, drained and
    finely chopped
a little syrup from the stem ginger jar

Cream the butter and sugar until light coloured and fluffy. Gradually beat in the egg. Sift the flour, ginger and salt together and fold into the mixture. Stir in the chopped pecans and stem ginger. Add sufficient syrup from the stem ginger jar to make a thick but cohesive dough. Turn on to a lightly floured board and, with floured hands, form into a sausage-shaped roll about 5cm/2 inches in diameter. Wrap in baking paper or foil and chill for several hours or overnight. (The dough will keep for several days in the fridge or for a month in the freezer).

Preheat the oven to 190°C/375°F/gas 5 and lightly grease a couple of heavy baking sheets. Using a sharp knife, cut off thin slices from the dough and lay on the baking sheets, leaving room for the biscuits to spread. Bake for 10–15 minutes until browned around the edges. Cool on a wire rack and store in an airtight tin.

Sweet tarts and pies have always been one of my favourite things to cook and eat. I hadn't quite realized how much I liked them until I came to sort through the recipes for this book and discovered that I had sufficient material for a whole chapter of these sweet pastry delights.

The French have it pretty well sewn up as far as fruit tarts are concerned. The window of even an average *patisserie* in France is full of deliciously tempting examples of *tarte aux pommes*, *tarte aux poires*, *tarte aux pruneaux*, and so on. The most famous of these French confections is surely *tarte Tatin aux pommes*, in which the apples are baked underneath a layer of sweet tart pastry and then turned out so that they gleam and glisten in all their burnished glory. It is unlikely that the Tatin sisters from Lamotte-Beuvron could ever have guessed that their upside-down apple tart was destined to be one of the most popular desserts ever conceived, but so it has turned out.

A RECIPE FOR TARTE TATIN

A *tarte Tatin* is simple to make. Melt about 50g/2oz unsalted butter in a wide, shallow frameproof baking tin, then add 75g/3oz caster or soft brown sugar. Let the butter and sugar bubble together to form a toffee-ish syrup, letting it brown and caramelize but not burn. Then add about 1kg/2lb Coxes apples, peeled, cored and cut into large wedges, turn them in the sugar and butter and sprinkle over 1 teaspoon wine vinegar or a little lemon juice. Cover with a layer of the sweet tart pastry given on page 154 then bake at 180°C/350°F/gas 4 for about 50 minutes. Loosen the sides of the tart, then turn out and serve with *crème fraîche*. A *tarte Tatin aux poires* made in the same way is arguably even more delicious. Sometimes with the pear version, I add a little syrup from a jar of preserved stem ginger to the fruit and scatter a little of the shredded ginger over the pears before covering with the pastry.

PASTRIES

Undoubtedly the basis of a good fruit tart is the pastry. The sweet tart pastry I give here (page 154) is the one I use most often for fruit tarts, as it produces a firm and biscuity shell, quite unlike the crumbly, short texture of British shortcrust pastry. Shortcrust pastry comes into its own for our double-crust pies but is a little too crumbly for a free-standing tart. Mixtures of fruit make delicious shortcrust pastry pies. Blackberry and apple is the most famous but try a mixture of damsons, blackberries and pears in the autumn or a Stateside mixture of rhubarb and strawberry earlier in the year.

Other pastries can be used to give quite different results. Flaky or puff pastry, rolled out thinly then covered with thin, overlapping layers of sugared fruit, brushed with butter, and baked at a high temperature, makes a crisp, fruity tart which should be eaten immediately with some homemade ice-cream.

Or make a softer, cakier pastry by using self-raising flour and more butter. (Use around 225g/8oz flour, 75g/3oz caster sugar and 175g/6oz unsalted butter, then bind with an egg yolk and lemon juice.) Press out to line a loose-bottomed cake tin, then pile on sliced, sugared and cinnamoned apples, drizzle over a little melted butter, and bake. The pastry will rise around the apples and the fruit juices will combine with the pastry to form a heavenly cake/tart. All these tarts are best served hot or warm with cream or ice-cream.

Previous page: cranberry and orange tart with cardamom-spiced pastry (page 156) This page: lemon, cardamom and almond tart (page 160)

I have experimented with other pastries, too, and I found that one made with a proportion of yellow corn (maize) flour is delicious, especially with sharp fruits. In this chapter I have included recipes for a Cranberry and Pear Pie (page 162) and a Cornmeal, Blackcurrant and Mint Pie (page 155) made with this cornmeal pastry which provides a crumbly, mellow-tasting foil to the sharp fruit fillings.

Another pastry I sometimes use for fruit tarts is a sweet, yeast pastry. It makes a good, substantial base for a fruit filling set in a sweet, scented custard or simply for sugared fruit piled on to the bready base. These are good dishes for outside eating or picnics. Wrap well in foil and some tea-cloths to keep warm.

Delicious fruit tarts and strudels may be made with frozen filo pastry. Layer 5–6 filo pastry leaves in a large, wide cake tin, letting the pastry overhang the rim. Brush melted butter and scatter some chopped, toasted almonds, walnuts or hazelnuts between the layers. Then heap on a filling of sugared, cinnamoned apples or pears with ginger. Sprinkle with a little calvados, whisky or brandy over the fruit if you like. Top with a few more pastry layers, then fold the overhanging pastry leaves over the top of the tart, crumpling and folding the pastry to make attractive swirls. Brush with more butter and sprinkle with sugar before baking at 190°C/375°F/gas 5 for about 40–50 minutes. This produces a crisp result similar to the *croustades* or *pastis* from Gascony in southwest France, though these would be flavoured with armagnac, prunes and orange flower water and traditionally made with goose fat. Strudels are made Swiss-roll fashion, and the fruit is usually heaped on to a layer of sweet, buttered breadcrumbs to absorb excess fruit juices and keep the pastry crisp.

FILLINGS

Classic French fruit tarts fill the pastry shell with a layer of confectioner's custard – *crème pâtissière* – before adding the fruit. This layer protects the pastry, preventing the fruit juices from making it soggy. Traditional *crème pâtissière* is thickened with ordinary plain flour, but I prefer to use cornflour as this makes a smoother, softer custard which doesn't run the risk of tasting of raw flour. For sufficient *crème pâtissière* to fill a 23–25cm/9–10 inch flan case beat together 4 egg yolks and 1 whole egg with 75g/3oz vanilla-scented caster sugar. When thick and light yellow beat in 40g/1½oz sifted cornflour. Bring 450ml/15fl oz milk to the boil then whisk the boiling milk into the egg and cornflour mixture. Return to the rinsed-out pan and cook, whisking all the time, for 2–3 minutes until thick.

Crème pâtissière may be flavoured with vanilla extract or a couple of spoonfuls of alcohol. Calvados, brandy or rum are good with apples, Armagnac is good with prunes, while Kirsch is excellent with plums, apricots and cherries. Delicious apple or pear tarts may be made by adding a thick layer of peeled, cored and sliced fruit on top of the custard-filled tart shell then baking until the fruit is cooked. Glaze with some plum or apricot jam. Grated orange or lemon zest is also a good flavouring for confectioner's custard, especially with strawberries.

Alternatives to *crème pâtissière* are *fromage frais*, well drained, or thick, creamy, strained Greek yoghurt. But assemble tarts with these fillings at the last moment or the pastry may turn soggy. Yoghurt is particularly good with raspberries or wild wood strawberries. Slightly sweetened mascarpone cheese makes an excellent base for barely cooked red- or whitecurrants or blueberries.

Compote of rhubarb, strawberries and orange (page 167) is delicious served with almond poppy seed tart (page 159)

FRUIT TARTS

The basic building block of a classic sweet tart is, of course, the pastry. *Pâte sucrée* is the classic French sweet pastry. It should be thin, crisp and biscuity – quite different to the short, crumbliness of classic British shortcrust. A great mystique has grown up around French pastry-making but the advent of food processors has put this 'skill' within the grasp of everyone. Remember to chill the pastry well before rolling it out, and this recipe is well nigh foolproof.

SWEET TART PASTRY

To line a 23–25cm/9–10 inch flan tin

175g/6oz plain, unbleached flour
40g/1½oz icing sugar
pinch of salt
90g/3½oz unsalted butter
1 egg yolk, size 2
lemon juice

Sift the flour, sugar and salt into the processor. Add the butter, cut into small pieces, and then process for 1 minute until the butter is thoroughly blended in. Add the egg yolk, lemon juice and 1½ tablespoons cold water. Process again until the pastry binds together. Turn on to a work surface and press the dough together. Knead lightly to create a ball of dough free from major cracks. Wrap in foil or waxed paper, then chill for 30–60 minutes. Soften for about 10 minutes at room temperature before rolling out.

See photograph opposite

PRUNE, ARMAGNAC AND WALNUT TART

The quality of this tart depends very much on the quality of the ingredients you use. Try to find French Agen prunes, which are moister and more richly-flavoured than run-of-the-mill prunes. If you can't find Agen prunes, plump up ordinary fruit by soaking in Earl Grey tea for a couple of hours. The walnuts you use should be light-coloured and sweet.

Serves 6–8

1 quantity of sweet pastry as above

FOR THE FILLING:
450g/1lb pitted prunes
3 tablespoons armagnac or cognac
75g/3oz unsalted butter, softened
75g/3oz caster sugar (preferably from the vanilla pod jar), plus a little extra
1 large egg, beaten
a pinch of salt
175g/6oz walnut halves
icing sugar to dust (optional)

Soak the prunes in the armagnac (or cognac) for at least 2–3 hours. Preheat the oven to 190°C/375°F/gas 5. Roll out the pastry to line a 23–25cm/9–10 inch metal flan tin. Line with paper and baking beans and bake blind for 10–12 minutes until the pastry rim is beginning to colour. Remove the paper and beans and cook for another 5–8 minutes until the pastry is a pale blonde colour. Remove the pastry case from the oven and reduce the oven temperature to 180°C/350°F/gas 4.

Drain the prunes, reserving the juices. Cream the butter and sugar together until pale. Beat in the egg gradually, then beat in the salt. Grind 100g/4oz of the walnuts in a processor. (Take care not to over-work the walnuts or they will turn very oily.) Beat the walnuts into the butter mixture, then gradually beat in the juices from the prunes. Spread the filling over the pastry base, then arrange the prunes over the filling. Finally scatter over the remaining walnut halves. Dredge with a little extra caster sugar. Bake for 35–45 minutes until the filling is risen, browned and set. Serve warm, dusted with icing sugar, if liked. Serve with *crème fraîche*.

CORNMEAL, BLACKCURRANT AND MINT PIE

A proportion of yellow cornmeal in the rich pastry for this pie gives a mellow, tender crumb that goes well with the tart fruit filling.

See photograph on
page 161

Serves 6–8

FOR THE PASTRY:
100g/4oz self-raising flour
100g/4oz yellow cornmeal (fine
* polenta)*
pinch of salt
100g/4oz caster sugar
175g/6oz unsalted butter, softened
finely grated zest of ½ lemon
1 egg, size 3, beaten

FOR THE FILLING:
225g/8oz blackcurrants
3–6 tablespoons caster sugar
10 mint leaves, shredded
caster sugar to dust (optional)

First make the pastry: place the flour, cornmeal, salt and sugar in a bowl. Rub in the butter until the mixture looks like breadcrumbs. Stir in the lemon zest and use the egg to bind to make a soft dough. Wrap in foil and refrigerate for 30 minutes. Preheat the oven to 190°C/375°F/gas 5. Cut off one-third of the dough and set aside. Roll out the remainder on a well-floured board and use to line the base of a 20–23cm/8–9 inch springclip cake tin (the pastry will be quite thick).

Mix the blackcurrants with the sugar and mint and pile on to the dough. Roll out the remaining portion of dough, cut into strips and use to make a lattice on the top of the fruit. Bake in the preheated oven for 30–40 minutes or until the fruit is bubbling and the pastry browned. Serve dusted with caster sugar if liked. Delicious served warm with thick cream.

**Apple tart with
cream and calvados
(top, page 156); and
prune, armagnac
and walnut tart**

APPLE TART WITH CREAM AND CALVADOS

There are many kinds of French apple tart and this one, based on the classic Normandy version, is perhaps my favourite.

Serves 6–8

1 quantity of sweet pastry (page 154)

FOR THE FILLING:
750g/1½lb eating apples (Coxes are excellent)
juice of ½ lemon
50g/2oz unsalted butter
65g/2½oz vanilla sugar
2–3 tablespoons calvados or whisky
3 egg yolks, size 3
200ml/7fl oz crème fraîche *or double cream*

Preheat the oven to 190°C/ 375°F/gas 5. Roll out the pastry to line a deep 23cm/9 inch flan tin, line with paper and baking beans, and bake blind for 10–12 minutes until the pastry rim is beginning to colour. Remove the paper and beans and cook for another 5–8 minutes until the pastry is a pale blonde colour. Remove the pastry case from the oven.

Peel and core the apples and cut into 6–8 wedges. Turn in the lemon juice. Melt the butter in a large, heavy frying pan. Cook the apples over a medium heat until they begin to brown. Scatter over a couple of tablespoons of sugar, raise the heat and cook, shaking the pan frequently, for 2 minutes to caramelize the sugar. Add the calvados (or whisky) and flame with a match, if you like.

Arrange the apple wedges in the flan case. Beat together the egg yolks, all but 1 tablespoon of the remaining sugar and the cream. Beat in any juices from the apples. Pour over the apples and scatter over the remaining sugar. Bake for 35–45 minutes until the filling is set and the apples fully cooked. Serve warm or at room temperature.

CRANBERRY AND ORANGE TART WITH CARDAMOM-SPICED PASTRY

This makes a delightfully sharp pudding around Christmas, when food tends to be heavy and very sweet. Serve the tart with plenty of whipped, sweetened cream or *crème fraîche*. A homemade ice-cream flavoured with ground cardamom would go very well too.

Serves 6–8

FOR THE PASTRY:
175g/6oz plain flour
40g/1½oz icing sugar
a pinch salt
50g/2oz unsalted butter, softened
50g/2oz curd cheese
½ teaspoon freshly ground cardamom
1 teaspoon finely grated orange zest
1 egg yolk, size 2

FOR THE FILLING:
½ teaspoon freshly ground cardamom
75g/3oz caster sugar, plus more to taste

200ml/7fl oz orange juice
225g/8oz fresh or frozen cranberries, thawed
5 medium-sized oranges
icing sugar to dust

First make the pastry: sift the flour, sugar and salt into a bowl. Rub in the softened butter and curd cheese until the mixture resembles fine breadcrumbs. Stir in the cardamom and orange zest. Beat the egg yolk with 2 tablespoons cold water and use to bind the pastry, adding a little more water if necessary. Form into a ball, knead very lightly, wrap in foil or waxed paper and chill for ½–1 hour.

Then take out of the fridge and allow to soften for 10 minutes.

Preheat oven to 180°C/350°F/gas 4. Roll out the pastry on a floured surface and use to line a 23cm/9 inch round flan tin, preferably with a loose base. Line the pastry with paper or foil and bake blind for about 12–15 minutes. Take out the paper and bake for a further 10 minutes until firm and cooked. As the pastry comes out of the oven, scatter the cardamom seeds from the filling over the still warm pastry. Set aside.

Now make the filling: heat the sugar and orange juice in a small, heavy pan until the sugar dissolves. Bring to the boil, toss in the cranberries, lower the heat and simmer for 5–10 minutes until the cranberries begin to pop. Finely grate the zest of 1 orange and stir into the cranberries. Allow the mixture to cool, taste for sweetness, adding a little more sugar if you like, then spoon into the flan case. With a sharp knife, remove all the zest and pith from the oranges, then slice about 5mm/¼ inch thick. Arrange the oranges on top of the cranberries and dust with icing sugar.

Cook in the oven for 20–30 minutes until the filling bubbles and the oranges are slightly browned. If necessary, dust with a little more icing sugar and brown under a hot grill. Delicious warm or cold rather than chilled.

Kumquat, vanilla
and chocolate tart
(page 158)

KUMQUAT, VANILLA AND CHOCOLATE TART

You could make this delicious, light tart with other fruit. Sliced pears poached in a vanilla syrup would be especially delicious, as would ripe sliced plums (use plum jam as a glaze) or, in season, poached fresh apricots or barely cooked blueberries or physalis (Cape gooseberries).

Serves 8

175g/6oz sweet shortcrust pastry (i.e. made with 175g/6oz flour)
75g/3oz bittersweet chocolate
150ml/¼ pint single cream
1 vanilla pod
2 eggs, size 2, separated
150g/5oz vanilla sugar
2 leaves (10g/¼oz, half a sachet) gelatine
175g/6oz mascarpone (or other soft, full-fat cream cheese)
½ teaspoon vanilla extract
350g/12oz kumquats, sliced and de-pipped

Preheat the oven to190°C/375°F/gas 5. Roll out the pastry to line a 25cm/ 10 inch round or a 23cm/9 inch square flan tin. Prick the base with a fork and line the sides with foil. Bake for 15–18 minutes until pale brown and fully cooked. Remove the foil strips halfway through cooking. Allow to cool. Melt the chocolate and brush over the inside of the pastry case. Put aside to set. Meanwhile, scald the cream with the split vanilla pod in a small pan, and set aside to steep for at least 15 minutes. Whisk together the egg yolks and 50g/2oz of the sugar until pale. Bring the cream back to the boil and stir on to the egg yolks. Cook the mixture over a small pan of barely simmering water until it coats the back of the spoon (about 10 minutes). Then remove the vanilla pod, wash and dry it and set aside.

Meanwhile, soften the gelatine in 3 tablespoons cold water for 10 minutes. Stir into the hot custard and stir until dissolved. (If using powdered gelatine, dissolve directly in the hot custard.) Allow to cool and to begin to set. Beat the mascarpone cheese in a bowl and gradually beat in the custard mixture, a little at a time. Stir in the vanilla extract. Whisk the egg whites in a grease-free bowl until stiff, then fold into the custard/cheese mixture. Pour into the flan case and allow to set.

Dissolve the remaining sugar in 300ml/10fl oz water over a low heat. Add the vanilla pod, raise the heat and boil for 3–4 minutes. Add the kumquats and simmer gently for 5–10 minutes until the kumquats are tender but not disintegrating. Using a slotted spoon, transfer to a plate and allow to cool. Boil down the syrup to form 4–5 tablespoons of sticky glaze. Arrange the kumquats on the tart and spoon/brush over the glaze. Chill until ready to serve.

ALMOND POPPY SEED TART

The flavour of this tart is much improved if you use whole, blanched almonds and grind them yourself in a processor or food mill rather than using commercially ground almonds, which often lack flavour. It is superb served with *crème fraîche* and a fruit compote, such as the Compote of Rhubarb, Strawberries and Orange on page 167.

See photograph on
page 153

Serves 6–8

FOR THE PASTRY:
175g/6oz unbleached plain flour
40g/1½oz icing sugar
90g/3½oz butter
1 egg yolk, size 3
juice of ½–1 lemon

FOR THE FILLING:
*2 rounded tablespoons blue poppy
   seeds*
100g/4oz ground almonds
2 amaretti biscuits, crumbled
100g/4oz unsalted butter, softened
90g/3½oz vanilla-scented caster sugar
2 eggs, size 3, beaten
75g/3oz slivered blanched almonds
25g/1oz icing sugar

First make the pastry: place the flour, icing sugar and butter in a food processor and blend until fine crumbs. (Or rub the butter into the flour and sugar by hand in a mixing bowl.) Add the egg yolk and the juice of ½ lemon. Blend again until the pastry begins to form. You may need a little more lemon juice. Tip out on to a work surface and knead lightly to form a cohesive dough, wrap in foil and chill for at least 30 minutes, which allows the pastry to relax and makes it easier to roll out.

Meanwhile prepare the filling: whizz the poppy seeds briefly in a clean coffee or spice mill. The aim is to break them up a little to release the flavour rather than reduce them to dust. Mix the poppy seeds with the almonds and crumbled amaretti. Cream the softened butter with the caster sugar until light, beat in a little of the egg followed by a couple of spoonfuls of the almond mixture. Continue until all the egg has been added, then stir in the remaining almond mixture. Set the oven to 180°C/350°F/gas 4. Roll out the pastry and use it to line a 23cm/9 inch loose-bottomed, metal flan tin. There may be a little pastry left over.

Spread the almond filling over the pastry and sprinkle over the slivered almonds. Dust with some of the icing sugar, then bake the tart in the centre of the oven for 30–40 minutes until the centre is risen and just firm. If necessary, protect the edges of the pastry with foil, dust the tart with more icing sugar and set it under a hot grill until the sugar caramelizes. Be careful, however, that the almonds do not scorch. Serve warm rather than hot.

VARIATIONS
1. If not serving the tart with a fruit compote, add a layer of sharp fruit jam or fruit purée under the almond cream filling.
2. Alternatively, omit the poppyseeds from the filling and top with a layer of fresh fruit rather than caramelized almonds. Use young, pink rhubarb, cut into small lengths, or sharp, green gooseberries. Allow about 225g/8oz fruit for a 23cm/9 inch tart, and sprinkle with a little caster sugar. Bake as above. Use a slightly deeper tart tin if adding fruit.

See photograph on
page 152

LEMON, CARDAMOM AND ALMOND TART

I love lemon curd. It is delicious on scones or bread and butter and makes an excellent cake filling. It is also good in a sweet tart. In this recipe, it is matched with citrus-fragranced cardamom and the tart is given crunch with a topping of caramelized almonds. It is excellent either warm or cold with chilled, thick pouring cream.

Serves 6–8

FOR THE PASTRY:
150g/5oz unbleached plain flour
50g/2oz caster sugar
pinch of salt
40g/1½oz ground almonds
*1 teaspoon freshly ground cardamom
    seeds*
grated zest and juice of 1 lemon
90g/3½oz unsalted butter
1 egg yolk, size 3

FOR THE FILLING:
25g/1oz ground almonds
*1 teaspoon freshly ground cardamom
    seeds*
1 tablespoon caster sugar
*300ml/10fl oz lemon curd (see recipe
    on page 20)*
90g/3½oz flaked or slivered almonds
icing sugar to dust

First make the pastry: sift the first three ingredients into a bowl and stir in the almonds, cardamom and lemon zest. Rub the butter into the flour mixture until the mixture resembles breadcrumbs. Beat together the egg yolk and 2 tablespoons lemon juice and use to bind the pastry. Use a little extra lemon juice or cold water if necessary. Work the pastry lightly until the dough is smooth and free from major cracks, then wrap in foil or greaseproof and chill for 45 minutes. Take the pastry out of the fridge and leave for 10 minutes, then roll out on a floured board and use to line a 25cm/10 inch metal flan tin with a removable base.

Preheat the oven to 190°C/375°F/ gas 5. Line the pastry case with greaseproof paper or foil and weigh down with baking beans or pulses. Bake in the oven for 10–15 minutes. Remove the paper and beans and return to the oven for 2 minutes. Take out of the oven and turn down the heat to 180°C/350°F/gas 4.

Now make the filling: mix together the almonds, cardamom seeds and sugar, and scatter over the still hot pastry. Spread the slightly warmed lemon curd over the almond mixture, then sprinkle with an even layer of flaked or slivered almonds. Dust lightly with icing sugar and bake for 20–25 minutes until the almonds are browned and the pastry cooked. If necessary, dust with more icing sugar and caramelize under a hot grill (protect the edges of the pastry with foil to prevent scorching).

LIME AND RASPBERRY TART

You could use loganberries or blackberries in this tart but I prefer the taste of lemon (use 3 of them) with these fruits to that of lime.

Serves 6–8

FOR THE PASTRY:
175g/6oz plain flour
40g/1½oz icing sugar
100g/4oz unsalted butter
1 egg, size 3, separated

FOR THE FILLING:
4 eggs, size 3
100g/4oz caster sugar
*finely grated zest and juice of 4
    limes*
150ml/5fl oz double cream
250g/9oz raspberries
icing sugar to dust

First make the pastry: place the flour, sugar and butter in a processor and whizz until the mixture resembles breadcrumbs. Add the egg yolk and 2 tablespoons iced water. Mix again until the dough coheres, adding a little more water if necessary. Turn out on to a work surface, knead lightly, wrap in foil and chill for 30 minutes.

Preheat the oven to 190°C/375°F/gas 5. Roll out the pastry to line a 23–25cm/9–10 inch flan tin with a removable base. Protect the sides of the pastry with strips of foil and bake blind for about 10 minutes. Remove the foil, brush the pastry with a little of the lightly beaten egg white and return to the oven for a further 5 minutes. Remove from the oven and allow to cool a little. Turn down the oven to 180°C/350°F/gas 4.

Meanwhile, make the filling: beat together the eggs and sugar until thoroughly blended but not frothy. Beat in the lime zest and juice. Beat in the cream. Place the flan tin on a baking tray. Arrange the raspberries on the pastry base. Carefully pour the lime custard into the pastry case, then return the tart to the oven and cook for 30–35 minutes until the custard is just set in the centre. Serve warm or cold, dusted with icing sugar.

Lime and raspberry
tart (left); and
cornmeal,
blackcurrant and
mint pie (page 155)

CRANBERRY AND PEAR PIE WITH A CORNMEAL AND AMARETTI CRUST

Much as I love Christmas plum pudding, I usually make at least one alternative dessert for the Christmas meal. The buttery cornmeal pastry in this pie makes a good foil for the refreshingly tart cranberry filling and the amaretti crumble topping makes it taste especially delicious. Serve with a little lightly sweetened whipped cream, topped with a crumbled amaretti biscuit or with a home-made vanilla or amaretti ice-cream.

Serves 8

FOR THE PASTRY:
75g/3oz plain flour
75g/3oz fine, yellow cornmeal
pinch of salt
40g/1½oz icing sugar
90g/3½oz unsalted butter, softened
1 egg yolk, size 2

FOR THE FILLING AND TOPPING:
350g/12oz fresh or thawed cranberries
75–100g/3–4oz caster sugar
3 large, just ripe pears, peeled, cored
  and cut into wedges
50g/2oz amaretti biscuits, roughly
  crushed
75g/3oz plain flour
25g/1oz ground almonds
50g/2oz caster sugar
50g/2oz unsalted butter, softened
50g/2oz chopped, blanched almonds

First make the pastry: sift the flour, cornmeal, salt and sugar into a bowl. Rub in the softened butter, then bind with the egg yolk beaten with 2½ tablespoons cold water. Knead lightly to form a ball of dough, wrap in foil and chill for at least 30 minutes.

Meanwhile, make the filling. Place the cranberries in a medium-sized non-aluminium saucepan with 6 tablespoons water. Heat over a medium heat until the cranberries start to burst (about 5 minutes). Add 75g/3oz sugar and the pears. Cook at a low simmer for 10–15 minutes. Taste for sweetness, adding more sugar to taste. Cool the filling.

Preheat the oven to 190°C/375°F/gas 5. Roll out the pastry to line a flan tin 25cm/10 inches in diameter. Scatter 3 tablespoons of the amaretti over the pastry, then spoon in the cranberry filling. Put the flour, ground almonds and sugar in a bowl and rub in the butter. Stir in the remaining amaretti and the chopped almonds. Scatter the mixture over the cranberry filling. Bake for 35–45 minutes until the pastry is cooked and the topping browned and crisp. Reduce the oven temperature after 25 minutes if the topping seems to be browning too much. Serve warm or at room temperature.

Cranberry and pear
pie with a cornmeal
and amaretti crust

The great majority of the puddings in this section are based on fruit. When I am thinking about how to end a meal, I usually take the season's fruits as my starting point. This seasonal approach is an instinctual way of cooking and thinking about food and menus. Few of us crave strawberries in February or a sticky date pudding in the blistering heat of July. By and large, seasonal fruits suggest the nature of the desserts and puddings we all feel like eating at specific times of year. There are sharp citrus fruits at the beginning of the year to cut through the winter doldrums; bright flavours like rhubarb and gooseberry announce the arrival of spring and lend themselves to hot puddings, like pies and crumbles, when the weather's cold, and to fruit compotes and fools when it turns warmer. All the summer fruits suggest icecreams, fruit tarts, fools, compotes and flummeries, all suitable for warm-weather eating. While autumn's harvest brings a wealth of apples, pears, quinces, damsons and plums which suggest comforting pies, cobblers and puddings for the colder, shorter days. Deep midwinter demands some substantial puddings made with the richer flavours of dried fruit and spices, and spiked with the occasional sharp taste of cranberries and, as the year comes full circle, with citrus fruits.

EXOTIC FRUITS

Of course there is a whole range of imported tropical fruits which interrupt and give variation to this seasonal pattern. Even though they are available throughout the year, I appreciate tropical fruits most in winter, when they are often at their best anyway, because they then provide a welcome note of sun and fresh flavour to brighten the long winter months. These fruits are best treated very simply, either served raw or very lightly cooked so that their essential flavours are not lost.

For a simple dessert, assemble a platter of peeled, stoned and sliced fruits like mango, papaya (pawpaw), guava, pineapple, persimmons and pitahaya. Serve sprinkled with lime juice or a lime and ginger syrup. Tropical fruits are delicious baked *en papillote* – in an envelope of baking parchment. Tuck in a piece of vanilla pod or cinnamon stick, sweeten with a little sugar and sharpen with a squeeze of orange, lime juice or a shot of dark rum. Mango, pineapple and banana are delicious cooked like this. Open the parcel at the table and eat with a scoop of good vanilla or coconut ice-cream.

Another simple idea for tropical fruits is to bake them, sliced and sugared, on a thin layer of bought puff pastry or a slice of buttered brioche. Baste with a little melted butter, sugar and lime juice and bake until the pastry or brioche is golden and the fruit is lightly caramelized. Mango, papaya and pineapple also make great upside-down puddings. Butter a baking tin generously and sprinkle with some brown sugar. Add the fruit and a sprinkling of lime juice, then bake them underneath either a layer of sponge cake (made with some ground almonds and flavoured perhaps with orange zest and cardamom seeds) or a rich, sweet pastry.

BANANAS

Bananas yield their most delicious aroma and flavour with the application of a little heat. Bake or grill with a little butter, some palm sugar (or light muscovado) or maple syrup. Add flavourings like lime or orange, dark Caribbean rum or bourbon whiskey, vanilla, cardamom or cinnamon. Bananas cooked in

Previous page:
ginger syllabub
(top, page 170)
served here with
buttered ginger
pears (page 175)
This page: carrot
and almond pudding
with amaretto
zabaglione sauce
(pages 166–167)

164

this way are delicious with *crème fraîche* and a slice of plain cake or toasted brioche. Or serve them with pancakes and ice-cream.

OLD-FASHIONED PUDDINGS

Some of my favourite ways to end a meal are unashamedly old-fashioned puddings. Dishes like bread and butter pudding, queen of puddings, fruit crumbles, cobblers and steamed puddings are all decadent treats and deserve to be made with the very best ingredients. They are puddings with a genuinely British heritage from an age when we were more lavish with good butter, fresh eggs and farmhouse cream than we are now. Of course, in these health-conscious times no one would suggest that we eat puddings like this after every meal, but for wintery Sunday lunches or high days and holidays, nothing cheers people like an old-fashioned baked or steamed pudding. These puddings are delicious served with a homemade custard (see page 190) or a scoop of good-quality vanilla ice-cream.

SUMMER PUDDINGS

It almost goes without saying that the best summer desserts are fruit-based. Think of fruit tarts with crisp, buttery pastry, custardy fillings, and masses of juicy berries; fruit fools with lightly cooked or crushed, raw fruit swirled into cream, *fromage frais*, yoghurt or, best of all, a mixture of cream and homemade custard. Then there are fruit compotes: mixtures of cooked and/or barely cooked fruits in scented syrups – cherries with cinnamon, peaches with vanilla or apricots with cardamom. Or try compotes of lightly poached red or white currants poured still warm over raspberries or skinned, ripe peaches. Flavour the syrup for these compotes with herbs like lemon grass, rosemary or lemon balm. Then there is the whole world of fresh fruit ice-creams and sorbets. Delicious ice-creams can be flavoured with the short-lived, evanescent scents of summer: try young blackcurrant or peach leaves, elderflowers, bay leaves or rose geranium leaves.

Simple mixtures of fresh berry fruits, served with cream or a soft, young cream cheese make a delicious summer dessert. Serve with a few crisp biscuits, like the Tuiles aux Amandes on page 145, brandysnaps, crisp, homemade meringues or a slice of sponge cake. For a more ambitious variation of this theme, try the delicious Orange and Almond Roulade with Summer Fruits on page 177.

STRAWBERRIES

The other quintessential English dessert for summer is strawberries and cream. As a raw description it begs several questions: what type of strawberries, how have they been treated, what type of cream should be used? For me, the strawberries have to be cut, even lightly crushed, and slightly sweetened so that they become juicy. The cream should be gently whipped to a soft, cloud-like consistency and again slightly sweetened (the addition of a little orange liqueur is also fine). *Crème fraîche* is good with strawberries too, but surely the best is sweetened, lightly crushed strawberries with thick, clotted cream as a filling for buttery scones in the fashion of the American strawberry shortcake.

By and large, though, there are things other than cream I'd rather put on my strawberries, all of which are quite well known: a few teaspoons of balsamic vinegar or port, a glass of fruity red wine or the juice of an orange, a couple of scooped-out passion fruits or, best of all, a slightly sweetened purée of sieved ripe raspberries. None of these really needs the addition of cream.

Steamed date and pecan pudding with maple toffee sauce (page 176)

165

POACHED PEACHES WITH RASPBERRIES AND REDCURRANTS

Serves 8

100g/4oz vanilla-scented caster sugar
300ml/10fl oz white wine
1 vanilla pod, split in half length-
ways
2 fresh bay leaves
8 ripe but not soft peaches
2 teaspoons redcurrant jelly
175g/6oz redcurrants
350–450g/12oz–1lb raspberries
lemon juice (optional)
a few fresh bay leaves to decorate
(optional)
crisp almond biscuits, to serve

Place the sugar, wine, vanilla pod and bay leaves in a non-aluminium saucepan. Add 900ml/1½ pints water and heat gently until the sugar dissolves. Simmer gently for 5 minutes, then add the whole peaches. Cook, half-covered and very gently, for 10–15 minutes. Remove the peaches with a slotted spoon to a plate and allow to cool, then remove the skin.

Meanwhile, remove the bay leaves and vanilla pod from the syrup and scrape some of the seeds from the pod into the syrup with the tip of a small knife. Boil the syrup steadily to reduce by at least half. Stir in the redcurrant jelly until it dissolves. Add the redcurrants, cover the pan and allow the currants to stand in the cooling syrup. When cool remove to a bowl with a slotted spoon. Liquidize half the raspberries and 2 tablespoons of the redcurrants, then rub through a sieve. Add sufficient vanilla syrup to create a sauce-like consistency. Fold in the remaining raspberries and redcurrants, and sharpen with lemon juice, if liked. Serve the peaches with a little syrup spooned over them and surrounded with the raspberry mixture. Decorate with fresh bay leaves, if liked. Serve with crisp almond biscuits and some strained Greek yoghurt or softly whipped cream.

See photograph on
page 164

CARROT AND ALMOND PUDDING

This fine-flavoured pudding makes an ideal alternative to Christmas pudding for those who want a lighter version of the traditional steamed pudding.

Serves 8

100g/4oz fine, fresh white bread-
crumbs
75g/3oz amaretti biscuits, crumbled
225g/8oz unsalted butter
175g/6oz caster sugar
4 free range eggs, size 3, beaten
175g/6oz unbleached self-raising
flour
175g/6oz peeled carrots, finely grated
75g/3oz candied lemon or orange
peel, chopped
finely grated zest of ½ lemon
75g/3oz blanched toasted almonds,
chopped
pinch of salt

Butter a 1.5–1.75 litre/2½–3 pint pudding basin or heatproof mould and line the base with a small disc of greaseproof paper. Mix the breadcrumbs and crumbled amaretti in a bowl. In a mixing bowl, cream together the butter and sugar. Gradually beat in the eggs a little at a time. Fold in the flour. Stir in the breadcrumb mixture. Then mix in the rest of the ingredients. Stir well, then pour into the prepared basin or mould. Cover with a pleated circle of greaseproof paper and an outer layer of foil, and tie with string. Steam the pudding in a large pan of simmering water, which comes halfway up the basin, for 2–2½ hours, making sure that the water is topped up regularly. Remove wrappings and turn out on to a heated serving plate. Delicious served with a homemade Real Vanilla Custard (see page 190) or the Amaretto Zabaglione Sauce opposite.

AMARETTO ZABAGLIONE SAUCE

Serves 8

5 free-range egg yolks
5 tablespoons vanilla-flavoured caster
* sugar*
85ml/3fl oz sweet white wine or
* marsala*
3–4 tablespoons amaretto liqueur
150ml/5fl oz whipping cream
1 amaretti biscuit, crumbled (optional)

Combine the egg yolks and sugar in a medium-sized heatproof bowl and whisk (a handheld electric whisk is ideal) until pale yellow. Add the wine or marsala, whisking constantly. Place the bowl over a pan of barely simmering water or use a double boiler. Cook, whisking constantly, until the zabaglione is thick, frothy and has doubled in volume (about 10 minutes). Remove from the heat and whisk in the amaretto liqueur to taste. Continue to whisk the mixture until lukewarm. In a separate bowl, whisk the cream into soft peaks. Gently fold the cream into the zabaglione. If liked, top with a crumbled amaretti biscuit before serving with the pudding.

COMPOTE OF RHUBARB, STRAWBERRIES AND ORANGE

See photograph on page 153

This recipe uses food writer Lynda Brown's excellent method of cooking rhubarb from *The Cook's Garden*, which prevents it collapsing into mush.

Serves 6

5 oranges (blood oranges look very
* pretty)*
450g/1lb young pink rhubarb,
* trimmed weight*
75–100g/3–4oz caster sugar
250g/9oz strawberries
2 tablespoons Cointreau or 2
* teaspoons orange flower water*

Remove the zest of 1–2 oranges with a vegetable peeler and cut into thin shreds (or use a citrus zester). Cut the rhubarb into 4cm/1½ inch lengths. Dissolve 75g/3oz sugar in 600ml/1 pint of water over a low heat in a non-aluminium saucepan. Bring to the boil, toss in the orange zest and boil for 2–3 minutes. Remove the orange zest with a slotted spoon and set aside. Add the rhubarb to the pan, bring back to the boil, turn down the heat and simmer for 1 minute. Cover the pan and switch off the heat. Allow the rhubarb to cool in the syrup – it should cook in the residual heat.

Meanwhile, remove all the peel and pith from the oranges and slice into segments with a sharp knife, removing all the pith and pips. When the rhubarb has cooled, remove to a serving dish with a slotted spoon, taste the rhubarb for sweetness and add the remaining sugar to the syrup if liked (but remember that reducing the syrup will concentrate its sweetness). Heat to dissolve, then boil down the syrup over a fierce heat until reduced and sticky. Add the reserved orange zest, cook for a further minute, cool a little and then pour over the rhubarb. Stir in the orange slices. Cool, cover and chill. Just before serving, hull the strawberries and, depending on size, either halve or quarter. Stir into the compote with the orange liqueur (or orange flower water).

VARIATIONS
Try other fruit with rhubarb. Loquats make their brief appearance in supermarkets and city fruit stalls in April and May. Halve the ripe fruit and remove the stones. Add to the rhubarb in its still-warm syrup (the gentle heat will release the loquats' subtle flavour), scent the syrup with lemon zest and/or fresh root ginger. Or try a compote of rhubarb and papaya, flavoured with shredded lime zest. Or follow a suggestion in Margaret Costa's inspirational *Four Seasons Cookery Book* and team poached rhubarb with fresh, ripe pineapple.

SPICED FRUIT COMPOTE WITH CINNAMON AND ROSEMARY

Serves 6

600ml/1 pint light, fruity red wine
175g/6oz white or brown sugar
2 x 5cm/2 inch pieces cinnamon stick
8 black peppercorns
6 cardamom pods, lightly bruised
couple of sprigs of fresh rosemary
1 orange
6 medium dessert pears, peeled but
　not cored
100g/4oz kumquats, halved
100g/4oz fresh or frozen cranberries,
　thawed
12 plump prunes
12 dried apricots
sprigs of fresh rosemary, to decorate

Place wine, sugar, spices, 1 sprig rosemary and a thick strip of orange zest in a small, deep, non-aluminium saucepan and heat gently to dissolve the sugar.

Bring to the boil and simmer for 10–15 minutes. Taste and remove the rosemary if the taste is strong enough (or leave in a little longer for a stronger taste). Add the pears and poach for 20–30 minutes until tender. Remove to a bowl, add the kumquats and poach for 5 minutes, then add the cranberries and poach carefully for a further 4–5 minutes until they are tender but still whole.

Remove all the fruit to the bowl with a slotted spoon. Reduce the syrup by about half by fast boiling, then pour over the fruit. (Leave the spices in the syrup). Add the second rosemary sprig, the prunes and apricots. Cool, cover and chill for several hours or overnight. Serve with some *crème fraîche*, Greek yoghurt or cinnamon ice-cream. Decorate with sprigs of fresh rosemary.

COMPOTE OF HUNZA APRICOTS WITH VANILLA AND LEMON

Hunza apricots look pretty unpromising in their dried state: like little buff-coloured pebbles. You will find them in most wholefood shops. They reconstitute to make a deliciously scented and flavoured fruit and are so sweet that they need little or no extra sugar. This compote is delicious served with plain baked puddings or with a real old-fashioned rice pudding. More simply, it is superb with creamy, Greek-style yoghurt.

Serves 4–5

175g/6oz hunza apricots
1 vanilla pod
1 lemon

Cover the apricots with 600ml/1 pint water and leave to soak for 1–2 hours. Turn into a non-aluminium saucepan and add the vanilla pod and a couple of strips of thinly pared lemon zest. Bring to the boil, lower the heat immediately and simmer gently for 15–20 minutes until the apricots are soft but not disintegrating.

Remove the apricots with a slotted spoon to a serving dish. Taste the syrup and remove the vanilla pod if you think the syrup is flavoured sufficiently, then reduce the syrup by fast boiling until it thickens a little. Add lemon juice to taste (1–2 tablespoons should be enough). Cool, then strain over the apricots. Serve cold.

VARIATION
To make a lovely, caramel-flavoured sauce to go with baked puddings, remove the stones from the cooked, drained apricots then blend in a liquidizer.

Add enough of the apricots' cooking syrup until you get a purée of the thickness you require.

PEAR AND BLACKBERRY QUEEN OF PUDDINGS

Serves 6

3 large, ripe pears
250g/9oz blackberries
175–200g/6–7oz caster sugar,
*   preferably from the vanilla pod jar*
300ml/½ pint single cream
300ml/½ pint full-fat milk
1 vanilla pod
90g/3½oz fresh white breadcrumbs
finely grated zest of 1 lemon
4 eggs, separated
½ teaspoon cream of tartar
pouring cream to serve

Peel, core and slice the pears. Put the pears and blackberries into a medium-sized, non-aluminium pan and cook gently for 10–15 minutes until the pears are tender. Sweeten to taste with caster sugar (2 tablespoons should be enough). Set aside.

Bring the cream, milk and split vanilla pod to the boil. Take off the heat and leave to infuse for 10 min-utes. Put the crumbs in a bowl with 50g/2oz of the sugar and the lemon zest. Pour the cream/milk mixture over, scraping out some of the vanilla seeds from the pod with the tip of a sharp knife. Leave to stand for 30 minutes, then beat in the egg yolks.

Preheat the oven to 180°C/350°F/ gas 4. Turn the mixture into a 1.2–1.5 litre/2–2½ pint shallow baking dish and cook for 30 minutes until the custard is just set. The pudding may be prepared in advance up to this point.

Turn up the oven to 190°C/375°F/ gas 5. Spread the pear/blackberry mixture over the custard. In a large, greasefree bowl whisk the egg whites and cream of tartar until shiny and thick, fold in the remaining caster sugar and pile on to the pudding. Bake for 15–20 minutes, or until the meringue is brown and crisp on the outside. Serve hot with chilled pour-ing cream.

Pear and blackberry
queen of puddings

See photograph on
page 163

GINGER SYLLABUB

Serve with the Buttered Ginger Pears (see page 175) or with Ginger and Pecan Biscuits (page 150).

Serves 4–5

25g/1oz caster sugar, plus more to
  taste
large pinch ground ginger and
  freshly grated nutmeg
finely grated zest and juice of
  ½ lemon
4 tablespoons amontillado sherry or
  sweet white wine
300ml/10fl oz double cream
2 globes stem ginger, finely chopped

a little syrup from the stem ginger
  jar (optional)

Place the first four ingredients in a bowl, cover, and leave to stand for a couple of hours in the fridge. Add the cream to the bowl and whip gently until it holds its shape but is not overly stiff.

Stir in the chopped stem ginger. Add more caster sugar or ginger syrup, if liked, to taste.

FRUIT FOOLS

At its simplest, a fruit fool is just a mixture of puréed or crushed fruit stirred into whipped cream, yoghurt or *fromage frais*. Raspberries, strawberries and blackberries are best in cream or Greek yoghurt fools. Crush some of the fruit and sweeten a little, then swirl it into the whipped cream or yoghurt. The famous Eton Mess mixes crushed strawberries and crushed meringues into the cream. Sharp fruits such as black- and redcurrants, gooseberries and rhubarb make delicious fools when cooked, puréed and folded into equal proportions of real egg custard and whipped cream. Rhubarb and cooked apricots, adequately sweetened, also make delicious fools swirled into thick, Greek yoghurt or *fromage frais*. For these little, creamy puddings use the best cream you can find – yellow, unpasteurized cream from Jersey herds has a delicious tang, or you can find organic double creams in most supermarkets these days. Serve fruit fools with thin, crisp biscuits or with a homemade sponge cake.

PASSIONFRUIT AND STRAWBERRY FOOL

Serves 4–6

5 passionfruit
65g/2½oz unsalted butter
100g/4oz caster sugar
2 eggs, beaten
120ml/4fl oz double cream
225g/8oz ripe strawberries

Halve the passionfruit and scoop out the pulp into a heatproof basin. Add the butter and sugar. Place over a pan of simmering water, ensuring that the water doesn't touch the bottom of the basin. Cook over a medium heat, stirring, until the butter melts, then add the well-beaten eggs. Cook the mixture, stirring often, until it thickens considerably – about 10–15 minutes.

Sieve, cool, cover and chill. Whip the cream until softly stiff, then fold into the passionfruit mixture. Slice or crush the strawberries – retaining a few for decoration, if liked – and fold into the fool. Pile into attractive glasses and decorate with strawberries.

VARIATION
1. Add the finely grated zest and juice of 1 lime to the passionfruit pulp. Omit the strawberries and fold in some mango purée. A large pinch of ground cardamom is good, too.
2. Freeze the mixture to make a delicious ice-cream. Either churn in an ice-cream machine or stir the mixture a couple of times during freezing to prevent ice crystals forming.

**Passionfruit and
strawberry fool (left)
and blackcurrant
fool (page 172)
served with Tuiles
aux Amandes (page
150)**

BLACKCURRANT FOOL

Tart fruits, like blackcurrants, need the extra sweetness of a custard base. They make the most delicious fool.

Serves 6–8

2 egg yolks, size 2
100g/4oz vanilla-scented caster sugar
150ml/5fl oz single cream
225g/8oz blackcurrants
250–300ml/8–10fl oz double cream

Whisk the egg yolks with 25g/1oz of sugar until pale. Heat the single cream until almost boiling, then whisk into the eggs. Place the bowl over a small pan of barely simmering water, ensuring that the water does not touch the base of the bowl. Cook, stirring frequently, until the custard thickens (about 10–15 minutes). Cool, stirring frequently to prevent a skin forming. (The custard cools more quickly if stood in a larger bowl of cold water.) Meanwhile, heat the blackcurrants with the remaining sugar until the juices flow and the blackcurrants are soft, and either purée or crush as preferred. Cool, then chill. Whisk the double cream until softly stiff, then fold in the custard. Finally, swirl in the blackcurrant mixture. Pile into attractive glasses and serve cold.

VARIATIONS
1. Use other tart fruit purées such as gooseberry, redcurrant or rhubarb. Add more or less sugar to taste. You will need about 450g/1lb gooseberries or rhubarb – drain after cooking so that the purée is not too wet.
2. The fool may be flavoured in various ways. Try flavouring the custard with a few crushed young blackcurrant leaves or peach tree leaves. For a gooseberry fool, try flavouring the fruit with elderflowers or a scented geranium leaf. A few dessertspoons of *crème de cassis* are a delicious addition to a blackcurrant fool.

APPLE DUMPLINGS WITH DATES AND PECANS AND BUTTERSCOTCH SAUCE

For a truly indulgent pudding, serve with chilled cream or a scoop of home-made vanilla ice-cream which will melt into the butterscotch sauce.

Serves 6

90g/3½oz lightly salted butter
175g/6oz light muscovado sugar
120ml/4fl oz double cream

FOR THE DUMPLINGS:
6 medium-sized dessert apples, such as
  Coxes
450g/1lb shortcrust pastry
25g/1oz shelled pecans, chopped
25g/1oz dates, finely chopped
½ teaspoon ground cinnamon
1 egg yolk, beaten with 2 tablespoons
  milk

First make the sauce: place all the ingredients in a small, heavy saucepan over a low heat. Stir until the butter melts and the sugar loses its graininess. Turn up the heat and boil the sauce for 2–3 minutes. Set aside.

Peel and core the apples. Roll out the pastry and cut into six circles about 7.5cm/3 inches larger than the apples. Place the pastry circles on a baking sheet, and place one apple on each circle. Mix together the pecans, dates and cinnamon. Half-fill the apples with some of the mixture, then add a spoonful of the butterscotch sauce, add more of the pecan mixture then spoon a little more sauce over.

Gather up the pastry to cover the apples and their filling, using the egg/milk mixture to seal the edges. Place seam down on a lightly greased baking tray. Use any pastry trimmings to decorate the apples if you wish. Brush with egg and refrigerate for at least 1 hour. Preheat the oven to 190°C/375°F/gas 5. Bake the apples in the middle of the oven for 30–40 minutes or until the apples are tender (test with a slim, metal skewer). Serve hot or warm with the remaining butterscotch sauce, gently reheated, and cream or ice-cream, if liked.

Apple dumplings
with dates and
pecans and
butterscotch sauce

PLUMS BAKED ON BRIOCHE WITH MARZIPAN AND ALMONDS

This is a version of a favourite French pudding given in *The Gentle Art of Cookery* by Mrs Leyel and Miss Hartley, published in 1925. The book is now out of print but it is well worth seeking out in second-hand bookshops. The pudding is quick to put together and needs little attention once in the oven. A brioche or chollah loaf will give an excellent result, otherwise use any fine-crumbed white bread. The recipe also works well with fresh apricots.

Serves 6

*6 slices of day-old white bread about
    2cm/½ inch thick*
100g/4oz unsalted butter, softened
750g/1½lb ripe plums
*100g/4oz caster sugar, preferably
    from the vanilla pod jar*
150g/5oz prepared marzipan
90g/3½oz slivered almonds
3 tablespoons Kirsch (optional)
    crème fraîche, *to serve*

Preheat the oven to 180°C/350°F/gas 4. Use almost all the butter to spread on the bread on both sides and lay the slices on a baking sheet. Halve and stone the plums and arrange as many halves as will fit on each slice of bread, cut-side uppermost, and dredge with half the sugar. Place a knob of marzipan in each plum cavity, scatter over the almonds and the Kirsch, if using. Sprinkle with a little of the remaining sugar and dot with the remaining butter.

Cover with a piece of buttered greaseproof paper and bake for about 40–45 minutes, uncovering and sprinkling with the remaining sugar halfway through cooking. The bread should be crisp and golden and the marizpan browned. Serve warm with *crème fraîche*.

Plums baked on
brioche with
marzipan and
almonds

PEAR AND GINGER CRUMBLE

I like crumbles baked in a fairly wide, shallow dish so that one gets a large proportion of crumbly topping to the slightly caramelized layer of fruit below, but some people prefer a deeper dish which gives a much juicier result.

Serves 4–5

*1kg/2lb just ripe pears, peeled, cored
   and sliced
juice and finely grated zest of
   ½ lemon
2 tablespoons soft brown sugar
2 pieces of preserved ginger in syrup,
   drained
75g/3oz slightly salted butter, plus a
   little extra for greasing
175g/6oz unbleached plain flour
50g/2oz ground almonds
scant tablespoon ground ginger
65g/2½oz soft brown sugar
75g/3oz flaked or chopped almonds*

Toss the pears as you slice them into the lemon juice, stir in the sugar and the finely chopped preserved ginger. Butter a 1.2 litre/2 pint capacity baking dish and pile in the pears. Preheat the oven to 180°C/350°F/gas 4.

Sift the flour, ground almonds and ground ginger into a mixing bowl, stir in the sugar then rub in the butter. Stir in the almonds and the lemon zest and spread the crumble mixture over the fruit.

Press down lightly then bake for about 40–45 minutes until the top has browned and the juices are bubbling through. This is at its very best served warm, rather than hot, with custard sauce or thick, pouring cream.

BUTTERED GINGER PEARS

See photograph on
page 163

Ginger and a little black pepper bring out the sweet flavour of cooked pears.

Serves 3–4

*40g/1½oz unsalted butter
4 large, just ripe dessert pears,
   peeled, cored and sliced
3 tablespoons vanilla caster sugar
freshly ground black pepper (optional)
2–3 tablespoons pear liqueur or
   calvados
2 globes of stem ginger, drained and
   finely shredded*

Melt the butter in a heavy-based, roomy frying pan over a medium-low heat. Add the pears and cook gently for about 10 minutes until they are tender. Raise the heat a little, sprinkle over the sugar and cook to caramelize the sugar. Add 1–2 grindings of black pepper, if liked, then add the liqueur and flame with a lighted match for a few seconds. Stir in the shredded stem ginger and serve immediately. Delicious served warm with the cold Ginger Syllabub (see page 170).

VARIATIONS

1. You can also try this recipe with apples, omitting the black pepper and using calvados or whisky to flame.

2. If you're not serving the pears with Ginger Syllabub, stir in 100ml/3½oz double cream and allow to bubble for a few minutes before serving with a slice of plain cake or toasted brioche as a quick, delicious pudding.

Steamed Date and Pecan Pudding with Maple Toffee Sauce

This is a complete indulgence, but worth splurging on once in a while even if you have to assuage your conscience by eating nothing but a salad beforehand. The anticipation of a steamed pudding bubbling gently away on the hob drives away all the cares and torments of the day. Serve, if your constitution can take it, with cream or homemade custard.

Serves 6

FOR THE TOPPING AND SAUCE:
50g/2oz unsalted butter
5 tablespoons maple syrup
3 tablespoons soft brown sugar
250ml/8fl oz/double cream
a little lemon juice

FOR THE PUDDING:
75g/3oz dates, chopped
175g/6oz unsalted butter, plus a
  little extra
100g/4oz soft brown sugar
3 eggs, size 3, beaten
120g/4½oz plain unbleached flour
1½ teaspoons baking powder
50g/2oz fresh white breadcrumbs
1 teaspoon finely grated lemon zest
100g/4oz pecan nuts, coarsely
  chopped
a few extra pecan nuts to serve

First make the sauce: place butter, syrup and sugar in a small, heavy saucepan and melt over a medium heat. Bring to a boil and gradually stir in the cream, bubble rapidly for a few minutes for the sauce to thicken. Add a few drops of lemon juice to taste. Set aside.

Now make the pudding: place the chopped dates in a bowl and pour over 100ml/3½fl oz boiling water, and leave to soak for 20 minutes. Cream the butter and sugar together until light and fluffy, then gradually beat in the eggs, adding a little flour to stop the mixture curdling. Sift the flour and baking powder and fold in with the breadcrumbs, pecans, lemon zest and soaked dates. Stir to mix.

Butter a large pudding basin and line the base with a circle of greaseproof paper. Pour in about 5 tablespoons of the sauce and swirl it round the basin. Spoon in the mixture and level off. Cover the basin with a circle of greaseproof paper and a circle of foil, and tie with string. Place in a large saucepan, pour in boiling water to come just over halfway up the basin, then cook at a gentle simmer for 2–2½ hours, topping up with extra boiling water when necessary. Just before serving re-heat the sauce, gently adding more cream if the sauce is too thick. Turn the pudding out on to a warm serving plate, pour over a little sauce and scatter with a few pecans. Serve any remaining sauce separately.

ORANGE AND ALMOND ROULADE WITH SUMMER FRUITS

This recipe is slightly adapted from one in the late Jeremy Round's essential book *The Independent Cook*. It is an excellent way of making a little fruit stretch a long way and you can vary the fruit you use according to availability. Currants of all kinds may be baked in the sponge, using the softer berry fruits in the filling. My favourite is either blackcurrants or blueberries in the cake and raspberries in the filling. Stoned cherries soaked in a little Kirsch-flavoured syrup are good as a filling, too.

Serves 8

melted butter for greasing the baking tin
90g/3½oz blanched almonds
4 eggs, size 2, separated
90g/3½oz vanilla-scented caster sugar
pinch of salt
finely grated zest of 1 orange
2 tablespoons orange juice
½ teaspoon cream of tartar
75–100g/3–4oz blackcurrants or blueberries

FOR THE FILLING:
300ml/½ pint double cream
1 tablespoon sifted icing sugar
2 tablespoons Cointreau or Triple Sec
a little finely grated orange zest (optional)
225g/8oz fresh raspberries
icing sugar to dust

Line a 25 x 33cm/10 x 13 inch (approximately) Swiss-roll tin with non-stick baking parchment or foil. Brush with melted butter. Preheat the oven to 180°C/350°F/gas 4. Toast the almonds until golden brown, cool, then grind in a clean coffee mill. Whisk the egg yolks and sugar (preferably with a hand-held electric whisk) until light, thick and increased in volume – set the bowl over a pan of hot water while you whisk. Fold the ground almonds, salt and orange zest into the egg yolk mixture, then stir in the orange juice. Whisk the egg whites and cream of tartar until stiff, then fold gently into the egg yolk mixture. Turn into the prepared tin and level off. Scatter the currants or blueberries over the surface, then bake immediately for 15–20 minutes until risen and browned.

Place a large sheet of baking paper on the work surface and scatter over a little caster sugar.

When the cake is cooked turn onto the paper, trim the short edges of the sponge then roll up the sponge loosely. Leave to cool. About 1 hour before serving, whisk the cream with the caster sugar and liqueur. Add the orange zest, if liked. Spread the cream over the unrolled cake, then scatter over the raspberries. Re-roll the roulade carefully, place on a serving plate and dust with icing sugar.

Orange and almond roulade with summer fruits

ORANGE AND ROSEMARY SAVARIN WITH SUMMER FRUITS

Serves 8–10

15g/½oz fresh yeast
300g/10oz unbleached strong plain
    flour
scant teaspoon salt
4 eggs, size 2, beaten
150g/5oz unsalted butter, softened,
    plus a little extra for greasing
25g/1oz caster sugar
100g/4 oz candied orange peel,
    chopped
1 orange

FOR THE SYRUP:
225g/8oz caster sugar
2 sprigs of fresh rosemary
120ml/4fl oz Grand Marnier liqueur

TO FINISH:
5 tablespoons apricot or plum jam,
    sieved
450g/1lb mixed summer fruits
    (currants, strawberries, raspberries)
sprigs of rosemary, to decorate

Mix the yeast with 100ml/3½fl oz of warm water and leave for 10 minutes. Sift the flour and salt into a warmed bowl and make a well in the centre. Add the yeast and the eggs and beat thoroughly for about 4–5 minutes. Cover the bowl and leave in a warm place for 1 hour to double in bulk.

Soften, but do not melt, the butter. When the dough has risen, beat in the softened butter, caster sugar, candied orange peel and the finely grated zest of ½ the orange. Butter a 1.25–1.5 litre/2¼–2½ pint capacity ring mould and spoon the mixture into it. Cover and leave to rise to the top of the tin (about 30–40 minutes). Meanwhile, preheat the oven to 200°C/400°F/gas 6. Bake the savarin for 20–25 minutes until browned and firm. Turn the savarin on to a rack placed over a deep plate.

While the savarin is baking (or warming if it was prepared in advance), make the syrup. Dissolve the sugar in 600ml/1 pint of water over a low heat. Add the rosemary and a couple of strips of orange zest and boil moderately for 5–6 minutes. Remove the rosemary and the orange zest, stir in all but 3 tablespoons of the liqueur and the juice of the orange. Gradually spoon the hot syrup over the warm savarin. Leave to stand, covered, until cool. Then sprinkle the savarin with the remaining Grand Marnier and brush with the warmed jam. Heap the fruit, sweetened if liked, into the centre of the savarin. Serve with *crème fraîche*, if liked, and decorate with fresh rosemary.

Orange and
rosemary savarin
with summer fruits

This is not a complete cookery manual. It does not pretend to give you a full account of all aspects of food and cooking, but in this section I have gathered together a few basic recipes for stocks and sauces which are referred to in other chapters. There are other building block recipes throughout the book, a recipe for pancakes on page 130 or one for sweet tart pastry on page 154 for example, but I make the assumption that you'll have other books which will contain basic recipes. For cooking techniques, explanations, trenchant observations, and countless inspiring ideas I can heartily recommend Lynda Brown's book *The Modern Cook's Manual*. Two books that are well worth searching for in second-hand book shops (they have been many years out of print) are Margaret Costa's *Four Seasons Cookery Book* and *The Observer French Cookery School* by Anne Willan and Jane Grigson. I refer to my well-splattered copies all the time.

STOCKS

I am not a cook who constantly has a stockpot on the simmer. Nor, I suspect, do many people outside the restaurant kitchen. If I am making a special dish that needs a good, homemade stock I have to make it, from scratch, for that dish. If I had a freezer (the omission is for reasons of space rather than snobbery), I should like to think that I'd have a store of frozen pots of ready-made stock to hand. Maybe. But in the home kitchen most cooks see making stock as an integral part of cooking a particular dish. So the bones from a duck will go to make a stock for a rich ballotine; the bones from the fish for a terrine will go to make the delicious jellied stock that binds the other ingredients together. This may be more work at the time, but as a process it does have a certain satisfying integrity.

CUBES & READY-MADE STOCKS

Making soups and sauces are two occasions when I wish I had fresh, homemade stock to hand. Delicious quick soups can be made on the basis of a good chicken or fish stock. Flavour the stock with ginger, soy, star anise or lemon grass, add a few vegetables, some meat or fish and perhaps a few noodles, and you have the makings of a delicious Oriental-style soup. You cannot really do this with a stock cube – however good and additive-free – and expect it to taste of anything very much apart from, well, stock cubes. Stock cubes and reduced stock pastes are best in powerfully flavoured dishes like casseroles and braised meats in which they will not dominate the flavour of the whole dish.

The fresh, liquid stocks you can buy in big supermarkets these days are a vast improvement on stock cubes or concentrated stock pastes, but they are expensive if you have to buy sufficient for a soup for 4 or more people. Where these liquid stocks do score heavily is in sauces, when you need only a few spoonfuls. In my experience, though, you should be wary of using them in reduced sauces where you reduce the stock by rapid boiling. Some of them develop rather unpleasant aftertastes if reduced too far.

I have included recipes in this section for three basic stocks: chicken, fish and vegetable.

CHICKEN STOCK

The method for chicken stock can be followed for any poultry or feathered game. For a light stock cook the bones from raw, for a darker stock brown the bones in a hot oven

Previous page:
stuffings and sauces
From the top:
traditional bread
sauce (page 189);
potato and chorizo
sausage stuffing
(page 188); rice and
fennel stuffing (page
188); Almond and
hazelnut sauce with
garlic and parsley
(page 187); fruited
couscous stuffing
(page 189); red
onion, kumquat and
cranberry relish
(page 190)

(220°C/420°F/gas 7) for about 30 minutes. The carcass from a cooked bird will give a very different, less fresh taste, but still one which will make a very good base for a soup. It is quite painless to get into the habit of making a pan of soup the day after you've had a roast chicken or duck or turkey.

FISH STOCK

Fish stock will be as good as the type of fish trimmings you use. Sole bones are the best, but most fish apart from the very oily ones will make fine stocks. Don't use mackerel, herring or sardines as they can give unpleasantly strong flavours. If you have some prawn, crab or lobster shells, these can be used to make a wonderfully flavoured stock which will make one of the best bases for a fish soup. Break up the shells as best you can before simmering with the vegetables and aromatics. Do not allow fish stock to boil – it should cook at a bare simmer.

VEGETABLE STOCK

Vegetable stock is endlessly variable and should be matched to the final dish you are making. For a mushroom dish, add some dried porcini mushrooms to the stock (or just use the liquid from soaking the porcini). Carrots will make the finished stock sweet, tomatoes add a sharper note. If you roast all the vegetables, turned in a little oil, until they brown around the edges, you'll end up with a much more deeply flavoured stock. Avoid too many green vegetables, especially cabbage and other members of the brassica family, as they can turn a stock into a murky, malodorous brew.

Most stocks are all the better for being reduced, by about half, by rapid boiling (or, in the case of fish stock, a steady simmer) after they have been strained. Do not add any salt before reducing a stock – or you could end up ruining your final dish through over-saltiness – and do not cook peppercorns for too long in a stock as they can turn it bitter.

SAUCES NEW & OLD

Sauces have changed beyond all recognition in recent years. Modern sauces are salsas – at their simplest, mixtures of raw, chopped vegetables and fruits with seasoning, spices and herbs – and a whole range of herb and nut pastes: Italian pestos, Catalan *picadas*, Spanish pepper and nut sauces (*romesco* is the most famous), and Greek sauces such as the garlicky *skordalia*. Thick warm or cold vinaigrettes, made with tomato, other vegetables and herbs, make delicious sauces for grilled fish or chicken. There are mayonnaise-based sauces and simple sauces of yoghurt and *crème fraîche* stirred through with herbs or diced, salted cucumber. Then there are Indian *raitas* and fresh herb and tamarind chutneys and South East Asian pastes of coconut and herbs and spices (see the Thai Green Curry Paste on page 132). All these sauces have one thing in common: they're quick to make and provide an essential contrast to the food you serve them with. Classic sauces tend to be an integral part of the main food – so you use the liquid from poaching fish or meat, say, to make a sauce to serve with it. We certainly shouldn't ignore the traditional flour and butter-based sauces in favour of the new saucery. Both have their point. See the recipes for two parsley sauces on page 186 for a good example of the two different types of sauces.

I have also included some recipes for stuffings in this section, together with several ideas for using them both in meat and poultry dishes and as stuffings for vegetables.

FISH STOCK

The best fish bones to use for fish stock are from the sole family. Dover sole or lemon sole make an excellently flavoured stock. Brill, turbot and halibut or the cheaper whiting are good too. Salmon heads and bones will make an excellently flavoured stock, but being an oily fish the stock will be slightly clouded. Avoid strong-tasting oily fish like mackerel or herring. The best method of making fish stock as clear as possible is to let the bones cool in the liquid before straining and do not let the stock cook for more than 15–20 minutes.

Makes about 600–750ml/1–1¼ pints

15g/½oz butter
1 leek, trimmed and roughly chopped
1 bulb of Florence fennel, trimmed
* and roughly chopped*
about 450g/1lb fish bones and heads
a few parsley stalks
1 bay leaf, torn in half or 1 stalk
* lemon grass, split in half*
175ml/6fl oz medium-dry white wine
* or dry vermouth*
10 whole white peppercorns

Melt the butter in a large pan and gently cook the leek and fennel for 5 minutes. Add the rest of the ingredients, except the peppercorns, to the saucepan and add 1.5 litres/2½ pints of water. Bring to the boil, skim, and simmer over a low heat for 15–20 minutes, adding the peppercorns for the last 10 minutes. Remove from the heat and leave to cool before straining into a clean saucepan. Discard the debris. Reduce by about half by steady simmering.

VEGETABLE STOCK

Vegetable stock is a movable feast. Alter the ingredients to suit the final dish, for instance a mushroom dish would benefit from a few dried porcini mushrooms simmered in the stock, for Chinese or Asian soup consider dried 'tangerine' peel, star anise, lemon grass and/or ginger. Avoid vegetables with overpowering flavours, such as cabbage, cauliflower and broccoli. I find a few spoonfuls of soy sauce do wonders for an insipid vegetable stock.

Makes about 900ml/1½ pints

1 tablespoon oil or 15g/½oz butter
1 onion, sliced
1 leek, sliced
2 carrots, sliced
the outside layer of 1 Florence fennel
* bulb or 2 sticks celery, chopped*
a few mushroom stalks
a few parsley stalks
a few thyme stalks
2 fresh bay leaves
salt
2 tomatoes
6 black peppercorns

Heat the oil or butter in a large pan over a low heat and add the vegetables and herbs up to and including the bay leaves. Stir, season with a little salt, cover, and sweat the vegetables in their own juices for 10 minutes, stirring once or twice and not allowing them to brown at all. Add the tomatoes and peppercorns and 1.5 litres/2½ pints water. Bring to the boil and simmer, half covered, for about 1 hour. Strain, pushing as much of the juices as you can through the sieve. Reduce by fast boiling until 900ml/1½ pints remain.

CHICKEN STOCK

If you use a whole chicken to make stock, you end up with some cooked chicken as well as the flavoursome broth. But you could use chicken wings (which many butchers will sell very cheaply) instead. For a browner, deeper-flavoured stock, brown the chicken wings and vegetables in a roasting tin in a hot oven, at 220°C/425°F/gas 7, for 30 minutes, before proceeding with the recipe.

Makes about 1.5 litres/2½ pints

*1 x 1.5kg/3lb free-range chicken, cut
    into joints or 1kg/2lb chicken wings
2 onions, sliced
1 carrot, sliced
2 stalks celery or half a celeriac,
    chopped
a few parsley stalks
1 fresh bay leaf
a few sprigs of thyme (lemon thyme
    is good)
10 black peppercorns*

Put all the ingredients apart from the peppercorns in a large saucepan and add 2 litres/3½ pints water. Bring to the boil, skim off any froth, and simmer, covered, for 25 minutes. Fish out the chicken breasts and pick off the flesh, set aside and return the bones to the pan. Simmer for a further 35 minutes, covered, then remove the other joints and pick off the flesh as before, returning the bones to the pan (the poached chicken may be used in a salad).

Add the peppercorns and simmer, covered, for another 30 minutes. Strain, then reduce the stock by hard boiling until about 1.5 litres/2½ pints remain.

MAYONNAISE

This is mayonnaise made by the classic (i.e. hand-beaten) method. It has a texture that no machine can reproduce. I use a small, coiled wire whisk when making mayonnaise. And I stand the bowl on a damp cloth to steady it while I whisk with one hand and dribble in the oil with the other.

Serves 4

*2 free-range egg yolks, size 2
½ teaspoon mustard powder
salt and black pepper
200–300ml/7–10fl oz pure olive oil, or
    a mixture of olive and grapeseed oil
lemon juice*

Make sure the egg yolks and oil are at room temperature. Place the egg yolks and mustard powder in a wide, roomy bowl and add a pinch of salt. Whisk to mix. Then, still whisking, add the oil a drop at a time (this is where an olive oil can or flask comes in useful). When about one-third of the oil is in, and the mayonnaise is thickening, the oil may be added in a thin stream. Stop when the mayonnaise is very thick. You may not need the full quantity of oil. Season to taste with black pepper and lemon juice.

ANCHOVY AND WATERCRESS MAYONNAISE

This mayonnaise is made by the processor method, which uses a whole egg for stability. It is lighter in texture and less rich than the classic mayonnaise on page 183. It makes a good accompaniment to rich, deep-fried foods.

Serves 4–6

1 small free-range egg
1 can anchovy fillets, drained
2 cloves garlic, peeled and coarsely
* chopped*
½ teaspoon mustard powder
150–175ml/5–6 fl oz olive oil
25g/1oz watercress, washed and
* trimmed*
freshly ground black pepper
lemon juice

Make sure the egg and oil are at room temperature. Place the egg, anchovies, garlic and mustard powder in a liquidizer or food processor. Blend briefly. Then, still blending, add the oil in a thin stream. Stop when the mayonnaise is quite thick. Transfer to a bowl. Blanch the watercress briefly in boiling water and drain thoroughly then squeeze dry. Chop the watercress and fold it into the mayonnaise. Season to taste with black pepper and lemon juice.

VARIATIONS
1. Try a sorrel mayonnaise made by adding a purée of barely cooked sorrel to a mayonnaise sauce (omit the garlic and anchovies from the above recipe). Or, for a similar effect, use a thick purée of cooked, drained green gooseberries or rhubarb.
2. Make a classic *sauce tartare* by stirring chopped shallots, parsley, chervil and tarragon into a mayonnaise, then add some chopped capers, gherkins and a little lemon zest.

ANCHOVY AND LEMON DRESSING

This makes a delicious accompaniment to roast or poached chicken, as in the Chicken Salmagundi on page 39, or with poached beef, hard-boiled eggs or potatoes.

Serves 4

2 hard-boiled egg yolks
6 anchovy fillets, drained
1 teaspoon salted capers, rinsed
1 teaspoon Dijon mustard
pinch of caster sugar
5 tablespoons olive oil
finely grated zest and juice of ½
* lemon*
15g/½oz finely chopped flat-leaved
* parsley*

2 tablespoons soured cream or crème
  fraîche
freshly ground black pepper

With either a mortar and pestle or a food processor, grind the first 5 ingredients together to make a smooth paste, then gradually work in the oil. Stir in the lemon zest, parsley and soured cream, and season to taste with lemon juice and pepper.

ROUILLE (GARLIC, SAFFRON AND RED PEPPER MAYONNAISE)

The simplest version of this well-known sauce, usually served with Mediterranean fish soups – most famously *bouillabaisse* – simply adds cayenne pepper and saffron to a basic aïoli or garlic mayonnaise. Even better, if totally unauthentic, is to add heat either through using a baked or grilled fresh red chilli or a purée of medium-hot, dried red chillis such as guajillo, chipotle (with a lovely smoky flavour) or guindilla. Rouille is great for livening up soups and stews of all kinds and for serving with simply cooked shellfish.

Serves 4–6

*1–2 fresh red chillies (or 1–2
    teaspoons of chilli paste made by
    soaking and puréeing any of the
    dried chillies mentioned above)*
a good pinch of saffron filaments
*4 large garlic cloves, peeled and
    halved*
sea salt
2 free-range egg yolks, size 2
*300ml/½ pint olive oil, or a half-and-
    half mixture of olive and
    grapeseed oils*
freshly ground black pepper
lemon juice

Preheat the oven to 220°C/425°F/ gas 7. Bake the fresh chillies for 15–20 minutes until the skin is blistered. Place the saffron in a small ovenproof dish and bake in the hot oven for 4–5 minutes to 'toast' lightly, then set aside.

When the chillies are done, cool, remove the skin and seeds and set aside. In a mortar and pestle, crush the garlic with a large pinch of sea salt to make a paste. Gradually work in as much chilli (or chilli-paste) as you like (err on the side of caution, you can always add more later). Gradually blend in the egg yolks. Drop by drop, add the oil, working it in with the pestle or a small whisk. When about half the oil is in, you can add the rest in a thin, steady stream, working the mixture all the time. Gradually crumble in the toasted saffron filaments. Then taste, adding more chilli, salt, pepper and lemon juice as required. Leave to stand, covered, for at least 30 minutes to allow the flavour of the saffron to develop.

PARSLEY SAUCES

The two recipes on the next page are very different parsley sauces, which neatly typify the split between the old and new regimes in the kitchen. The first is a French *sauce poulette* made with stock and enriched with egg yolk and cream, the second an Italian sauce, basically a thick viniagrette of herbs and oil. Both are good.

PARSLEY SAUCE (1)

This sauce is excellent with poached lamb or chicken, use the poaching liquid, de-greased, as the stock. For a parsley sauce to go with Good Friday fish, use either all milk or a mixture of fish stock and milk and add any juices from cooking the fish to the sauce at the end.

Serves 4–6

25g/1oz butter
1½ tablespoons plain, unbleached flour
300–450ml/½–¾ pint stock
1 egg yolk
100ml/3½fl oz double or whipping cream
15g/½oz fresh parsley, chopped
salt and freshly ground black pepper
lemon juice

Melt the butter in a medium-sized, heavy saucepan and stir in the flour, cook for a few minutes over a low heat, stirring all the time. Heat the stock, then gradually stir 300ml/10fl oz of it into the roux, and whisk briskly to produce a smooth sauce. Cook the sauce over a very low heat (use a heat diffuser if necessary) for 15–20 minutes, stirring regularly. Add more stock if the sauce seems to be too thick.

Whisk the egg and cream together in a small bowl, then whisk in a few tablespoons of the hot sauce. Add the cream mixture to the pan and cook for a few minutes over a very gentle heat. Stir in the finely chopped parsley, then season to taste with salt, pepper and lemon juice. The sauce should have an easy, pouring consistency; if it is too thick, thin with a little more stock.

PARSLEY SAUCE (2)

This thick, vinaigrette-type sauce goes well with poached and grilled meats, and also grilled fish such as tuna and swordfish.

Serves 4–6

2 large shallots, peeled
15g/½oz fresh parsley
15g/½oz fresh mint leaves
1 tablespoon salted capers, rinsed
finely shredded zest of ½–1 lemon
1 teaspoon Dijon mustard
4–5 tablespoons extra virgin olive oil
salt, freshly ground black pepper and caster sugar
1–2 teaspoons lemon juice or wine vinegar

Roughly chop the shallots and herbs. Process all the ingredients down to the mustard in a food processor or liquidizer. Blend in enough olive oil to make a thick sauce, scrape out into a bowl and season to taste with salt, pepper and a pinch of sugar. Stir in lemon juice or wine vinegar to taste.

VARIATION
By using more olive oil and all parsley (with a sprig of tarragon) rather than any mint, this sauce makes a delicious dressing for cold, rare-roasted or poached beef. This quantity will dress at least 750g/1½lb of meat. Add some crushed garlic to the dressing, if liked, and use tarragon mustard and tarragon vinegar to flavour.

ALMOND AND HAZELNUT SAUCE WITH GARLIC AND PARSLEY

Medieval sauces tended to be thickened with pounded nuts or breadcrumbs rather than flour. A modern-day remnant of this tradition is bread sauce, which we usually serve with roast chicken or turkey. This sauce, which incorporates the liver from the bird, is akin to the Catalan and Spanish *picadas* and nut-thickened sauces. It is delicious with poultry and game birds. Serve it in small quantities, more as a relish than as a sauce.

Serves 4–6

4 tablespoons olive oil (or fat from
   the roasted bird)
3 peeled cloves garlic
1 x 1cm/½ inch slice good white bread
50g/2oz poultry livers, trimmed
   (include the liver from the chicken
   or turkey)
40g/1½oz blanched almonds, toasted
40g/1½oz toasted skinned hazelnuts
2 tablespoons finely chopped parsley
1–3 teaspoons sherry vinegar or
   balsamic vinegar
salt and freshly ground black pepper
2–3 tablespoons poultry stock or
   cooking juices from the roasted
   bird

Heat half the oil or fat in a small frying pan over a medium heat and cook the whole garlic until just browning (about 4–5 minutes), then remove to a plate. Add the bread to the pan and fry until golden on both sides, then set aside with the garlic. Add the remaining oil or fat and quickly cook the liver until just cooked (about 2–3 minutes).

Pound the garlic, bread and nuts in a mortar and pestle until paste-like, then gradually work in the liver (and the oil or fat in the pan) and parsley. When the mixture is smooth, work in the vinegar (start with 1 teaspoon then add more to taste) and season to taste. Thin with a little stock or cooking juices if liked. If using a processor, grind all the ingredients together to make a smooth paste, thinning with stock or cooking juices.

SPICED PEPPER AND HAZELNUT SAUCE

See photograph on
page 134

This delicious sauce is based on the Spanish *romesco* sauce from the province of Tarragona. In Spain, fresh tomatoes would be included; in this version the sun-dried variety adds the depth of flavour that our winter tomatoes cannot match. It is delicious served with battered and deep-fried vegetables like those on page 133 or with simply steamed cauliflower or boiled potatoes or pasta.

Serves 4

½–1 dried red chilli
1 fresh red pepper, halved and
   de-seeded
4 cloves of garlic
4 sun-dried tomatoes in olive oil, drained
50g/2oz hazelnuts, skinned and
   toasted
2 tablespoons fresh parsley, chopped
1–2 tablespoons sherry vinegar or red
   wine vinegar
50–85ml/2–3fl oz olive oil
salt and freshly ground black pepper

Preheat the oven to 200°C/400°F/gas 6. Soak the de-seeded dried chilli in a little hot water for 15 minutes. Place fresh pepper and garlic on a baking sheet and bake for 15 minutes or until the pepper looks blistered. Cool, skin the pepper and garlic. In a processor or food mill, grind all the vegetables, the tomatoes, the nuts and the soaked, drained chilli. Add the parsley and beat in vinegar to taste and add sufficient oil, a bit at a time, to make a thick sauce. Season to taste and set aside.

See photograph on
page 179

RICE AND FENNEL STUFFING

This is a delicious stuffing for a boned turkey or chicken. Or try it stuffed into blanched, hollowed-out onions then baked. Or bake it in a separate dish, moistening with a little of the cooking juices from the roasting bird.

Makes enough for 1 medium-sized boned turkey or 10–12 stuffed onions

salt and pepper
225g/8oz Italian arborio rice
450g/1lb fresh spinach, washed and
*   trimmed*
freshly grated nutmeg
25g/1oz butter
1 tablespoon olive oil
100g/4oz pancetta or thick-cut bacon,
*   chopped*
175g/6oz Florence fennel, chopped
*   (reserve any feathery tops)*
100g/4oz onion, chopped
1 teaspoon fennel seeds, lightly
*   crushed*
1 dessertspoon chopped fresh thyme
grated zest of ½ lemon
1 large beaten egg

Bring a large pan of salted water to the boil and throw in the rice. Cook for 12–15 minutes until just tender. Drain thoroughly and place in a large bowl. Rinse out the pan and cook the roughly chopped spinach, covered, for about 5 minutes until it collapses. Add to the rice and mix, seasoning well with salt, pepper and a good grating of nutmeg.

Heat the butter and oil in a frying pan over a medium heat. Cook the pancetta (or bacon), fennel, onion and fennel seeds together for 10–15 minutes. Stir frequently and do not allow to over-brown. Mix into the rice and spinach, then add all the remaining ingredients. Stir to mix and adjust the seasoning to taste.

VARIATIONS
1. Add some garlic or 225g/8oz cooked, skinned chestnuts, roughly chopped.
2. Leave out the pancetta or bacon. Add 50–75g/2–3oz freshly grated Parmesan cheese and bake in a shallow, wide baking dish, drizzled with a few tablespoons of olive oil, for about 30 minutes at 180°C/350°F/gas 4. Serve as a vegetarian main course supper dish with salad.

See photograph on
page 179

POTATO AND CHORIZO SAUSAGE STUFFING

This makes a delicious accompaniment to roast chicken, guinea fowl or pheasant. When the bird has about 30 minutes cooking time to go, drain off the fat and juices, add the stuffing to the roasting tin, then sit the bird back on top and finish cooking, basting with the reserved juices from time to time.

Serves 6

2 tablespoons olive oil
1 medium-sized onion, chopped
450g/1lb waxy potatoes, peeled and
*   cut into 1cm/½ inch cubes*
100g/4oz celery, chopped
1 clove garlic, finely chopped
1–2 teaspoons mild paprika
liver from the bird, chopped (optional)
225g/8oz chorizo sausage, skinned
*   and crumbled into rough 1cm/½*
*   inch pieces*
1–2 teaspoons chopped fresh rosemary
zest of ½ lemon
salt and freshly ground black pepper

Heat the oil in a heavy frying pan over low to medium heat, then fry the onion for 5–10 minutes until soft and golden. Add the potatoes and celery, and cook for a further 5–10 minutes. Add the garlic, paprika and liver (if using). Cook for 2–3 minutes more. Take off the heat and stir in the sausage, rosemary and lemon zest. Season with salt (the sausage will contain some salt) and lots of freshly ground black pepper. As the vegetables are almost cooked, this stuffing doesn't require much extra cooking – 20–25 minutes at 190°C/375°F/gas 5 should be sufficient.

See photograph on
page 179

FRUITED COUSCOUS STUFFING

This is a lovely light stuffing for boned pheasant or duck, or as an accompaniment to roast goose, pork or even lamb. It is also delicious as a stuffing for vegetables. Try red or yellow peppers, hollowed-out onions or fennel bulbs. These would make a wonderful vegetarian alternative for Christmas lunch.

Makes enough for a large roast, serving 6–8

225g/8oz couscous
50–75g/2–3oz dried apricots, diced
50g/2oz dried cherries or currants
juice and finely shredded zest of
*   1 orange*
2 medium-sized red or yellow peppers
3 tablespoons olive oil
100g/4oz red or yellow onion,
*   chopped*
1 clove garlic, finely chopped
2.5cm/1 inch piece fresh ginger,
*   finely chopped*
½ teaspoon ground cardamom
1 teaspoon ground coriander seeds
3 tablespoons chopped fresh coriander
salt and freshly ground black pepper
75–100g/3–4oz blanched, toasted
*   almonds*

Measure the couscous in a measuring jug, tip into a bowl then add just under twice the volume of warm water. Add the apricots, cherries (or currants) and the orange juice. Leave to soak and absorb the liquid. Halve and de-seed the peppers and grill, skin-side up, until the skin blisters and blackens (about 10–15 minutes). Place in a paper bag or covered bowl and allow to steam for 10 minutes. Remove the skin, slice the peppers and set aside.

Heat the oil in a medium-sized frying pan over a low to medium heat. Then cook the onion for 5 minutes until beginning to soften, add the garlic, ginger and ground spices, and cook for 5 minutes more. Fluff up the couscous with a fork, then stir in the orange zest, peppers, and the onion/ginger mixture. Stir in the fresh coriander and season well with salt and pepper. Add the almonds.

TRADITIONAL BREAD SAUCE

See photograph on
page 179

Pay particular attention to the seasoning in bread sauce or the finished sauce will taste bland and uninteresting. Use a good, dense-textured loaf.

Serves 6

450ml/15fl oz full-fat milk
1 small onion, cut into quarters
1 stick celery
1 bay leaf, torn in half
1 teaspoon allspice berries
4 cloves
1 blade of mace
90g/3½oz good day-old white
*   breadcrumbs*
salt, black pepper and freshly grated
*   nutmeg*
25g/1oz butter

Place milk, onion, celery, bay leaf and spices in a small, heavy pan and bring to the boil. Half-cover and leave to steep for 1 hour. Strain, and place the milk in a liquidizer with the onion (discard the rest of the debris in the sieve). Blend, then return the milk to the rinsed-out saucepan and bring back to the boil. Add the breadcrumbs and stir until the sauce thickens considerably. Simmer for 2–4 minutes. Season to taste with lots of salt, pepper and freshly grated nutmeg. Just before serving, stir in the butter. Serve warm rather than hot.

RED ONION, KUMQUAT AND CRANBERRY RELISH

This is an excellent sharp and fruity relish to serve alongside fatty meats – try with pork, duck or goose.

Serves 6–8

2 tablespoons extra virgin olive oil
*3 medium-sized red onions, halved
    and sliced*
1 teaspoon crushed coriander seeds
*½ teaspoon freshly ground cardamom
    seeds*
*100g/4oz kumquats halved and
    de-pipped*
100g/4oz fresh cranberries
*2 tablespoons sherry or balsamic
    vinegar, plus more to taste*
*juice and finely shredded zest of
    1 orange*
3–4 teaspoons muscovado sugar
salt and freshly ground black pepper

Heat the oil in medium-sized heavy saucepan over a low heat. Add the onions and cook, covered, for 15–20 minutes. Stir often and do not allow to brown too much. Add the spices and cook for 2 minutes more. Add the kumquats, cranberries, vinegar, orange juice and zest, 2 teaspoons of the sugar and 3 tablespoons water. Season well with salt and pepper. Cook, covered, for another 15 minutes.

Uncover, raise the heat a little and cook, stirring often, until the liquid evaporates. Taste and adjust the seasoning to taste, adding more vinegar and/or sugar to taste.

REAL VANILLA CUSTARD

We should take it as the ultimate culinary compliment that the French know this delicious sauce as *crème anglaise*. If I'm using the custard as the basis of an ice-cream or in a trifle, I tend to use single cream, otherwise full-fat milk.

Serves 6

*600ml/1 pint single cream or milk or
    a mixture of the two*
1 vanilla pod
4–5 egg yolks
40g/1½oz vanilla-scented caster sugar

Place the cream and/or milk with the split vanilla pod into a saucepan and bring to the boil. Turn off the heat and allow to steep for 15 minutes. Meanwhile, beat the egg yolks with the sugar until light coloured. Bring the cream/milk back to the boil and pour on to the egg yolks, stirring constantly. Place the bowl over a pan of barely simmering water, making sure that the water doesn't touch the base of the bowl. Cook, stirring frequently, until the custard thickens. The custard is ready when a finger, drawn across the back of the stirring spoon, leaves a clear trail. This will probably take about 10–15 minutes.

Strain to remove the vanilla pod. If little blobs appear in the custard it has overheated. Immediately plunge the base of the bowl into cold water and whisk the custard. Strain through a fine, non-metallic sieve and the custard should be okay.

VARIATIONS
1. A real vanilla custard is the basis of the best real vanilla ice-cream. Chill the finished custard, then fold in 300ml/10fl oz lightly whipped double cream. Either freeze according to the directions of your ice-cream machine or freeze in a polythene freezer box, beating the mixture 2–3 times at 1–1½ hour intervals.
2. Custard picks up and amplifies flavours wonderfully. Use a couple of torn bay leaves or a piece of cinnamon stick in place of the vanilla pod.
3. An even more wickedly indulgent sauce can be made by whipping ¼ pint of double cream and folding into the chilled custard.

ACKNOWLEDGEMENTS

The publisher would like to thank the following sources for providing the photographs for this book:

Robert Harding Syndication/*Homes & Gardens* magazine/Laurie Evans 28,35,40,44, 57,64,126; /Gus Filgate 88,100,123; /Michelle Garrett 31,33,65,72,74,111,161,169,171,177; /Norman Hollands 102,119; /Graham Kirk 50,76,89,92,164; /Jess Koppel 9,11,18,19,47, 49,83,85,91,113,122,125,153; /Vernon Morgan 24,27,78,87,107,109,110,116; /James Murphy 12,15,23,32,37,75,80,94,98,121,130,137,138, 142,144,165; /Simon Smith 30,43,48,99,104; /Roger Stowell 63,68,134,147,150,151,157, 172,173,174,179; /Philip Webb 162; /Frank Wieder 41,42; /Philip Wilkins 21,36,128; /Huw Williams 70,163.

Laurie Evans 108,139,145
Roger Stowell 69,152
Pictures on pages 180,181,183,185 reproduced courtesy of Mary Evans Picture Library

The publisher is also grateful for permission to reproduce Shaun Hill's Apricot and Hazelnut Bread from *Shaun Hill's Cook Book*, published by Pan Books.

SELECT BIBLIOGRAPHY

This is a short list of books referred to in the text or which I find indispensable.

Stephanie Alexander, *Stephanie's Feasts and Stories* (Allen & Unwin, 1988)

Lindsey Bareham, *In Praise of the Potato* (Michael Joseph, 1989)

Frances Bissel, *The Real Meat Cookbook* (Chatto & Windus, 1992)

Raymond Blanc, *Recipes from Le Manoir aux Quat'Saisons* (MacDonald Orbis, 1988)

Arabella Boxer, *Book of English Food* (Hodder & Stoughton, 1991)

Jennifer Brennan, *Thai Cooking* (Warner Books, 1991)

Lynda Brown, *The Modern Cook's Manual* (Michael Joseph, 1995)

Anna Del Conte, *Entertaining all'Italiana* (Bantam, 1991)

Bruce Cost, *Food from the Far East* (Century, 1990)

Margaret Costa, *Four Seasons Cookery Book* (MacMillan, 1981)

Elizabeth David, *English Bread and Yeast Cookery* (Penguin, 1979)

Elizabeth David, *French Provincial Cooking* (Penguin, 1970)

Elizabeth David, *Spices, Salt and Aromatics in the English Kitchen* (Penguin, 1970)

Silvija Davidson, *Loaf, Crust and Crumb* (Michael Joseph, 1995)

John Evelyn, *The Salad Calendar*, reprinted in Jane Grigson's *Food with the Famous* (Grub Street, 1991)

Hannah Glasse, *The Art of Cookery made Plain and Easy* (Reprinted, Prospect Books, 1983)

Jane Grigson, *English Food* (Penguin, 1988)

Jane Grigson, *Fruit Book* (Michael Joseph, 1982)

Jane Grigson, *Good Things* (Michael Joseph, 1990)

Sophie Grigson, *Eat Your Greens* (Network Books, 1993)

Sophie Grigson, *Sophie Grigson's Ingredients Book* (Pyramid, 1991)

Sophie Grigson, *Sophie's Table* (Michael Joseph, 1990)

Shaun Hill, *Shaun Hill's Cookery Book* (MacMillan, 1995)

Simon Hopkinson, *Roast Chicken and Other Stories* (Ebury, 1994)

Diana Kennedy, *The Cuisines of Mexico* (Harper & Row, 1972)

Joy Larkcom, *The Salad Garden* (Frances Lincoln)

C.F. Leyel and Olga Hartley, *The Gentle Art of Cookery* (Chatto & Windus, 1974)

Deborah Madison, *The Greens Cook Book* (Bantam Books, 1987)

Deborah Madison, *The Savory Way* (Bantam Books, 1990)

Barbara Maher, *Cakes* (Penguin, 1982)

Mark Miller, *Coyote Café* (Ten Speed Press, 1989)

Joyce Molyneux, *The Carved Angel Cookery Book* (Collins, 1990)

Jill Norman, *The Complete Book of Spices* (Dorling Kindersley, 1990)

Sri Owen, *The Rice Book* (Doubleday, 1993)

Claudia Roden, *A New Book of Middle Eastern Food* (Penguin, 1986)

Jeremy Round, *The Independent Cook* (Barrie & Jenkins, 1988)

George and Cecilia Scurfield, *Home-made Cakes and Biscuits* (re-issued by Serif, 1994)

Nigel Slater, *Real Fast Food* (Michael Joseph, 1992)

Michael Smith, *Fine English Cookery* (Faber, 1977)

Annie Somerville, *Fields of Greens* (Bantam Press, 1993)

Patricia Wells, *Bistro Cooking* (Arrow, 1992)

Anne Willan, *The Observer French Cookery School* (MacDonald, 1980)

INDEX